Herbert L. Welch

Herbert L. Welch

Black Ghosts and Art in a Maine Guide's Wilderness

GRAYDON HILYARD
AND LESLIE HILYARD

STACKPOLE
BOOKS
Guilford, Connecticut

DEDICATION

*To the Palmers of Sagamore Lodge,
Saviors of History*

STACKPOLE
BOOKS

Published by Stackpole Books
An imprint of The Rowman & Littlefield Publishing Group, Inc.
4501 Forbes Blvd., Ste. 200
Lanham, MD 20706
www.rowman.com

Distributed by NATIONAL BOOK NETWORK
800-462-6420

Pencil sketches by John Swan. Poetry by Linda Warren. Cover and fly leaf art by Alexander Kouznetsov. Color photography by John MacLeod unless otherwise noted.

British Library Cataloguing in Publication Information available

Library of Congress Cataloging-in-Publication Data available

978-0-8117-3776-0 (hardcover)
978-0-8117-6761-3 (e-book)

™ The paper used in this publication meets the minimum requirements of American National Standard for Information Sciences—Permanence of Paper for Printed Library Materials, ANSI/NISO Z39.48-1992.

Printed in the United States of America

Sagamore Lodge, John Swan.

CONTENTS

ACKNOWLEDGMENTS

Special thanks to Jeffery I. Knapp of Portland, Maine.

We owe a debt to the following institutions for access to collections: American Antiquarian Society; Art Students League of New York; Bethel, Maine Historical Society; Brigham Young University; Clinton, Maine Historical Society; Diamond Library, University of New Hampshire; Dwight D. Eisenhower Library; Free Library of Philadelphia; Clinton, Maine Historical Society; History and Philosophy Newspaper Library, University of Illinois; Houghton Library, Harvard University; *Lewiston Sun Journal*; Library of Congress; Maine Central Institute; Martin and Osa Johnson Safari Museum; Museum of Comparative Zoology (Departments of Icthyology, Ornithology, and Vertebrate Paleontology), Harvard University; National Gallery of Australia; New England Historic Genealogical Society; Penobscot Marine Museum; Pittsfield, Maine Historical Society; *Portland Press Herald*; Rangeley Sporting Heritage Museum; Rangeley Public Library; and the Society for Post-Medieval Archaeology.

Thanks also to Margaret Anderson, Marc Aroner, Barbara Arthur, James R. Babb, Pamela Bates, Douglas Beal, Coleen Bean, Jennifer V. Beane, Ellen Belyea, Randall H. Bennett, Nancy Betz, Anna Bowditch, Judith Bowman, David Biesler, Peter Biesler, Ralph Billingsley, Stanley Bogdan, Richard Brescani, Tom Browne, Cynthia Burgher, Olivia Burgher, Love Call, Chris Capstick, Harry Carey, Robert A. Carlson, John Carville, Stephanie Cassidy, Jenna Caswell, Christine Clark, Robert Cook, Cathi Cooper, Paul Cote, Stephanie Chu-O'Neil, Steven Crandall, Michael Decoteau, Chris Del Plato, Mary Dette, Harold K. Duley, Warren Duncan, Cy Eastlack, Edward Evers, Earle Fletcher, George Fletcher, David Footer, Julie Footer, Robert Fransden, Wanda Gonzalez, Peter Gribben, Arthur Guerin, Fred Harnden, William Hartigan, Andrew Herd, Raejean Herrin, Gerald Hilyard, Suzanne Hilyard, Augustus S. Hinds II, James C. Higgins, Mike Hiza, Jay S. Hoar, Mike Houle, John Hoyt, Kevin Johnson, Jillian Jones, Ronn Jones, Harland Kidder, Jeff Knapp, Adelaide Knight, Robert Kohrman, Larry Koob, Susan Koob, Alexander Kouznetsov, Lefty Kreh, William B. Krohn, Nancy Lacompte, J. Edson Leonard, Lynn Lewandowski, Danielle Libby, Harvey Libby, Robert Mahoney, Henry R. Martin, Charles McLaughlin, Henry Mehegan, Julie Mehegan, Peter Mehegan, Wesley A. Miller Jr., Wesley A. Miller Sr., King Montgomery, P.A. Morris, Scott Morton, John Mundt, Luther of Newfoundland, Wilfred "Sonny" Noel, Gertrude O'Brien, Robert Oldmixon Sr., Donald Palmer, Jack Palmer, Kathy M. Palmer, Stephanie Palmer, Ted Patlen, Albert Pflueger Jr., Stephen Philbrick, William Pierce, Archer Poor Jr., Harold Porter, Gary Priest, Jim Procter, Tom Rideout, William Roy, Peter Sang, Charles Schaaf, Daniel Schmidt, Paul Schullery, Anne Simmons, Bradford Smith, Richard Smith, James Stone, John Swan, Marie Tille, Michael Tolaven, Karen Touchette, Talon van Howten, Jefferson Voorhees, Allan Walker, Bob Warren, Linda Warren, Rick Weik, Hal Wert, Art Wheaton, Eleanor White, James "Bud" Wilcox Jr., Andrew Williston, and Donald Wilson.

APOLOGIA

To those who have waited long and patiently for our work on Herbert Leon Welch, we apologize.

Life rarely follows a logical, linear path, and the same is true of the writer. Among the detours on our trail to Welch: a triple bypass, a pacemaker, and the removal of any organs deemed unnecessary by the medical community. As time consuming as those events were, they paled in comparison to the time spent on a book named *Bogdan*.

Having completed our book *Carrie Stevens: Maker of Rangeley Favorite Trout and Salmon Flies*, we knew eventually we'd want to follow it up with a book on Herbert Welch, creator of the famed Black Ghost streamer. And so we did.

Rumor had it that celebrated fly reel maker Stan Bogdan had been a friend of Welch. Getting an interview with him was tougher than getting a papal audience, but for once there was truth in rumor. Bogdan credited Welch as an early source of encouragement for his designs. Moreover, Welch was the first to sell the Bogdan reels commercially, at his legendary sporting goods store at Haines Landing on Mooselookmeguntic Lake in Oquossoc, Maine. For ten years, Bogdan fished those waters while staying at Camp Antlers on the eastern shore. And so on and on our interview with Bogdan went—for years.

While we apologize for the delay, Bogdan never did. "C'mon now," he would say. "I'm eighty-six. I don't buy green bananas anymore. Herb won't mind waiting." Bogdan was the first to tell us that being called "Herbie" would have not sat well with Welch. He preferred "Herb." Following an adolescent test run with "Bert," Welch started using "Herb" in his letters, on his paintings, and on his 1948 Upper Dam Fish Log entry documenting a 5-pound salmon caught on a brown-and-white bucktail. Accordingly, we will obey his wishes except to eliminate the early vogue of quote marking nicknames. And Herb, for that we do apologize.

A misguided willingness to leave previous writers unchallenged can lead to flawed notions—repetition in print does not make something true. Such was the case in *Carrie Stevens* when we attributed the origin of the Pink Lady to her, and parrotted the longstanding George Shephard Page–Louis Agassiz brook trout connection (see Chapter 2). As to the Pink Lady origins, we would be firmly rebuffed by Carrie speaking from the long-sealed Welch files. Another example is the fashionable term Rangeley Style, used to describe the work of any New England tier using a long-shanked hook. While there is a distinctive style best known as the Carrie Stevens Method (based on the use of staggered material), there is no Rangeley Style. Regional tiers including Bud Wilcox, Dick Frost, Frank Case, Maurice Bauer, and Elizabeth Duley all used the eastern method of tying all material in at the head—a method in no way limited to Rangeley.

Given the scarcity of documentation, we believe that it is not our place to reconstruct the intimate details of Welch's life. This may disappoint some who are more concerned with the inner workings of a life than with achievements, and while we have sympathy for that view, we do not apologize for our approach. Far better not to know than to be misled.

When Herb's second wife, Dorothy, died, the Welch residence descended to the Voorhees family. They left the house as they found it in 1964: painting supplies still filling the cabinets, easels standing

Herb dispensing medical advice, c. 1936. Over the years, he advertised for Jeep, Bass Shoe, and Ashaway Line and Twine.

SATURDAY EVENING POST

in corners, oils by Herb draping the walls where mounted fish loom large. Roughed out pine forms for fish mounts line a taxidermy workbench sealed by years of paint and stain. It looks as if Herb has just run down to the Mooselookmeguntic House to put a carton of Chesterfields on his running charge. (He advertised for Camels, but he smoked Chesterfields.)

Ambiance aside, the Welch house contained row after row of shop invoices and the stacks of ledger-bound canceled checks. With permission granted, we immersed ourselves in a sea of yellow paper. We are still mesmerized by the scope of the inventory, which involved hundreds of American, Canadian, and European vendors, such as Hardy, Hawes, Percy, Wheatley, Bogdan, F.E. Thomas, Parker, and Winchester.

Anything you needed for summer could be found at Welch's store: clothing by Pendelton, moccasins by Bass, blankets by Hudson Bay, pottery by Roseville, sporting goods by Spalding, games by Milton Bradley, and photo supplies by Kodak. If something was out of stock, Bernice or Dorothy Welch would order it. The store was their domain, with Herb only occasionally there for color, since his summers and autumns were dominated by guiding and his winters by taxidermy and the sportsman show circuit.

A final word on the dangers of assumptions: From *Carrie Stevens* on, we have thought it only fair to warn readers that the Hilyards are gloriously free of the world of academic writing. No writer's workshop has ever tarnished our work. In fact, our Newfoundlands are better schooled than we are. We may be devout fly fishers, enamored of all things Rangeley, but we have never abandoned our day jobs for the lure of royalties.

The vehicle we've chosen for our mea culpa is the apologia, a bit of Greek, stolen by the Romans, and usurped by the English, all meaning the same thing. Or so we assumed. Recently, we found that while an apology is exactly that, an apologia is a defense or justification of behavior—not a humble plea but a gauntlet thrown down. Uh-oh. Curious how words can mutate over time, leaving presumers floundering.

So will this mark the end of the Hilyard apologias? No more Greek or Latin? No more embellished confessions of various shortcomings? Probably not. After all, if this were a logical world, men would ride sidesaddle.

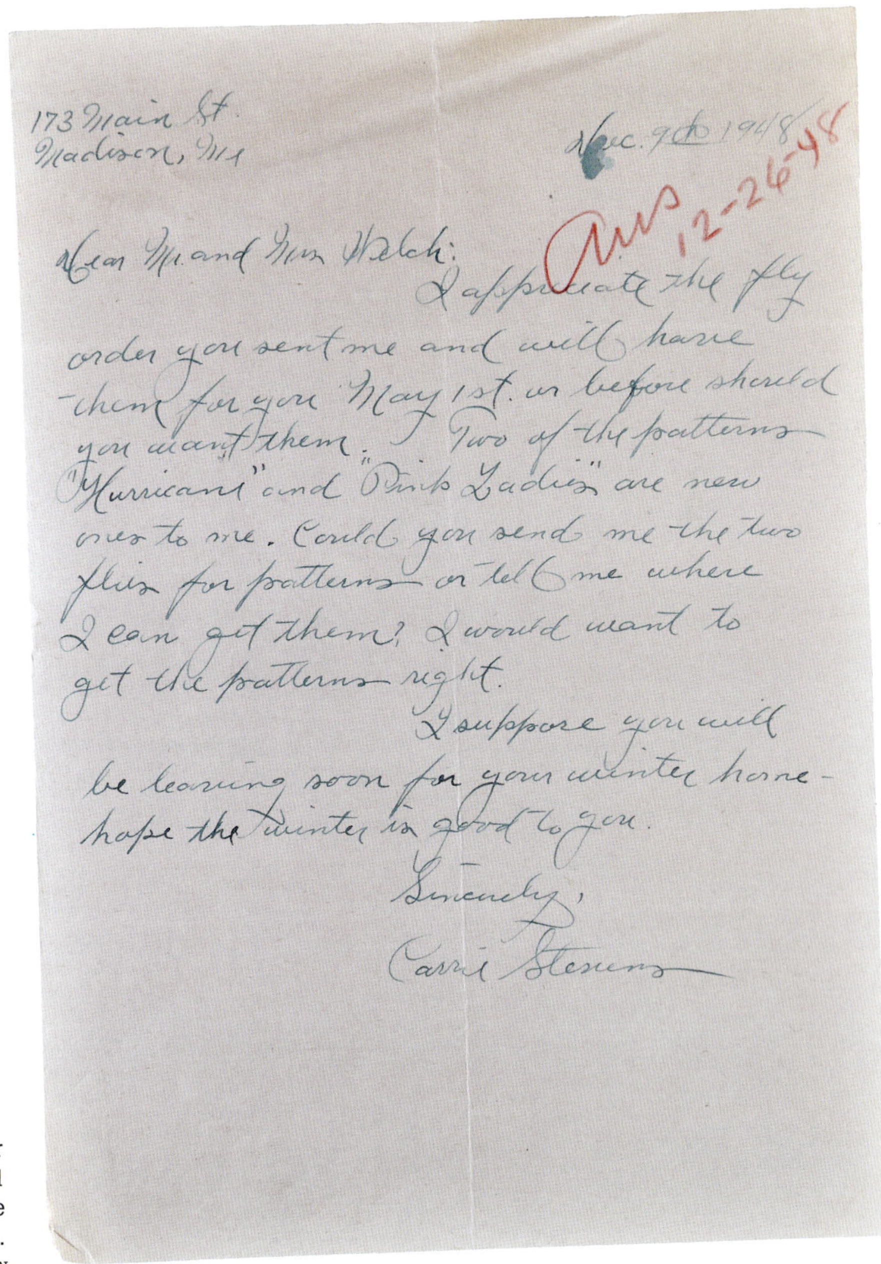

173 Main St.
Madison, Me

Dec. 9th 1948

Ans 12-26-48

Dear Mr. and Mrs. Welch:

I appreciate the fly order you sent me and will have them for you May 1st. or before should you want them. Two of the patterns "Hurricane" and "Pink Ladies" are new ones to me. Could you send me the two flies for patterns or tell me where I can get them? I would want to get the patterns right.

I suppose you will be leaving soon for your winter home - hope the winter is good to you.

Sincerely,
Carrie Stevens

Research is rarely finished. This letter proves the dangers of assumptions and proves Carrie Stevens did not originate the Pink Lady as earlier thought.
VOORHEES COLLECTION

Swan

FOREWORD

Herb Welch. I first met him sixty-six years ago, and to this day, he remains one of my heroes. Over the years, I have met many fascinating and wonderful people, but none of them can take Herb's place.

Taking the old Boston & Maine Railroad down from Nashua to North Station in Boston, I first met Herb at the old Mechanics Hall Sportsmen's Show in 1936. That was back when sportsmen shows were really sportsmen shows. Maine guides competed in log-rolling contests, Penobscot Indians roamed about, sporting celebrities like Jim Thorpe and the boxer Jack Sharkey held court. So much was going on that you needed a master of ceremonies, which every year was Chief Needabah, all decked out in full Indian regalia.

All of the really important people at the show hung out at the Ashaway Line & Twine Co. booth owned by Julian Crandall. This was where I met Herb, and we hit it off immediately. Now this was long before I was known as a reelmaker and I was just a kid, but he still took me under his wing and patiently answered all my questions, some probably not too well thought out. Rich or poor, famous or not, Herb always had time for everyone.

In 1939 I met Ted Williams at the Ashaway booth through Herb, who actually taught Ted how to fly cast at the show. Of course, with his athletic coordination it did not take him long to become a good fly caster, more on the power side than finesse. He and Jack Sharkey would give casting demonstrations (with Ted probably being the better of the two), but neither could compete with Herb. Boy, could he throw a line. At the shows I saw, he used a 10-foot bamboo rod made by Merganser with an Ashaway silk line. What a showman. When he entered a room, all eyes went to him. People just seemed to sense that they were in the presence of someone special. And he could fish too. Not many people remember that he held the *Field & Stream* record for bonefish, a 12-pound 4-ounce bone that he caught on a streamer somewhere in Florida.

Herb invited me to Haines Landing in 1936, and going there got to be a bit of a habit. Even after I married Phyllis in 1944, we visited every year for two weeks until the early '50s. We always stayed at Camp Antlers on Mooselookmeguntic, just down the shoreline from his home and shop. Back then, it was owned by Jack Lawrence. What a character he was. I once made knives for these guys and engraved their names on them—the only two knives that I ever made. You have to wonder if they might still be around after all of these years. Probably not.

We would fish Mooselook over to Upper Dam in the mornings and evenings and often spend the afternoons with Herb at his shop. His art studio was filled with beautiful paintings, many of fish, but some nice landscapes too. And to this day, he is still the best trout taxidermist that I have ever seen, and I have been all over the sporting world. But maybe what I remember best was that big glass bowl on his showcase, a monstrous thing more than a foot wide, almost totally round, and full of Carrie Stevens streamers at a dollar apiece.

Life has been so good to me and I have few regrets after all these years. But I sure do wish that I had stocked up on Carrie's streamers and Herb's brook trout.

Stanley E. Bogdan (1918–2011)
Nashua, New Hampshire
2004

A 2-by-3-inch promotional stamp for the first Campbell and Fairbanks sportsman show in 1927.
DEL PLATO COLLECTION

THE BOSTON HERALD, TUESDAY, FEBRUARY 4 1947

TED WILLIAMS AT SPORTSMEN'S SHOW chats with Chief Needahbeh of Old Town, Me., left, and Herb Welch of Rangeley Lakes, Me., New England fly-casting champion, center.

After the December 7, 1941, attack on Pearl Harbor, a twenty-six-year-old Ted Williams joined the Marines and became a fighter pilot. At age thirty-three, he served again in Korea, flying thirty-nine missions and surviving a 200 mph crash landing on February 16, 1953. Despite the wars costing him five seasons, he finished his career with 531 home runs. He is still known as the "last of the .400 hitters." But he would not know all of this during his 1947 conversation with Chief Needebah (left) and Herb Welch (center). RANGELEY SPORTING HERITAGE MUSEUM

PART I

FROM DARK FOREST TO CITY LIGHTS

CHAPTER 1

Travels

History does not record any seismic tremors on September 6, 1879. Nor does it mention glitter from a lingering meteor shower or that the sun or moon were eclipsed from earthly sight.[1]

Yet, for us enamored of blood sport history, the day was stellar. For on that date, Herbert Leon Welch was born in the provincial hamlet of Brownville, Maine.

While readers seek answers, sometimes writers can only offer questions. Such is the case with Welch's genealogy. Birth, marriage, and death records were not required by Maine law until 1892, and even when such records exist, some states release them only to descendants. Voter registration lists are useless for tracking the maternal line since they reflect the dismal fact that only males could vote prior to 1920. Incomplete state and federal documents full of misspelled names must suffice, while newspapers do their part to confuse as well. Personal correspondence was rarely kept, and if there are obituaries, they often tell us only what we already know—that the deceased is dead.

A young Herb c. 1895. RANGELEY SPORTING HERITAGE MUSEUM

Combine this with the fact that neither Herbert Welch (1879–1960) nor his only sibling, Adelaide (1874–194?), had children, and tracking family history is laborious, although not impossible. By scouring town and federal population records, town and state business registers, school and family documents, historical newspapers, and magazines, profiles began to emerge.

Three generations of birth records in Canaan, Maine, reveal that the Welches had deep Maine roots: Herb's great-grandfather, David, born in 1805; his grandfather, Oliver, in 1833; and his father, Ansel, in 1853. Ansel would marry Arvella Martha Brown on November 20, 1873, in nearby Skowhegan, Maine. Adelaide, better known as Addie, was born in November 1876, sharing her mother's Skowhegan birthplace. Pursuing work, the family moved to Brownville, Herb's birthplace, where Arvella found employment at E.M. Johnson's Millinery and Fancy Goods business. On Mrs. Johnson's retirement in 1882, Arvella took over the business.[2]

Herb's mother, Arvella,
an entrepreneurial spirit c. 1882.
RANGELEY SPORTING HERITAGE MUSEUM

A cabinet photo of Herb's sister, Adelaide, c. 1895.
RANGELEY SPORTING HERITAGE MUSEUM

Herb's father, Ansel,
a man of presence c. 1882.
RANGELEY SPORTING HERITAGE MUSEUM

The 1880 federal census has Ansel employed as a mortiser of shovel handles and keeper of horses. This could not have been an altogether satisfactory arrangement, as records consistently identify him as a horse trainer, a vitally important vocation prior to the automotive age. His not being fully involved would have had to chafe.

Nonetheless, the Welches remained in Brownville until around 1886, when the August 10 edition of the *Bangor Whig and Courier* reported: "Mr. Johnson who runs the extensive shovel handle business at Brownville is to dispose of his interests there, the change being made on the account of the scarcity of stock. The business may be removed to New Hampshire." Johnson was the sole manufacturer of shovel handles in Brownville. The "scarcity of stock" was a lack of available ash, which was considered the finest wood for handles.

The Welch name next appears in the 1891 edition of the *Maine Register and Legislation Manual*, which records a Mrs. A.M. Welch as a dressmaker and co-owner of a millinery and fancy goods store in Pittsfield, Maine. This location makes perfect sense, as Pittsfield was known as a "trotting town," with extensive harness-racing venues and breeding operations where Ansel's skills would be useful.[3] Additionally, Pittsfield borders Clinton, home to Arvella's family for generations.

While the Welches are not listed in any Pittsfield census, evidence of them is found in the records of the Maine Central Institute. Still functioning, this prestigious preparatory school was founded in Pittsfield in 1866 as a Free Baptist gateway school for Bates College of Lewiston, Maine.[4]

Both Herb and Addie are listed in the 1895 catalogue as residents of Pittsfield. Herb is registered as Third Class, College Preparatory, which places him in the final year of a three-year program. By any standards, this was a challenging program, requiring studies in Latin prose composition, Virgil, Homer, algebra, geometry, elocution, and Xenophon's *Anabasis*, a study of the 401 B.C. Greek military advance across Asia Minor, led by Cyrus the Younger.

Addie graduated from Maine Central Institute in 1895. In their *1897 History of M.C.I. Alumni and Alumnae*, we find her studying elocution with a leading teacher of the day, Marie Ware Laughton, owner of the Boston School of Expression in Boston's Copley Square. The *History* noted that "she read at the dedication of Powers' Hall of M.C.I. in February of 1897 and her Pittsfield friends had reason to feel proud of her talent. She was assigned the part of Cyril in *The Princess* when it played in Boston in the Spring of 1896." Addie would continue to impress, with the 1898 M.C.I. catalog listing her as an instructor in physical culture (an early term for physical education) and elocution (an oratory art focused on gesture, vocal production, and delivery).

By 1903, we find Addie living with her mother in Allston, Massachussetts, after her father died at age 50.[5] While there, Addie attracted the attention of Warren A. Seavey, son of a prominent Massachusetts family that traced it roots to colonial America. On December 31, 1903, a Boston justice of the peace joined them in marriage—one that would be promptly annulled.[6] (Warren would graduate from Harvard Law School in 1904 and soon

Ansel Welch at work as a horse trainer. RANGELEY SPORTING HERITAGE MUSEUM

The Maine Central Institute provided secondary education for Herb and Addie, who would later teach there. It recently passed its 150th year of operation.
PENOBSCOT MARINE MUSEUM

The Brownville school provided elementary education for Herb and Addie.
PENOBSCOT MARINE MUSEUM

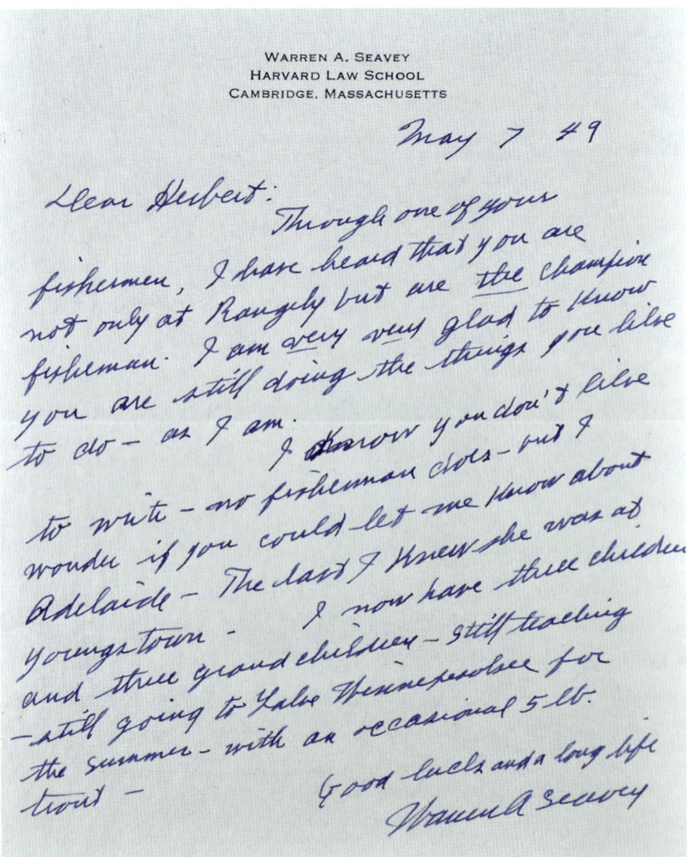

WARREN A. SEAVEY
HARVARD LAW SCHOOL
CAMBRIDGE, MASSACHUSETTS

May 7 49

Dear Herbert:
Through one of your fishermen, I have heard that you are not only at Rangely but are *the* champion fisherman. I am very very glad to know you are still doing the things you like to do – as I am.
I know you don't like to write – no fisherman does – but I wonder if you could let me know about Adelaide – The last I knew she was at Youngstown.
I now have three children and three grandchildren – still teaching – still going to Lake Winnepesaukee for the summer – with an occasional 5 lb. trout –
Good luck and a long life
Warren A Seavey

Memories linger... On May 11th Herb responded to Warren's 45 year old wistful thoughts saying?...
VOORHEES COLLECTION

afterward became a professor of law at the Imperial Pei Yang University in Tientsin, China. Eventually he returned, joining the Harvard Law School faculty, where he taught from 1925 until 1955.)[7]

Sometime between 1905 and 1910, Addie would marry a Kentucky-born man named Truman Woodward. Per the 1920 census, they resided in Austintown, a suburb of Youngstown, Ohio, where Truman worked as a chemist for a manufacturing facility. We know they had no children and that her mother lived with them from 1921 to 1925, returning to Portland where she died in 1926, but we hear no more of Addie.

It seems unlikely that the late-night prank of stuffing a cow into the belfry at the Maine Central Institute would be sufficient grounds for expulsion.[8] Nonetheless, the first inkling of the Welch family's arrival at 154 Clark Street in Portland, Maine, surfaces in the Portland High School records noting Herb's transfer and enrollment on September 29, 1895. Voter registration records indicate that Ansel preceded the family in 1893. The Panic of 1893, a serious depression causing nationwide bank failures, had destabilized the economy of small town Pittsfield and may well have put the family on the road again.

Although included in the 1895 football team photo, Herb's stay in school was brief. School records have him being "discharged on March 12, 1896." Whatever the reasons for Herb's decision not to complete his studies, a shortage of drive and determination was not among them. From 1897 to 1904, the Portland City Directory lists him as a crayon artist with a studio on Congress Street, the primary business district both then and now. These listings demonstrate his entrepreneurial spirit and substantiate family lore that he was involved in art from an early age.

Like most artists, Herb required a day job, and that was provided by the Boston Store, located just down Congress Street from his art studio. A leading department store owned by Porteous, Mitchell, and Braun, it sold dry goods, shoes, and home furnishings. This venerable landmark survived well into the 1970's, only to be crushed by the arrival of a mall.

One of Herb's tasks was to act as a window dresser, creating displays to draw in passersby. This task would prove pivotal for his future, as one such display drew in Walter D. Hinds, Portland's leading taxidermist. Part of the Boston Store's wide inventory had been brook trout that had given up the ghost. Rather than

Herb is found in the center row on the right. VOORHEES COLLECTION

The Portland Maine Bulldogs 1895 high school football team. Herb is found in the back row, second from the left.
PORTLAND EVENING EXPRESS

waste them, Herb decided to create a window display by skinning them and gluing them to canoe paddles. As Herb knew nothing of preservation techniques and how to pickle skins before mounting, it was not a stunning success. In the heat generated by a plate glass window, the fish quickly shriveled and stunk. Impressed by the creativity, if not the skill, Hinds immediately hired Herb.[9] By 1906, the Portland City Directory listed him not as a crayon artist but as a taxidermist, working from a Hinds owned building at 72 Pine Street.

Despite all his industry, it was Herb's participation in sports that captured Portland's attention. Granted, his football experiences playing right guard were limited to four games, and even less is known of his role in the 1899–1900 Portland YMCA basketball championship.[10] But baseball was a different story. Long before the days of megamillion dollar contracts for utility infielders hitting .200, there were the minor league ball yards scattered across America. While a few large cities could support the majors, it was small-town minors such as the New England League that gave baseball its national identity. According to the *New York Times* edition of April 5, 1901, the league was founded in 1886 but reorganized in 1901, creating a circuit of teams from Lowell and Haverhill, Massachusetts; Manchester, Dover, and Nashua, New Hampshire; and Bangor, Lewiston, and Portland, Maine.

Most minor leaguers of the era walked to the park, covered their own expenses, and prayed that they would not get hurt. Back then, gloves were more like mittens, spikes were really spikes, and helmets were for the military. Hopes of making it to the big leagues may have seemed delusional, but Herb would not be deterred—and for good reason.

On May 19, 1901, opening day was front-page news for the *Portland Sunday Telegram* as Portland trounced Haverhill, 19–4. Reports that "Welch retired the side by catching a flyball that was started for a hit" must have put a smile on the young shortstop's face. If not, the box score noting that he went 4 for 5, assisted in 2 double plays, and stole a base surely did. On May

Herb is found in the front row, third from the left. HILYARD COLLECTION

Although Herb owned the catcher's mitt on his jersey, he played shortstop. BOB WARREN

22, 1901, a competing Portland paper, the *Daily Eastern Argus*, reported that, once again, "Welch made quite a record with the stick, putting in 4 singles out of 5 times at bat," in a defeat of Lowell. On May 25, 1901, "the *Argus* this morning prints the averages of the Portland players up to date. Welch leads the team with a remarkable average of .476 and a fielding average percentage of .937." Rumors were circulating that the majors had interest.

On June 18, the *Argus* ran the headline:

> NERVOUS FINISH
>
> Umpire Wheelock in need of the services of an optician…
>
> The credit of the victory belonged to a young man by the name of Herbert Welch. With 3 on base in the 6th he made a stop and double play unassisted which fairly took the spectators off their feet. In the

The Welch's Clark Street home in Portland, 1895–1903.
JEFF KNAPP

> 8th, he stopped a hard drive back of second which looked way out of his reach. Each play prevented runs by Bangor.

On July 8, the *Argus* would report that enthusiasm for the intrepid shortstop was waning:

> Our infield with Welch in the game is the equal of any in the league, and our outfield, even if we are obliged to play a pitcher in the right garden, will do very well. The one uncertain point in the team at the present time is at shortstop. Welch has covered short in grand style up to date for a youngster on his first out, but now he complains of ill health and wants a vacation. This is a request management cannot afford to grant. If Welch is sick his illness has not affected his work, but of course if he does not feel able to play ball and desires to lay off, why that is his business. If Welch insists on a vacation, Manager Maehis will be obliged to go out and sign another shortstop... It is to be hoped that Welch may be able to continue in the game. For he is a pleasant, gentlemanly player with a baseball future before him.

But Welch would not return and his absence was felt immediately, as the Portlanders experienced a ten-game losing streak. They would recover to win the 1901 pennant, but inexplicably, would not field a team the following year. Seeking redemption, Herb joined the Nashua (New Hampshire) nine in 1902, recording a less impressive .203 batting average.

To this day, rumors credit Herb with having played for the Boston Red Sox, founded in 1901 as the Boston Americans. However, our conversations with Richard Brescani, VP of Red Sox Publications and Archives, and his associate, Henry Mehegan, assistant to Brescani, fail to support the claim.

Despite having no financial stakes in them back then, the majors used the minors as farm teams, raiding them at will. Scouting was sketchy at best, and there would have been no paper trail showing team interest until a player was wearing a major-league uniform. Brescani and Mehegan did confirm that a Herbert Welch briefly played shortstop for the Red Sox from September 15, 1925, until October 1, 1925, but those dates are far too late for our Herb.

That Tennessee-bred Herbert who played for the Red Sox would be only one of four other Herbert Welches we encountered in our research: one a painter from Michigan, one a wrestler from Arkansas, and one a registered Maine Guide from Skowhegan. All contemporaries, all with parallel interests, all contributing to the confusion.

So what would cause a young ballplayer on the threshold of the majors to walk off the field? Did any mysterious issues linger to haunt him in that dismal 1902 season played in Nashua? The February 16, 1936, *Hartford Courant* reports:

> Welch's baseball career was cut short by his love of the game. At the age of 17 he was playing for Portland's Pine Tree nine in the old New England League. He was slated to go on with the Boston Red Sox but before reporting, he went into the woods for a brief vacation. A torn knee ligament received in a guide's pickup game at Rangeley laid him up for a long time and it was 8 years before he touched a ball again.

A late-life interview Herb gave prior to the Connecticut Sportsmen's and Boat Show does not clear things up. Herb does not mention Nashua, nor why he could not play in Portland but could play in the Rangeley woods. At this late date, the hunt for answers is unlikely to yield a revelation. Perhaps it is best to be grateful that one shattered dream did not discourage Herb from pursuing others.

ENDNOTES

1 David McWilliams Ludlum, *The Country Journal Weather Book*, Boston: Houghton Mifflin Company, 1976, p. 36.
2 William R. Sawtell, *Slate, Rails, and Men*, vol. ii, Brownville, Maine, pp. 137–138.
3 Sanger Mills Cook, *Pittsfield on the Sebasticook*, Bangor, Maine, 1966, pp. 69–73.
4 W.H. Bunting, *A Day's Work, 1860–1920, Part II*, Thomaston, Maine: Tilbury House, 2000, p. 134.
5 "Ansel Welch Obituary," *Portland Daily Advertiser*, March 21, 1903.
6 New England Historical Genealogical Society, *Massachusetts Vital Records, 1840–1911*, No. 151, Boston, December 31, 1903.
7 Warren Abner Seavey, *Who Was Who in America with World Notables*, Marquis Who's Who, Inc., vol. iv, 1961–1968, p. 845.
8 Margaret Anderson, interview with author, July 12, 2010.
9 David A. Footer, interview with author, November 11, 2014.
10 Peter E. Gribben, *First Century of Portland High School Football*, Portland, Maine: Dale Rand Publishing, 1989, p. 6.

CHAPTER 2

Arrivals

By 1905, when Herb Welch arrived on the shores of Mooselookmeguntic Lake in the western mountains of Maine, the pioneer days were over, but not by much. Only fifty-one years had passed since the Town of Rangeley was incorporated, named for its founder, Squire James Rangeley, who owned the 30,720 acres surrounding Aquassac Lake.[1] Rangeley's pioneering enthusiasm had waned following the tragic death of his nineteen-year-old daughter, Sarah; however, his early pioneering was enough to fix his name to the Androscoggin chain of lakes and their Aquassac headwaters (Aquassac meaning "at the place of trout" in the Abenaki language).[2] Bereft of leadership and ravaged by the Civil War, growth stalled. By 1900, Rangeley had achieved a year-round population of a mere 971.[3]

While the Aquassac became Rangeley Lake, the Cupsuptic ("hemmed in by rocks"), Mooselookmeguntic ("where hunters watch moose by night"), and Umbagog ("shallow water") retained their Abenaki identities. Not so the Molechunkamunk ("crooked water") and Welakennebacook ("red water") Lakes;[4] it was another pioneer named George Frost Richardson (1790–1845) who arrived in 1832 and renamed them after himself as the Upper and Lower Richardsons. Apparently, the Allegundabagog Lake connecting the upper and lower lakes offered no such temptation to be renamed. With the raising of the Middle Dam on the Lower Richardson in 1883, the Allegundabagog would disappear, leaving behind the Narrows of today.

Richardson remained on his lakes for three years, farming and attempting development, but he was

A view of Rangeley c. 1860. RANGELEY SPORTING HERITAGE MUSEUM more speculator than pioneer. In 1835, he sold the bulk of his 24,480 acres surrounding the lakes to William Willis. Richardson's profit of $48,044 would be about $1,310,000 in today's currency. Twenty-four hours later, Willis sold out to a consortium at his same purchase price.[5]

Many believe the Andros portion of the Androscoggin River's name refers to an early Massachusetts colonial governor, Sir Edmund Andros (1637–1714), but according to *The Comparison of Indian Geographical Names* published in 1870 by J. Hammond Trumbell, the name Androscoggin appeared in print as early as 1639. This was long before the governor's arrival and his failed attempt to eradicate the Eastern Abenakis, and it explains why contemporary Andros biographies make no mention of the presumed honor.

A rare 1822 map of Maine by Moses Greenleaf in the collection of the Rangeley Sporting Heritage Museum in Oquossoc accurately depicts the chain of lakes, but only Umbagog and Mooselookmeguntic are identified by name. Not until 1888 would Maine maps consistently identify the Androscoggin Lakes by their anglicized names.

Charming as the Abenaki names are, it is best not to read too much into their translations. The Abenaki language existed only in an oral tradition and has long been dead. What little that has come down to us has been filtered through French and English ears. For example, the Androscoggin River, which may have started as the Ammerascaegin, suffered at least fifteen variants on its way to its current spelling. Most of those Abenaki variants generated by European ears are thought to translate to "fish coming in springtime."

When we corresponded with Ne-Do-Ba, a Lewiston-based Native American organization founded to maintain all things Abenaki, they replied: "We applaud your desire to 'finally get things right,' but this is an instance where it is not possible, and, in our opinion, it is best not to address place names at all."

Despite the achievements of the Englishman to the north and the Scotsman to the south, the efforts of these pioneers had little impact on Herb Welch's location, which was between those two territories. Following the structure of a five-act play, Mooselookmeguntic Lake culture would evolve from commercial enterprise rather than agrarian settlement. The stage was set around 1853 when Coe and Pingree of Salem, Massachusetts, imported Italian workers, granite, and oxen to construct the formidable Upper Dam to separate the Mooselookmeguntic from the Upper Richardson. Its purpose was to facilitate log drives from their timber holdings, ranging from the lakes region to the northwest Québec border. Prior to the dam's construction, adequate water flow from snow melt and spring rains was unpredictable, making log drives difficult. Without a sufficient push of water, it could take four years to complete a log drive from Mooselookmeguntic to Lewiston on the Androscoggin River.[6] By building and rebuilding the Upper Dam again in 1883, the Mooselookmeguntic and Cupsuptic water levels rose 11 feet, radically changing shorelines and inadvertently creating a world-renowned brook trout fishery known as the Upper Dam Pool.[7] Act I of Mooselookmeguntic's evolution was about to begin.

Prior to 1853, fishing in the Rangeley Lakes had been for subsistence, carried out by nomadic Abenakis and pioneering farmers who battled six months of winter and endless rocks. One such farmer was Joshua Gross Rich (1820–1897), who arrived from Roxbury, Massachusetts, in 1844 to settle at Stony Batter Point across the water, west of Haines Landing on Mooselookmeguntic Lake.[8] Rich quickly moved on and eventually established the Angler's Retreat on Welokennebacook Lake in 1860. Now known as the Lakewood Camps on the Lower Richardson, it remains in business, a modern holdover from an earlier golden age.

A man of many talents, Rich wrote locally for Maine newspapers and nationally for leading sporting periodicals. As a self-trained naturalist and fur broker, he dealt directly with Louis Agassiz, then the world's leading ichthyologist and the founder of Harvard University's Museum of Comparative Zoology.

The earliest known image of Upper Dam c. 1853. Recent changes have led to fears for the future of the legendary fishery.
RANGELEY SPORTING HERITAGE MUSEUM

Do not search for an imposing rock. Indian Rock is more accurately called Indian Ledges, a low-lying shelf of rocks across from the Oquossoc Angling Association.
RANGELEY SPORTING HERITAGE MUSEUM

Better known today as the Agassiz Museum or the MCZ, the museum still displays a mounted caribou supplied by Rich in the mid-1800s.

Well grounded in fishery matters, Rich's comments on early fishing methods are telling:

> We will now go back 40 years (ed. 1843), and take a look at all these trout… In those days, all of us, Natives and hunters, used a fish pole cut from the shore nearest the pools we were to fish, without, landing-net or fly-hook… We used to spear them, too—I am sorry to say, (for I am now converted)… It was a rare excitement with a big iron jack and pitch pine kindling, a small boat… one man with a paddle in the stern and another with a spear in the bow… One night at Trout Cove… Leverett and myself took in one night 100 beauties, which weighed the next morning 600 pounds. Those we sold to old Pearly Smith, the trap maker, at four cents a pound salted, and took our pay in steel beaver traps.[9]

H.O. Stanley and some of his tackle innovations. The Rangeley Spinner that he originated is still being sold today.

KNAPP COLLECTION

Theo Page (left) and H.O. Stanley (right) on the Haines Landing dock. Stanley originated the Stanley Smelt in 1895. Much later, the Stanley Streamer was originated by Leslie Hilyard.
HILYARD COLLECTION

A May 25, 1894, article in the *Industrial Journal of Bangor* established both the Reverend Zenas Thompson (1804–1882) and Joseph Ellis Ware of Farmington, Maine, as early fly fishers on Rangeley waters in 1829. Ware had recently immigrated from England and would instruct the Reverend Thompson in the use of the fly rod. Lumbermen reports of exceedingly large trout lured them to the Rangeley Lakes.

Another article in the May 15, 1909, *Lewiston Journal* by the minster's son, Fred Thompson, established their destination as "Indian Rock country." This places their location at the confluence of the Kennebago and Rangeley Rivers feeding into Cupsuptic Lake.

> It was up in the Indian Rock country where father cast the first fly. A heavier rod and not so fine a one as they use now. I have always kept it and think a good deal of it. How is it made? It is a four jointed rod, the three upper joints made of lancewood and the main part is like the English maple... I have heard Mr. Ware say that the rod he gave father dated back to the times of the Old English fishing.

These articles, published fifteen years apart and long after 1829, contain identical phrasing, and they may derive in part from the same source material. We hoped our reading of Reverend Thompson's memoirs (compiled by his grandson in 1934) would shed more light on his fishing experiences, but his writings understandably focused on his work as a Universalist minister throughout Maine and his Civil War experiences as a chaplain in the 6th Regiment of Maine Volunteers. Both of his sons served in the war as well, with one surviving and one dying in the Third Battle of Winchester in 1864. The reverend would feel guilty about this for the rest of his life, as he had prodded the fallen son into enlisting.[10]

The Stanley family of Dixfield, Maine, would prove to be the link between subsistence and recreational fishing in the Rangeley Lakes. As with the Upper Dam's creation of a premier fishery, the process was inadvertent. In 1823, Isaac Newton Stanley (1804–1881) arrived in Dixfield on the banks of the Androscoggin River. As a fur and hide broker, he made annual fall trips to Rangeley as early as the 1830s. In addition to buying bearskins, he caught brook trout by the barrel and pickled them in salt brine as part of the family's winter food supply.

In 1841, Isaac was joined by his oldest son, Henry Orville Stanley (1829–1913), who would become one of Maine's first two fish and game commissioners in 1872. With the exception of 1880, Henry would serve in that capacity until his retirement in 1905. Receiving more prestige than money from the appointment, Stanley used his entrepreneurial skills. Over the years, he derived his principal income from ownership of a general store, a grist mill, a wool carding factory, fishing tackle manufacturing, and a partnership in a fish hatchery.[11]

In a January 1908 article for Carleton's *State of Maine Sportsmen Journal* entitled "An Invaluable Scrapbook," H.O. Stanley described his early treks:

> The first time I ever saw Mooselookmeguntic and Cupsuptic Lakes there was but a narrow channel which I could wade across... The Rangeley Stream during Sept. and Oct. was the favorite resort of the large trout which came there in large numbers, and weighing 5–10 pounds each. About the 15th of October, the stream would be full of the Blueback trout... They are extinct now...
>
> In those days, no parties from out of state ever visited to my knowledge. The first one I knew to come there was my cousin, George Shephard Page of New York. He happened to visit me in Dixfield in September, I think early in the 60's. As it

H.O. Stanley, one of the the very efficient Fish Commissioners of Maine, to whom we are indebted for many favors writes at recent date:

"I am somewhat extensively engaged in fish culture outside of what I am doing for the State. I have a hatching-house here at Dixfield, where I hatch 150,000 salmon for the State, and turned into the Androscoggin River this season, and am expecting to increase the amount the coming year. I have also just established a large hatching-house (in company with Mr. George Shephard Page and George O. Hayford) at Bemis Stream, on the Mooselookmeguntic Lake, where we intend to take hundreds of thousands of spawn from the finest trout in the world. We shall hatch and turn into the lake twenty-five per cent of all we take. Shall also hatch a large amount of land-locked salmon and turn into the lake. The balance of the trout eggs, after turning in twenty-five per cent, we shall sell at a very low price to anyone wishing to stock other waters."

Forest & Stream
Sept. 18, 1873

George S. Page and his fly patterns. The upper pattern is the Page and the lower is the New Page, both tied by Leslie K. Hilyard.
HILYARD COLLECTION

An interior view of the Oquossoc Angling Association developed from a John Bicknell glass plate negative, a photographic technique that preceded film.
MORTON COLLECTION

> happened, I had arranged to go to the Rangeley's the next morning. So he joined our party and went along with us. We found plenty of large trout. He went home and took a dozen or more of these fish with him. They created considerable interest among the sportsmen of New York and many could, or would not, believe they were really brook trout until some were shown to Prof. Agassiz who pronounced them the common brook trout.

Act II was about to begin...

When George Shephard Page (1833–1892) arrived in Dixfield in 1860, he was a young businessman dealing in the chemical by-products of coal tar. Born in Readfield, Maine, to Samuel and Margaret Page, he was educated in Chelsea, Massachusetts, where his father pioneered chemical work in coal tar and paraffin varnishes. The younger Page would soon hold patents in his field and memberships in the American Chemical Society and the American and New York Pharmaceutical Societies.[12]

Yet, George Shephard Page's achievements in business would soon be overshadowed by his achievements in the national and international fisheries community. Foremost among the latter were his founding of the American Fish Cultural Association and membership in the Societie d'Acclimation of Paris and Germany's Deutsche Fischerei-Verein, two of Europe's most prestigious fisheries organizations. On his frequent consultations in Europe, Page represented the interests of the Smithsonian then focused on the science of fish propagation.[13]

International prestige notwithstanding, it was Page's work on the Mooselookmeguntic that truly defined him. Page, along with his brother, Theo, and cousin, H.O. Stanley, established fish hatcheries on Bema Stream and later at the mouth of the Rangeley River. Their techniques became the gold standard of the industry, and they would supply brook trout and blueback trout ova to the Rangeley Lakes and beyond.

Another testament to Page's abilities is the founding of the Oquossoc Angling Association, which still exists today. Prior to its 1870 organization, regional accommodations were few and spartan, often consisting of nothing more than tents and

A view of the Oquossoc Angling Association sent by Page to Hannibal Hamlin, who was vice president under Lincoln during his first term. As a gesture to the South, Andrew Johnson of Tennessee replaced Hamlin in Lincoln's second term and would later become one of two American presidents to be impeached.
RANGELEY SPORTING HERITAGE MUSEUM

lean-tos. Since September snows are not uncommon in those western mountains, this arrangment was not satisfactory. Page organized a group to lease the land at the confluence where the Kennebago and Rangeley Rivers meet Cupsuptic Lake. The group bought existing buildings on the site owned by C.T. Richardson, who stayed on as the first camp manager. The association was formally incorporated in 1870 as a private entity, with George Shephard Page as president.[14] Now, almost 150 years later, it remains the oldest organization of its kind in continuous operation.

For all his achievements, George Shephard Page will be best remembered for ushering the Rangeley brook trout fishery onto the world stage. His 1863 offering of eight brook trout, ranging from 5 to 8½ pounds each, to the editors of the *New York Times*, the *New York Evening Post*, and the *Spirit of the Times* would draw the attention of both the national and international fishing community to the Rangeley Lakes.[15]

The recent arrival of the railroads would connect urban fishers with the rustic cabins and urbane hotels that would soon line the wilderness shores. Greenheart fly rods and silken lines would replace spears and nets. Indian Rock boats that would assume the Rangeley name and guides to row them became the order of the day. The pursuit of weighty spangled brook trout irrevocably shifted the fishing of the region from the subsistence to the recreational, and Rangeley's gilded age began.

In 1876, the United States would hold its first world's fair in Philadelphia. Held on the centennial of the nation's birth and opened by President Ulysses S. Grant, it was a resounding success. Some thirty-eight nations and many states created pavilions that required two hundred acres to house them all. Thousands of objects representative of this age of invention and scientific inquiry were on display. One such display was described as follows:

> *Salvelinus fontinalis*. (Mitch) Gill & Jordan 26792. Mounted (male) Rangeley Lakes, Me. George

Shephard Page, weight 10 pounds. The largest Brook Trout on record. Taken by Geo. Shephard Page in 1867. Transported alive in a box of water (which also contained a female trout weighing 8¼ pounds) to Stanley, Morris Co. New Jersey.[16]

Seven generations of Pages and 140 years later, this same brook trout is on display at the Rangeley Sporting Heritage Museum in Oquossoc.

As the Adirondack brook trout rarely exceeded 3 pounds and their Rangeley counterparts often exceeded 8, arguing weight superiority was pointless. So the Adirondack gentry did what they could to deny the validity of the Rangeley species. Obviously the Rangeley brook trout was not a true *Salvelinus fontinalis*; at best, they were lowly lake trout. The gauntlet had been thrown down.

It has long been thought that Page's 1863 report set off a firestorm between Rangeley and the Adirondacks that was soon squelched when Louis Agassiz voted for Rangeley. While the common myth is that Agassiz was impressed by a large trout caught by Page or J. Parker Whitney of Boston, a closer reading of the archival record reveals that it was a trout caught by Senator William P. Frye of Lewiston in 1883, some twenty years after the initial New York City news reports.

This explains why our review of Harvard's Museum of Comparative Zoology fish registers dating from 1842 shed

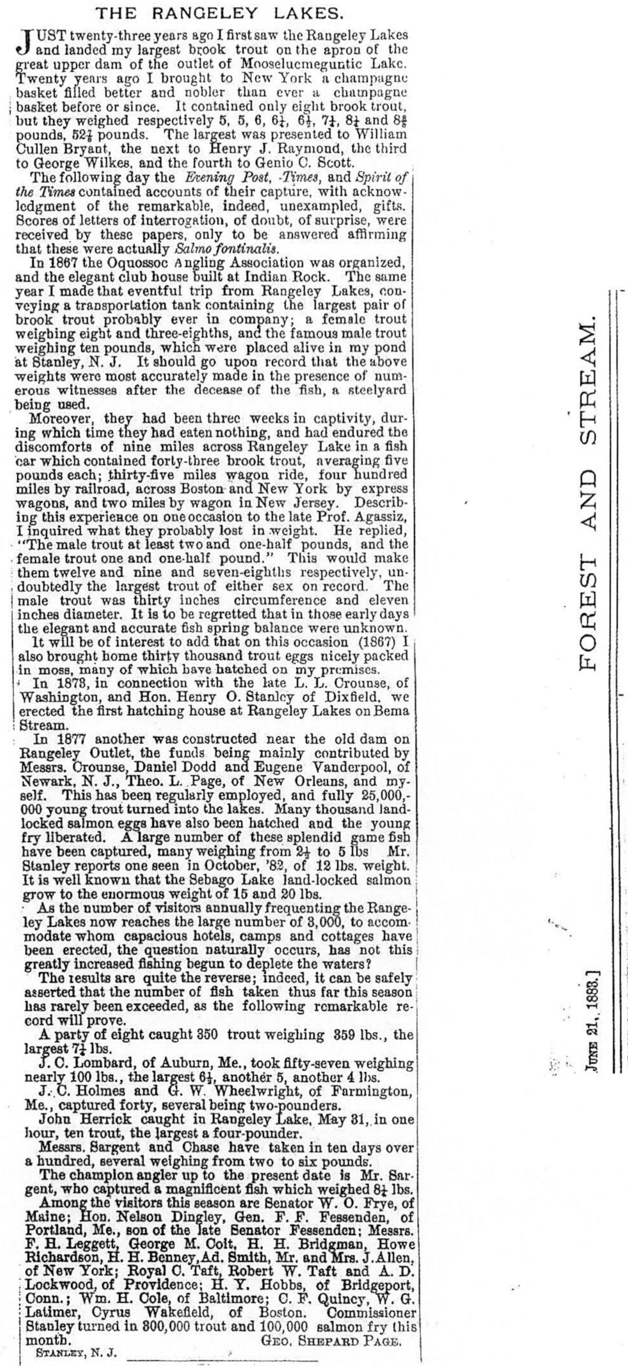

FOREST AND STREAM. June 21, 1883.

THE RANGELEY LAKES.

JUST twenty-three years ago I first saw the Rangeley Lakes and landed my largest brook trout on the apron of the great upper dam of the outlet of Mooselucmeguntic Lake. Twenty years ago I brought to New York a champagne basket filled better and nobler than ever a champagne basket before or since. It contained only eight brook trout, but they weighed respectively 5, 5, 6, $6\frac{1}{4}$, $6\frac{1}{2}$, $7\frac{1}{4}$, $8\frac{1}{4}$ and $8\frac{3}{8}$ pounds, $52\frac{7}{8}$ pounds. The largest was presented to William Cullen Bryant, the next to Henry J. Raymond, the third to George Wilkes, and the fourth to Genio C. Scott.

The following day the *Evening Post*, *Times*, and *Spirit of the Times* contained accounts of their capture, with acknowledgment of the remarkable, indeed, unexampled, gifts. Scores of letters of interrogation, of doubt, of surprise, were received by these papers, only to be answered affirming that these were actually *Salmo fontinalis*.

In 1867 the Oquossoc Angling Association was organized, and the elegant club house built at Indian Rock. The same year I made that eventful trip from Rangeley Lakes, conveying a transportation tank containing the largest pair of brook trout probably ever in company; a female trout weighing eight and three-eighths, and the famous male trout weighing ten pounds, which were placed alive in my pond at Stanley, N. J. It should go upon record that the above weights were most accurately made in the presence of numerous witnesses after the decease of the fish, a steelyard being used.

Moreover, they had been three weeks in captivity, during which time they had eaten nothing, and had endured the discomforts of nine miles across Rangeley Lake in a fish car which contained forty-three brook trout, averaging five pounds each; thirty-five miles wagon ride, four hundred miles by railroad, across Boston and New York by express wagons, and two miles by wagon in New Jersey. Describing this experience on one occasion to the late Prof. Agassiz, I inquired what they probably lost in weight. He replied, "The male trout at least two and one-half pounds, and the female trout one and one-half pound." This would make them twelve and nine and seven-eighths respectively, undoubtedly the largest trout of either sex on record. The male trout was thirty inches circumference and eleven inches diameter. It is to be regretted that in those early days the elegant and accurate fish spring balance were unknown.

It will be of interest to add that on this occasion (1867) I also brought home thirty thousand trout eggs nicely packed in moss, many of which have hatched on my premises.

In 1873, in connection with the late L. L. Crounse, of Washington, and Hon. Henry O. Stanley of Dixfield, we erected the first hatching house at Rangeley Lakes on Bema Stream.

In 1877 another was constructed near the old dam on Rangeley Outlet, the funds being mainly contributed by Messrs. Crounse, Daniel Dodd and Eugene Vanderpool, of Newark, N. J., Theo. L. Page, of New Orleans, and myself. This has been regularly employed, and fully 25,000,000 young trout turned into the lakes. Many thousand landlocked salmon eggs have also been hatched and the young fry liberated. A large number of these splendid game fish have been captured, many weighing from $2\frac{1}{2}$ to 5 lbs Mr. Stanley reports one seen in October, '82, of 12 lbs. weight. It is well known that the Sebago Lake land-locked salmon grow to the enormous weight of 15 and 20 lbs.

As the number of visitors annually frequenting the Rangeley Lakes now reaches the large number of 3,000, to accommodate whom capacious hotels, camps and cottages have been erected, the question naturally occurs, has not this greatly increased fishing begun to deplete the waters?

The results are quite the reverse; indeed, it can be safely asserted that the number of fish taken thus far this season has rarely been exceeded, as the following remarkable record will prove.

A party of eight caught 350 trout weighing 359 lbs., the largest $7\frac{1}{4}$ lbs.

J. C. Lombard, of Auburn, Me., took fifty-seven weighing nearly 100 lbs., the largest $6\frac{1}{2}$, another 5, another 4 lbs.

J. C. Holmes and G. W. Wheelwright, of Farmington, Me., captured forty, several being two-pounders.

John Herrick caught in Rangeley Lake, May 31, in one hour, ten trout, the largest a four-pounder.

Messrs. Sargent and Chase have taken in ten days over a hundred, several weighing from two to six pounds.

The champion angler up to the present date is Mr. Sargent, who captured a magnificent fish which weighed $8\frac{1}{4}$ lbs.

Among the visitors this season are Senator W. O. Frye, of Maine; Hon. Nelson Dingley, Gen. F. F. Fessenden, of Portland, Me., son of the late Senator Fessenden; Messrs. F. H. Leggett, George M. Coit, H. H. Bridgman, Howe Richardson, H. H. Benney, Ad. Smith, Mr. and Mrs. J. Allen, of New York; Royal C. Taft, Robert W. Taft and A. D. Lockwood, of Providence; H. Y. Hobbs, of Bridgeport, Conn.; Wm. H. Cole, of Baltimore; C. F. Quincy, W. G. Latimer, Cyrus Wakefield, of Boston. Commissioner Stanley turned in 300,000 trout and 100,000 salmon fry this month.

GEO. SHEPARD PAGE.

STANLEY, N. J.

George Shepherd Page recounts twenty-three years of Rangeley memories.

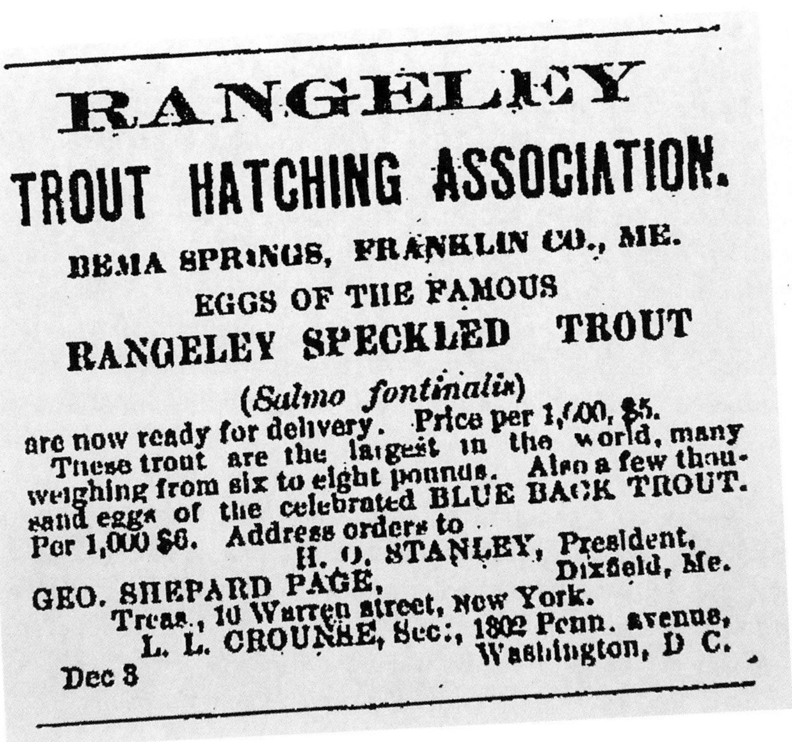

An 1875 *Forest & Stream* advertisement for Rangeley genetic stock. Early on, the importance of blueback trout was recognized.

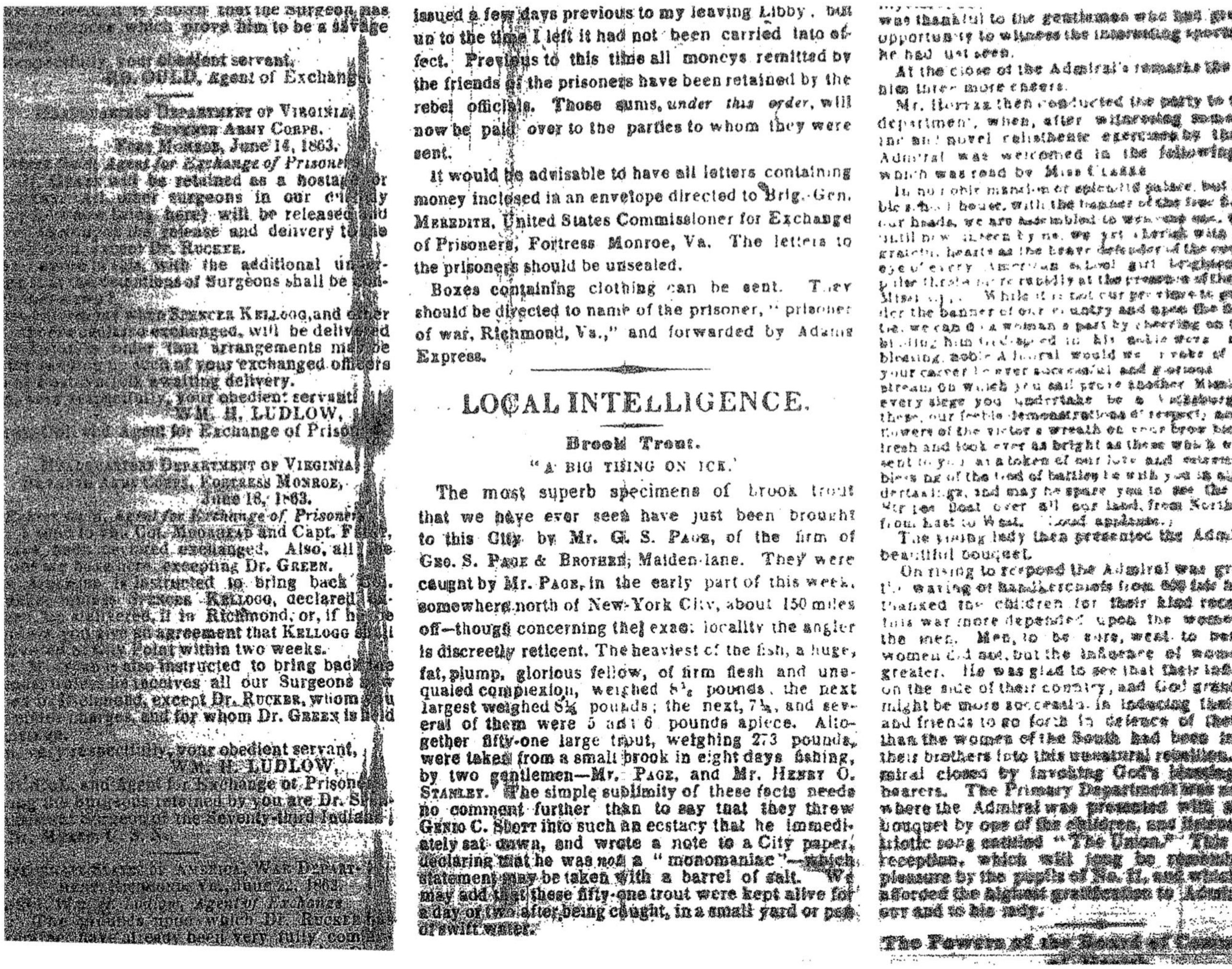

issued a few days previous to my leaving Libby. But up to the time I left it had not been carried into effect. Previous to this time all moneys remitted by the friends of the prisoners have been retained by the rebel officials. Those sums, *under this order*, will now be paid over to the parties to whom they were sent.

It would be advisable to have all letters containing money inclosed in an envelope directed to Brig.-Gen. Meredith, United States Commissioner for Exchange of Prisoners, Fortress Monroe, Va. The letters to the prisoners should be unsealed.

Boxes containing clothing can be sent. They should be directed to name of the prisoner, "prisoner of war, Richmond, Va.," and forwarded by Adams Express.

LOCAL INTELLIGENCE.

Brook Trout.

"A BIG THING ON ICE."

The most superb specimens of brook trout that we have ever seen have just been brought to this City by Mr. G. S. Page, of the firm of Geo. S. Page & Brother, Maiden-lane. They were caught by Mr. Page, in the early part of this week, somewhere north of New-York City, about 150 miles off—though concerning the exact locality the angler is discreetly reticent. The heaviest of the fish, a huge, fat, plump, glorious fellow, of firm flesh and unequaled complexion, weighed 8½ pounds, the next largest weighed 8¼ pounds; the next, 7¾, and several of them were 5 and 6 pounds apiece. Altogether fifty-one large trout, weighing 273 pounds, were taken from a small brook in eight days fishing, by two gentlemen—Mr. Page, and Mr. Henry O. Stanley. The simple sublimity of these facts needs no comment further than to say that they threw Genio C. Scott into such an ecstacy that he immediately sat down, and wrote a note to a City paper, declaring that he was not a "monomaniac"—which statement may be taken with a barrel of salt. We may add that these fifty-one trout were kept alive for a day or two after being caught, in a small yard or pen of swift water.

The *New York Times* reporting that launched the Rangeley's gilded age, October 17,1863. NEW YORK PUBLIC LIBRARY

no light on the first responder's identity. We had been warned that the registers were not necessarily definitive, as only fish kept by the ichthyology department were logged. Many fish came and went without a trace, and when the collection was purged in 1938, many logged physical specimens were lost as well. No matter; there is still something inherently seductive about the museum's leatherbound pages where a flowing script records the presence of a Seth Green, J.G. Rich, A. Nelson Cheney, Spencer F. Baird, and George B. Goode of the Smithsonian, and Agassiz, father and son. Equally entrancing is the geographic scope, with the registers recording specimens from East India, Europe, Cuba, Singapore, Java, Bavaria, Arabia, Zanzibar, the Gulfs of Maine and Mexico, the Cape of Good Hope, and the world's largest lake, Siberia's Baikal. No ivory tower recluse, Agassiz haunted the Boston and Fulton fish markets, sailed to the Galapagos Islands in the wake of Darwin, and ventured up and down the Amazon in search of unknown species.

Closer to home, Agassiz organized an 1858 Adirondack expedition to which renowned poet Henry Wadsworth Longfellow was invited. But when Longfellow asked, "Is it true that Emerson was going to take a gun?" and was told yes, he responded, "Then somebody will be shot" and refused to go along.[18]

So not only have we contemporary writers gotten the Rangeley trout to Agassiz attribution all wrong, but we are also guilty of changing the chronology of events. What we saw as a brief skirmish between the warring states of Rangeley and the Adirondacks turns out to have been a twenty-year war. And when a young genealogist named Jack Palmer of Long Island, New York, shook the dust from some New York Public Library archives, he emerged with the opening volley in the Rangeley-Adirondack War, a New York Times report not seen since October of 1963.

In the winter of 1869, a seventeen-year-old Andover lad named Fred C. Barker (1852–1933) with seventy-four cents in his pocket snowshoed the frozen Richardsons to Upper Dam in search of work. Finding none, he pushed on through the night another 7 miles across Mooselookmeguntic Lake to a logging camp at Bemis Stream. There, he attracted the attention of Squire John Toothaker, the region's leading timber baron. Impressed by the motivation and stamina of the 75-pound lad, he offered a college education, with the promise of a bookkeeping position on graduation. But Barker was focused on woodcraft, trapping, and guiding, so he politely declined. However, the Squire would not forget him. In 1876, when Barker need a $175 loan for a steamboat purchase, Toothaker immediately granted it. Act III on Mooselookmeguntic Lake was about to begin.

After seven years of guiding, trapping, and running log drives in the Rangeley Lakes region, young Barker had both the capital and the experience to unleash his entrepreneurial spirit. He obtained a State of Maine master's license to captain a growing fleet of steam vessels, which would ultimately connect his three enterprises that defined the Mooselookmeguntic shoreline for decades.

In the fall of 1876, Barker bought the steamer *Mollychunkamunk* from Captain C.W. Howard of Rangeley. Renaming her the *Oquossoc*, he ran the steamer about the Mooselookmeguntic, using Indian Rock and the Oquossoc Angling Association as headquarters. The steamer made daily trips to the Upper Dam, connecting with boats on the Rangeley and Upper Richardson Lakes.[19]

Barker acquired the *Reindeer* in 1884, but due to the steamer's insufficient size, he quickly sold it to Captain Elmer Thomas, who transported it to Kennebago Lake. Renamed the *Caribou*, it steamed between the Kennebago Lake House and the Kennebago Falls and connected to Seven Ponds near the Québec border.[20] That same year its 45-foot replacement was built and named *Metalluk*, for the last survivor of the band of Abenakis who had lived around the Richardson Lakes. A roadside marker in Stewartstown, New Hampshire, now notes Metalluk's passing, while more permanent tributes are found on the Lower Richardson, where a mountain, an island, and a brook bear his name.

Per a Phillips Phonograph newspaper account dated April 14, 1886, Barker's next steamer was named the *Mollelocket* and was towed by horses across a frozen Rangeley Lake to Bemis Camps on Mooselookmeguntic Lake. This 20½-mile trip took only four hours and eight minutes. With its arrival, Barker eliminated the original *Oquossoc* from his fleet.

The Barker image is the frontispiece to his autobiography, *Lake and Forest As I Have Known Them*, written in 1903. The Captain Barker Streamer was orginated and tied by Leslie K. Hilyard. HILYARD COLLECTION

While no firm date exists, per Captain Barker's *Lake and Forest As I Have Known Them*, he continued his custom of naming ships after members of local indigenous tribes and called his next steamer the *Oozalluc*. Mollelocket was a member of the Pequawket tribe and a well-regarded midwife who assisted in the birth of Susan Merrill, the first white child born in Andover, Maine.[21] Adding symmetry to the earlier ship *Metalluk*, the *Oozalluc* was named for Metalluk's second wife. While these Native Americans preceded Captain Barker by a generation, they were well known to his Andover relatives.

Steamboats on Mooselookmeguntic Lake were small compared to those on Moosehead and Sebago, Maine's largest lakes. This was a result of their environment, as the landing sites were tight, shallow, and guarded by rocks. Although the construction of Upper Dam had raised water levels 11 feet, that level was only maintained during log drives.[22] Hazards to navigation abounded the rest of the time, requiring great skill and fervent prayers that the wind would stay down.

In 1896, Florence E. Barker christened the 65-foot flagship of her father's fleet the *Florence E. Barker*. It must've been a time of mixed emotions for the Captain. While the vessel was named for his young daughter, Florence E. Barker, that name had also belonged to his young wife who died giving birth, a tragedy reminiscent of his own mother's death when he was only one. As the young Captain never remarried, it is doubtful that his pain was ever interred.

The final steamship in the Barker fleet was the *Senator William P. Frye*, bought from C.W. Howard in 1908 for $1,300. The Captain had long been friendly with the congressional senator from Maine, so he retained the steamer's original name.

The *Florence E. Barker* and her namesake, the captain's only child. HILYARD COLLECTION

A view of Bemis Camps c. 1880 (note the cleft rock) where young Barker often slept when on log drives from Bemis to Upper Dam. MCLAUGHLIN COLLECTION

The interior of the Bemis station. The inside hanging of an evergreen is known as "topping out." It is symbolic of a completed structure and remains a time-honored tradition in the construction trade. RANGELEY SPORTING HERITAGE MUSEUM

By 1879, Captain Barker's steamship routes were so firmly established that he could give up guiding. However, competition was encroaching and there was no room for expansion on adjacent lakes. The Rangeley Lake routes were locked in by friends whom he had no interest in alienating. As to the Richardsons, Maine had given a monopoly to Charles Farrar of Massachusetts to operate passenger steamships from 1877 through 1888.[23] Again, the Barker entrepreneurial spirit surfaced when he realized that by creating shoreline destinations, he could control the passenger and freight service to them.

Attaching dates to Captain Barker's early life can be a fool's errand. Not even he would attempt to give specific dates in his autobiographical *Lake and Forest*, written in 1903. Nonetheless, we feel compelled to do what we can, extrapolating dates from credible sources and buoyed by sole access to unpublished documents contained in the Barker-Harnden and George Shephard Page family archives.

If some dates appear to be too close to one another, remember that Barker had a full calendar in every season. Spring was for log driving, summer was for guiding, fall was for education, and winter was for

The Birches on Students Island that fell to fire in 1925. The few remaining camps were hauled across the ice to join the Barker Hotel. HARNDEN COLLECTION

either Massachusetts factory work or Maine trapping. Often, the work seasons would overlap. From age twelve on, Fred C. Barker was at full throttle and immune to sleep.

A review of land deeds indicates that Captain Barker signed a five-year lease at $75 a year with L.L. Crouse, E.S. Coe, and David Pingree in 1880. That deed gave him the rights to build camps and roadways on and to lumber the land surrounding his recently purchased Buckfield and Canton Railroad Camps at the mouth of Beema Stream entering Mooselookmeguntic Lake.[24]

Originally, the railroad camps had been built by L.L. Crouse, H.M. Hutchinson, and George Shephard Page to escape the heavy fishing pressure on both the Rangeley and Kennebago Rivers flowing to their Oquossoc Angling Association. The pressure became so heavy that the state shut the rivers down from 1877 to 1881 to allow the stocks to replenish. Concerned by the fishery depletion and sensing a business opportunity, Page, Crouse, and H.O. Stanley constructed the first fish hatchery on the lakes in 1873, some 2 to 3 miles up Beema Stream.[25] Having taken over the Beema Stream area lease, Barker took charge of the upstream hatchery in 1876 since by then Page and Stanley had moved their hatchery operation to the mouth of the Rangeley River. A November 1895 *Rumford Falls Times* interview with Barker notes:

> the spring and hatch house are full of trout and he finds it necessary to keep two men there in charge of the place in order to keep the Italians and other railroad laborers from slaughtering the fish. He is not shipping any eggs this fall, but is letting nature take its course after which they will be taken out of the spring and placed in the lake.

Over time, Beema Stream became Bema, but not necessarily the Bemis of today, which initially referred to the hamlet that grew beside the railway tracks of the standard-gauge Rumford Falls & Rangeley Lakes Railroad. Despite its past prominence in Mooselookmeguntic Lake culture, and despite Bemis Mountain to the south, the source of the name Bemis remains cloudy. The September 12, 1902, edition of the *Maine Woods* (from Phillips, Maine) notes that the ticket agent at Bemis posted a sign saying "the camp was named for an old hunter that camped here." Other than that, we have not found any other reference to the Bemis surname.

Accessing Barker's Camp Bemis—located on a broad expanse of Mooselookmeguntic Lake called Bemis Bay, which is still famous for its northwest gale winds—was not for the faint of heart. However,

the Barker charm paired with an excellent fishery prevailed. The original camps were soon replaced by nine log cabins and a six-room lodge with a capacity of sixty guests. With the construction of the railroad in 1896, arrival became less harrowing.

While today Bemis is a quiet grouping of quiet camps, it was not always so. Back then, there were no roads. Instead, the company store, dance hall, boardinghouses, school, and a cluster of homes bordered both sides of a standard-gauge railroad track. Initially, the railroad's function was to transport wooden products made from birch logs boomed across Mooselookmeguntic to the mills at Bemis. However, it did not take long for management to recognize the value of tourism, and passenger cars were added to the freight. Under Captain Barker's supervision, the Bemis train station was built of logs. It would become the focal point of the wilderness hamlet until it burned in 1921 and was rebuilt in the Arts and Crafts style.[26]

The Bemis train station designed and built by Captain Barker c. 1896. It is often described as the only log train station in America, which seems unlikely.
RANGELEY SPORTING HERITAGE MUSEUM

Both refined and rustic, the Barker Hotel and Camps were Mooselookmeguntic's premier destination from 1902 until 1966. HARNDEN COLLECTION

With Camp Bemis consistently at capacity, Captain Barker signed a five-year lease at $50 per year with Coe and Pingree in 1885. This granted him a northerly lot on Students Island, a 100-acre island 4 miles offshore from Camp Bemis and roughly in the center of Mooselookmeguntic Lake. Subsequent leases at the rate of $300 per year gave him rights to the entire island.

Students Island took its name from three Yale students who had built a camp there around 1850. Students being students, the name did not conjure up images of idyllic reverie. No stranger to marketing, the Captain changed the name of the camps from Students Island to the Birches, after the trees that lined the shores of the northern part of the island. Later, when there were twenty-eight camps and a main lodge capable of housing 125 guests, fire struck. With eleven cabins and the lodge in ashes, the Birches shut down in 1925.

Fire was not the major cause of change, however. Captain Barker sensed that his guests were beginning to prefer a more genteel style of vacationing. More and more, he was fielding questions about the accommodations, the dining, and the availability of social activities. More and more, he was greeting people who would never set foot in a Rangeley boat. Once again, his entrepreneurial drive and foresight would serve him well.

The 1901 extension of the Rumford Falls and Rangeley Lakes Railroad from Bemis to Oquossoc gave the Captain an opportunity. In 1902, on his earlier purchase of 1,300 feet of Mooselookmeguntic shoreline at Sandy Point, the Barker Hotel opened. With Bald Mountain looming in the background, the three-and-a-half-story structure offered thirty-five rooms of shelter to guests and staff. With a Queen Anne shingle style reminiscent of coastal resorts, the hotel's towering glass-enclosed cupola offered majestic views of New Hampshire's Mount Washington. Fanning out below, thirty-two cabins lined the white birch-lit lawns sloping to the water's edge, where a 135-foot wharf met the *Florence E. Barker*, the *Senator Frye*, and other private launches. Graced by a well-trained staff, the elegant dining room was flanked by great rooms full of books, billiard tables, and grand pianos. Noble game mounts gazed down from the wooden walls at contented guests, who could number over 200. Unquestionably, the Barker was the crown jewel of the Captain's life's work.

Captain Barker was not alone on Mooselookmeguntic Lake. Others had preceded him as camp and hotel owners, offering both opportunity and competition. The primitive Upper Dam Camps, where Barker had first sought work in 1869, had expanded into the Upper Dam House and adjacent camps that were capable of housing 60 guests and overlooked the Upper Dam Pool, which harbored many of America's largest brook trout.

In 1877, George Soule of Rangeley built the first public house at Haines Landing. In 1884, his son, Billy Soule, built the Pleasant Island Camps on Cupsuptic

An image of the Barker Hotel c. 1904, developed from a Bicknell glass plate negative. Per Barker, its construction was prompted by a desire "[t]o leave something in the troubled wake, to show that we have passed."
MORTON COLLECTION

An image of the Upper Dam House and Camps c. 1904, developed from a Bicknell glass plate negative. Due to its remoteness, the hotel raised its own food supply, stabled horses and cows, and raised poultry. MORTON COLLECTION

A hand-colored photograph by Bicknell of the remaining three log cabins on the waterfront at Haines Landing that were originally built in 1898. BEISLER COLLECTION

Advertisement from 1909 for Bald Mountain Camps found in *Maine Woods* and *Maine Sportsman*. PHILBRICK COLLECTION

Lake, from which he ran two steamers: the *Maysie* and the *Cupsuptic*. Two years later, Rufus Crosby and Walter Twombly bought George Soule's fifty-room hotel and re-named it the Mooselookmeguntic House. Combining a camp experience with hotel amenities, three log cabins were added in 1898 that were linked by a shared porch.[27] In 1890, Samuel Hano of Allston, Massachusetts, completed construction of the Birch Island Camps on Cupsuptic Lake. When he moved on in 1892 to build Sagamore Lodge on Quimby Pond, he sold the five camps to Billy Soule.

In 1897, Edward Whorff opened the Bald Mountain Camps on the eastern shore, which consisted of six log

This Mooselookmeguntic House at Haines Landing image c. 1904 was developed from a Bicknell glass plate negative. MORTON COLLECTION

An interior view of the Mooselookmeguntic House c. 1910. Early interior shots are rare, as wide angle lenses were not readily available until the late 1920s. PALMER COLLECTION

cabins in the shadow of Bald Mountain. A half-mile hike to the summit offered guests a panoramic view of Rangeley and Mooselookmeguntic Lakes.

While Mooselookmeguntic's far shore was slow to develop due to Coe and Pingree's land lease–only policy, it was not so on the eastern shore. In 1903, John Decker of Weld, Maine, bought 17,927 feet of shoreline ranging from Haines Landing to Bugle Cove from his employer, Hugh Chisolm, president of the International Paper Company in Rumford, Maine. Known as the Decker Purchase, it was divided into 158 lots to be sold, not leased.[28] This did not mean that 158 camps would eventually crowd the shoreline; many buyers purchased multiple adjacent lots to build on for one family, if at all.

Founded on two preexisting camps built in 1902, Arthur Gautier's Camp Wildwood was faith-based. Hidden behind Shelter Island on the west shore diagonally across from Haines Landing, Camp Wildwood and its chapel were accessible only by water. Nonetheless, a church bell called the faithful for a daily 7:30 morning Mass and a 10:00 Mass on Sunday. Built in 1917 by Arthur Gauthier's half brother, Rev. Eugene Trombley of Chicoutimi, Québec, the chapel design reflected his Québécois origins. An

Sabbath on Mooselookmeguntic Lake

For most nine-year-old kids, their first brush with freedom comes with their first bicycle. Not mine, however. I grew up at Bald Mountain Camps, owned by my grandparents, Rose and Ronald Turmenne. That meant my dooryard was Mooselookmeguntic Lake and my first "bicycle" was a Rangeley boat.

Weather permitting, every Sunday I set off 7 miles to Upper Dam to pick up Lynwood Johnson and take him to church at the Wildwood Cove Chapel. Sometimes it was foggy, sometimes windy, but I was brought up Catholic and getting to Mass was important. When I got older, I became an altar boy, and so getting to Wildwood Cove became even more important. A 10-horse Johnson motor on a Rangeley boat can be slow going in rough weather, but Father Boucher and the ten to fifteen people in the chapel always waited for us, singing hymns while I changed into my robes.

Considering Mooselook's temperamental nature and how that Sunday crossing was about an 18-mile round-trip, maybe the young boy was not alone as much as he thought he was.

Stephen Philbrick
Bald Mountain Camps
Mooselookmeguntic Lake
2015

The Wildwood Cove Chapel, built in 1917 by Rev. Eugene Trombley. Recently disassembled and stored, it awaits funding for restoration and relocation on a more accessible site.
TURMENNE COLLECTION

An interior view of the chapel. The two seraphim now kneel in Oquossoc's Lady of the Lakes Chapel, founded in 1909 by Cornelia "Fly Rod" Crosby.
TURMENNE COLLECTION

unpublished manuscript entitled *Wildwood Remembered*, written by family member Dennis Breton, describes the chapel best:

> Its log construction was unusual for the area in that the logs were perpendicular to the ground rather than the customary parallel log construction... approximately 12 feet wide, 15 feet high, and 22 feet in length...
>
> Furnishings included: a pair of angel statues that were placed on either side of the altar, a statue of the Sacred Heart, candlesticks, a bell for the belfry, chimes to be used at the consecration, vestments, hand carved stations of the cross, pump organ, and oil cloth altar front intricately painted with the likeness of Saint Joseph...
>
> Father Trombley built the altar, mainly from mahogany salvaged from a sunken boat. While the chapel did not have stained-glass windows, the windows were attractively painted with religious motifs.

Reuben G. Allerton c. 1870, founder of the Oquossoc Angling Association and author of *About Brook Trout.*
OQUOSSOC ANGLING ASSOCIATION

Two camps of note far preceded the Decker Purchase, built in 1875 by Allerton and Frye, two founding members of the Oquossoc Angling Association. Reuben G. Allerton (1834–1877) of New York City, established his lodge high on a 50-foot bluff overlooking Bugle Cove on the eastern shore of Mooselookmeguntic. A deeply religious man, as well as the first treasurer of the Oquossoc Angling Association and treasurer of the Goodyear India Rubber Company of New York City, he remains best known for his book *About Brook Trout*. Published in 1869 and dedicated to George Shephard Page, its fifty illustrated pages give a detailed account of a week-long fishing trip to the Oquossoc Angling Association.

While the menus amuse (with their descriptions of birch bark napkins and trout rib toothpicks), the results of the eight fishers' six days of fishing astound. They took thirty brook trout, weighing a total of

With its embossed gold trout and lettering, *About Brook Trout* covers are also found in red and brown leather.
HILYARD COLLECTION

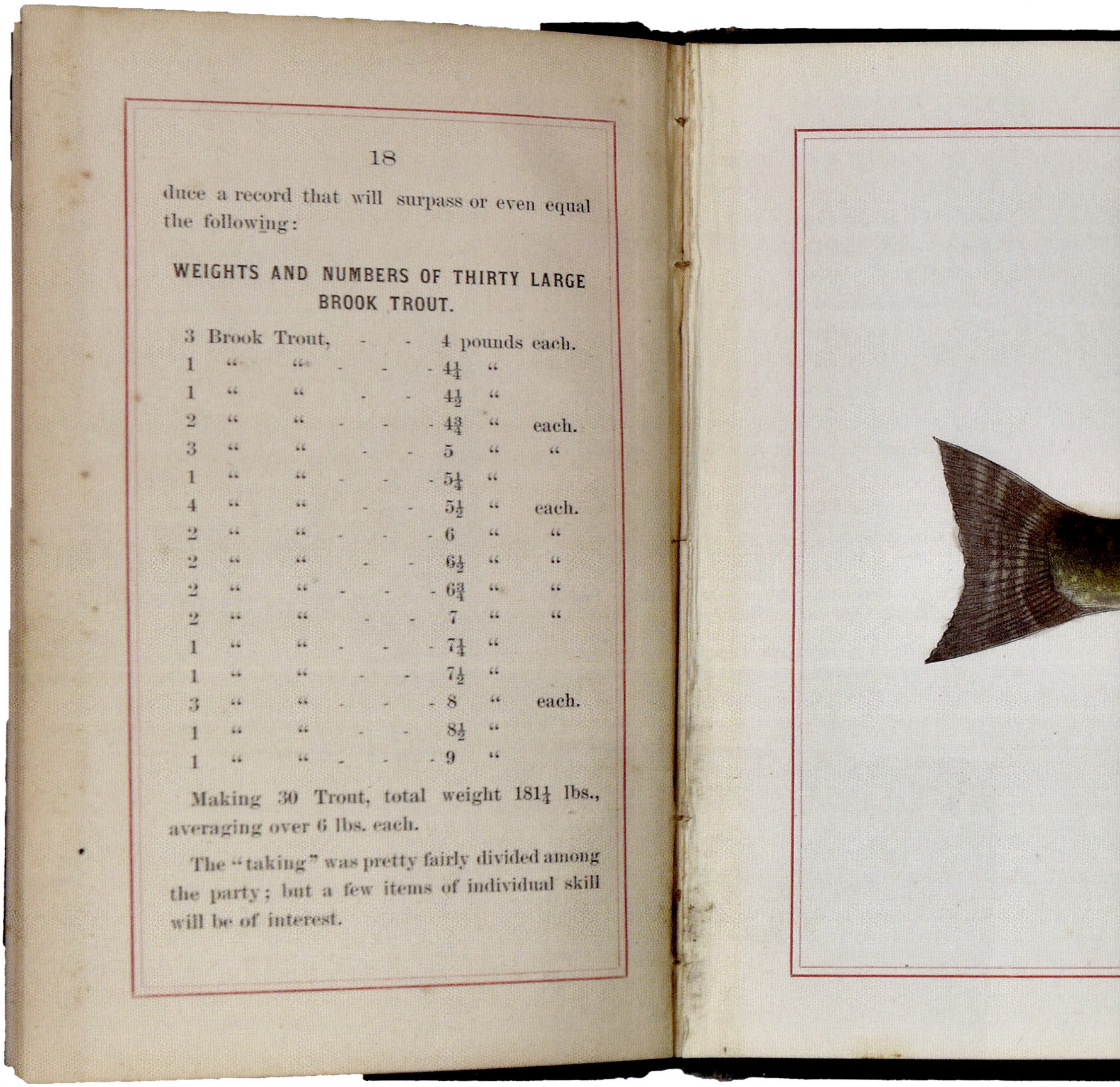
18

duce a record that will surpass or even equal the following:

WEIGHTS AND NUMBERS OF THIRTY LARGE BROOK TROUT.

3 Brook Trout,	- -	4 pounds	each.
1 " "	- - - -	4¼ "	
1 " "	- -	4½ "	
2 " "	- - - -	4¾ "	each.
3 " "	- -	5 "	"
1 " "	- - - -	5¼ "	
4 " "	- -	5½ "	each.
2 " "	- - - -	6 "	"
2 " "	- -	6½ "	"
2 " "	- - - -	6¾ "	"
2 " "	- -	7 "	"
1 " "	- - - -	7¼ "	
1 " "	- -	7½ "	
3 " "	- - - -	8 "	each.
1 " "	- -	8½ "	
1 " "	- - - -	9 "	

Making 30 Trout, total weight 181¼ lbs., averaging over 6 lbs. each.

The "taking" was pretty fairly divided among the party; but a few items of individual skill will be of interest.

181¼ pounds. The smallest weighed in at 4 pounds while the largest was 9 pounds. Volumes have been written on the Rangeley Lakes, but *About Brook Trout* remains the most sought-after by collectors. A centerfold watercolor painting of a brook trout titled *The Angler's Pride* by Helen D. Findlay adds to its appeal. According to Allerton's advertising, each painting in each book is exactly that: an original painting and not a print. How many of these rare leather-bound books still exist is unknown. The low hundreds is a reasonable estimate, each going today for over $1,000. It would be far better if you could still order directly from R.G. Allerton, who would have charged you $1.50 for a copy. The 7-inch-by-11-inch brook trout image was available separately for $1.00, and framing was offered for an additional $1.50.

By 1875, William P. Frye (1831–1911) was rising through Maine's political ranks, starting in the House of Representatives and ending as Attorney General. He then spent ten years in the national House of

The Angler's Pride, painted by Helen D. Findlay. Sadly, the image is often cut out of Allerton's book reducing its value.
HILYARD COLLECTION

Representatives before moving on to the Senate for another thirty years. Seven of the Senate years were spent as Vice President, following the death of a sitting Vice President and the assassination of William McKinley. When not in Congress, Frye could be found fishing from his Camp Frye, built in 1875 on a small island bordering Cupsuptic Lake and guarding the entrance to the Mooselookmeguntic.

In 1906, Garret Hobart built Abenaki Lodge adjacent to Camp Frye. The camps were linked closely as were the families, bound by Republican politics and marriage. Sadly, as President pro tempore, Senator Frye would replace the dying Garret Hobart as Vice President of the United States in 1899.

No matter what their achievements, some people are best remembered for seemingly lesser accomplishments. Such is the case for Senator Frye, who

Louis Agassiz, founder of Harvard's Museum of Comparative Zoology. Harvard recruited Agassiz away from Frederick Wilhelm IV of Prussia in 1847 by offering the chair of zoology and geology and an annual salary of 1,500 dollars. HOUGHTON LIBRARY

was confronted by Professor Louis Agassiz in a classic case of the academic versus the layman:

> Prof Agassiz Was Convinced.
>
> In the first speech Senator Frye made after being elected to the Senate he made mention of the very large brook trout caught in the Rangeley lakes, weighing from 1 to 7 or 8 pounds, and when on his way to his hotel Professor Agassiz overtook him and congratulated him on his speech, saying it was a very credible effort, but advised him that whenever hereafter he mentioned the brook trout, the speckled trout, or the squaretailed trout, not to have them quite so large, as there was never a brook trout that weighed over 3 pounds. The Senator asked him if he was open to conviction, and he said if he saw one weighing more he would believe it, not otherwise. When Congress adjourned the Senator went home

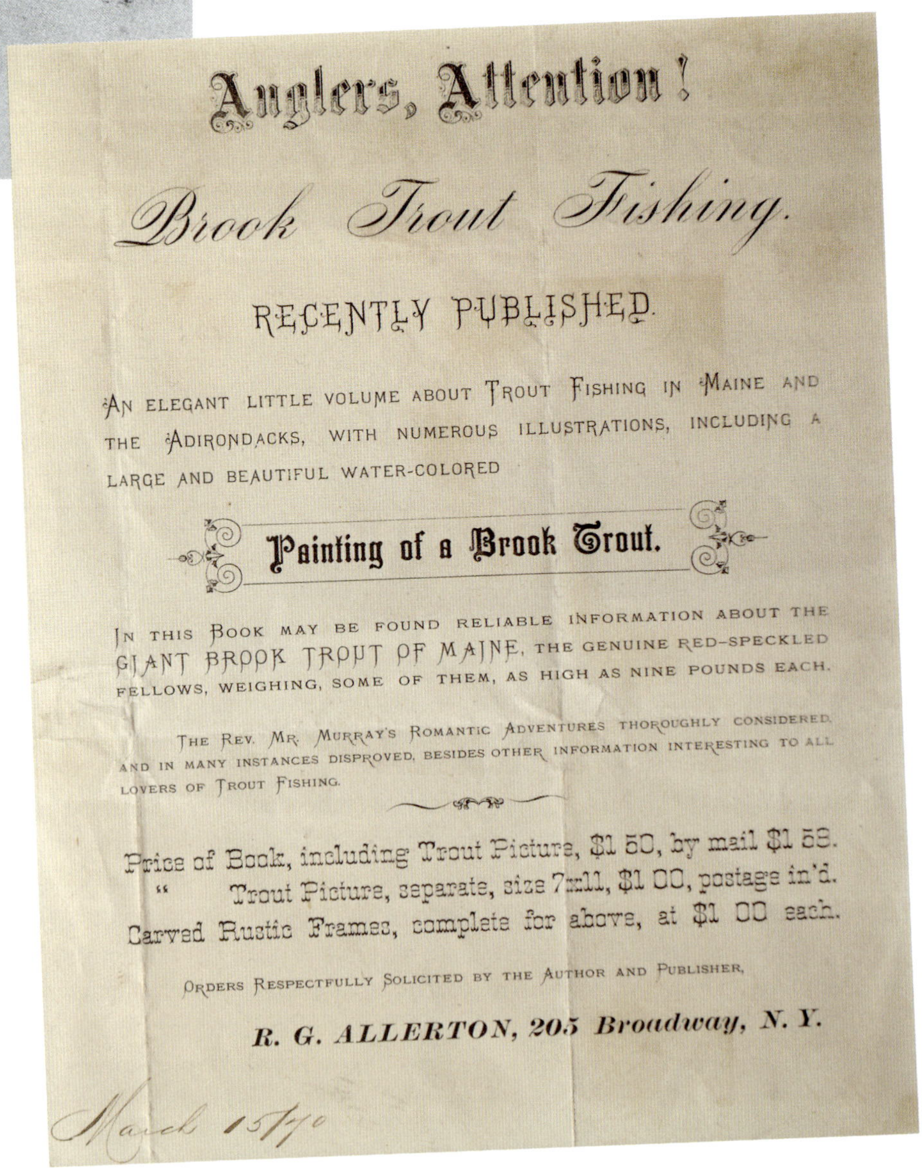

Anglers, Attention!

Brook Trout Fishing.

RECENTLY PUBLISHED.

AN ELEGANT LITTLE VOLUME ABOUT TROUT FISHING IN MAINE AND THE ADIRONDACKS, WITH NUMEROUS ILLUSTRATIONS, INCLUDING A LARGE AND BEAUTIFUL WATER-COLORED

Painting of a Brook Trout.

IN THIS BOOK MAY BE FOUND RELIABLE INFORMATION ABOUT THE GIANT BROOK TROUT OF MAINE, THE GENUINE RED-SPECKLED FELLOWS, WEIGHING, SOME OF THEM, AS HIGH AS NINE POUNDS EACH.

THE REV. MR. MURRAY'S ROMANTIC ADVENTURES THOROUGHLY CONSIDERED, AND IN MANY INSTANCES DISPROVED, BESIDES OTHER INFORMATION INTERESTING TO ALL LOVERS OF TROUT FISHING.

Price of Book, including Trout Picture, $1 50, by mail $1 58.
" Trout Picture, separate, size 7x11, $1 00, postage in'd.
Carved Rustic Frames, complete for above, at $1 00 each.

ORDERS RESPECTFULLY SOLICITED BY THE AUTHOR AND PUBLISHER,

R. G. ALLERTON, 205 Broadway, N. Y.

March 15/70

The prospectus for *About Brook Trout* also speaks to the rivalry between the Adirondack and Rangeley fishers. HILYARD COLLECTION

to Lewiston and, with a friend, went to his camp in the Rangeleys, and while there one day they each caught a trout weighing about 7 pounds, which they sent on to Professor Agassiz. In a few days the Senator received a few lines from the professor, and this is what he wrote: "The theory of a lifetime kicked to death by a stubborn fact."
Boston Herald[29]

So, the stage was finally set at Haines Landing when Herbert Leon Welch arrived in 1905. Due to the railroads, these wilderness lakes were now accessible to more than just an adventurous few. This, combined with all the publicity it was receiving, connected Oquossoc, Maine, with Boston, New York City, Philadelphia, and even Europe.

The initial 1863 New York City newspaper reports brought about by George Shephard Page had been followed by accounts reporting on fabulous brook trout caught by prominent people. Founded in 1873, rarely did an issue of *Forest & Stream* fail to mention the Rangeley Lakes. Even the Fulton Fish Market on the New York City waterfront promoted the name by selling Rangeley Lakes blueback trout as well as mountain trout, which were actually nothing more than whitefish.

In 1876, Captain Charles A.J. Farrar published *Farrar's Guide Book to the Androscoggin Lakes*. It was 357 pages in hardcover and ran for fourteen editions. In February 1877, *Scribner's Monthly Illustrated*

"Fly Rod" Crosby Reports from Madison Square Garden

Next comes the finest display of taxidermist work ever seen in New York City and I am proud to say this is the work of Walter D. Hinds of Portland, who is ably assisted by Mr. and Mrs. H.L. Welch, G.W. Pickel, James C. Norton and Thomas Canadian and they are selling many of the mounted heads and fish. There is an 80 pound tarpon, a 36 pound salmon and beautiful trout...

It is here thousands of copies of the *Maine Woods* are given away, and that Capt. Fred C. Barker, one of the best known and most popular men in the Rangeleys, shakes hands hour after hour with old friends and is introduced to many, who come to arrange for their summer outing at his attractive log camps where many distinguished people tarry for weeks...

...The small mouthed black bass of the New Preston, Conn., hatchery in large glass tanks attract many who watch them for hours, but were there tanks from some of our Maine hatcheries with a 5 pound trout and salmon, the black bass would be lonely...

Maine Woods
March 6, 1908

The Senator Frye Lake Fly was originated and tied by Leslie K. Hilyard. HILYARD COLLECTION

Maine made its presence felt at the third Madison Square Garden sporting exposition in 1897. RANGELEY SPORTING HERITAGE MUSEUM COLLECTION

Fuel for Walter Hinds' rapid expansion. Family money underwrote many of Hinds' ventures. HILYARD COLLECTION

Magazine published Edward Seymour's lengthy *Trout Fishing in the Rangeley Lakes*. In June of 1877, *Harper's New Monthly Magazine* countered with a fifteen-page article by Edward Abbott titled "The Androscoggin Lakes." Not until the 1890s would the name Rangeley Lakes be universally accepted.

No one, however, did more to promote the Rangeley Lakes than Cornelia Thurza Crosby (1854–1946), better known as "Fly Rod" Crosby. As publicity agent for the Maine Central Railroad (which connected to all points in the Maine wilderness), she preached the splendors of the Rangeley Lakes with evangelical fervor. From 1892 through the 1920s, her columns were published locally in the *Phillips Phonograph*, which became the *Maine Woods* in 1900 and later the *Maine Woods and Sportsman* in 1908. She also wrote nationally for two of the major New York City fishing journals: *Shooting and Fishing* and *Forest & Stream*, which became *Field & Stream* in 1930.

In 1895, Crosby represented Rangeley at the first New York Sportsmen Exposition, held in Madison Square Garden. Extremely charismatic, she held court before a log cabin named Camp Maine Central, which was attended by Maine guides, an Indian maiden in tribal dress, and a black bear cub. It didn't hurt that Crosby's friend, famed sharpshooter Annie Oakley, frequently dropped by. Crosby's performance was credited with attracting 5,000 visitors

The *Ethel May* launch tied up at Lagomonte Lodge. Built by A.S. Hinds, the lodge was passed down to Ethel May (Hinds) Bisbee, then to A.S. Hinds II, then to Larry and Susan Koob of Oquossoc.
HINDS COLLECTION

With Charles F. Orvis, A.N. Cheney was co-author of *Fishing with the Fly,* published in 1883. Charles' daughter, Mary Orvis Marbury, expanded on it in 1892 with her *Favorite Flies and Their Histories.*

to Maine that following summer. With the passage of the Maine Guide Bill in 1897, Crosby's influential lobbying was recognized with the grant of the first Registered Maine Guide license. This gesture was purely ceremonial, as there is no evidence that she ever guided professionally.

Another one of the early camp builders on Mooselookmeguntic Lake was Aurelius Stone Hinds of Portland, Maine. It is not surprising, as Camp Bemis guest registers record him and his sons, Charles, Walter, and Harry, as frequent guests since 1890.

Taking advantage of new fashions that exposed more female skin to the sun, A.S. Hinds amassed a fortune patenting an early version of sunscreen. Marketed worldwide as Hinds' Honey and Almond Cream, this cream sold by the gallon until Hinds wisely sold out to Lehn & Fink of New Jersey—just before Procter & Gamble took over the market.[30]

In 1902, Hinds spent much of his fortune importing Italian craftsmen to build his palatial home on Mooselookmeguntic, which he called Lagomonte (Italian for "lake and mountain"). Masons spent months creating a towering fireplace made of fossil laden limestone from Europe. Carpenters spent months laying floors and creating walls and ceilings from southern yellow pine. Pioneering electricians spent weeks installing a dynamo, driven by a kerosene engine and backed up by sixty-five storage

The majestic Mooselookmeguntic Lake and its shoreline remains much the same today due to preservation by the Rangeley Lakes Heritage Trust, founded in 1991. MACLEOD COLLECTION

Built in 1908, Camp Ridlon has recently been restored by the Higgins family of Milton, Massachusetts.
PENOBSCOT MARINE MUSEUM

batteries capable of powering seventy-five lights. A lofty water tower gravity-fed the plumbing. Named for his daughter, Ethel May, his steam launch was pulled and launched using an iron railway system. All told, the summer home contained fourteen rooms, with separate quarters for the guides and staff. Nothing would challenge Lagomonte's status as the most magnificent private home on any of the Rangeley Lakes.

Others joined the eastern shore land rush, many calling their camps by their family names, a tradition that still continues. Names such as Taylor and Ridlon carry historical significance: Ruel Taylor Sr. was the first stationmaster at Bemis in 1896 where the baggage room served as birthplace for his daughter, Neva,[31] and Frank Ridlon of Brookline, Massachusetts, was a pioneer in electrical installation and an early developer of Haines Landing. In 1904, Ridlon bought ten lots from Theo Page and added them to the camps already on site. Of this original complex, five camps remain on the side lawn, while Camp Ridlon, originally known as Wellesmere, continues to dominate the Haines Landing shoreline as it has since 1908.[32]

So in 1905, when young Herb stood on the Haines Landing dock, he had much to see and ponder.

A Bicknell glass plate negative image of the five camps at Haines Landing originally called the Circle Camps, built c. 1904.
MORTON COLLECTION

Before him lay Mooselookmeguntic Lake, 11 miles long and flecked by islands, with Bald Mountain in the background and New Hampshire's distant White Mountains casting a long shadow in the foreground. Behind Herb, the Mooselookmeguntic House was the centerpiece of a thriving waterfront. With Bald Mountains Camps far to his left and the Birches five miles out on Students Island, Camp Bemis was just beyond. Out of sight, the presence of the legendary Upper Dam and the Angler's Retreat could be felt, as were the Kennebagos. Wealthy campers, delivered by trains and horses, spent entire summers in private camps and hotels. And where trains and horses could not go, the steamships would. Mooselookmeguntic's star was rising. With Herb's arrival on stage, Act IV was about to begin...

ENDNOTES

1 Edward Ellis, *The Journal of Squire Rangeley*, Horsham Valley Graphics, 1990, p. 10.
2 "Indian Trails of New Hampshire," *New Hampshire Archaeologist Journal*, 1967.
3 "Greenville and Donham," *Maine Register*, Portland, Maine, 1900.
4 Edward Ellis, *A Chronological History of the Rangeley Lakes Region*, Trevose, Pennsylvania: Rangeley Lakes Region Historical Society, 1983, p. 6.
5 Herbert P. Shirrefs, *The Richardson Lakes: Jewels in the Rangeley Chain*, Bethel, Maine: Bethel Historical Society, 1995, p. 113.
6 Union Water Power Company, "Operation of the Andoscoggin Storage System," Lewiston, Maine, revised, 1975, p. 2.
7 Ibid.
8 William B. Krohn, *Joshua Gross Rich: The Life and Work…*, Orono, Maine: Maine Folklore Center, p. 24.
9 J.G. Rich, "The Trout of Maine Waters, 7th Paper," *The American Angler*, April 14, 1883.
10 Zenas Thompson, *Memoirs of Reverend Zenas Thompson*, Roslindale, Massachusetts, 1934.
11 William B. Krohn, "Henry O. Stanley and His Fishing Tackle Business," Dixfield Historical Society Newsletter, June 2012, p. 1.
12 George Shephard Page, *Forest & Stream*, New York, May 1882, p. unknown.
13 Ibid.
14 Samuel L. Lambert Jr., *The Oquossoc Angling Association, 1870–1970*, 1970, p. 15.
15 George Shephard Page, "The Rangeley Lakes," *Forest & Stream*, New York, June 21, 1883.
16 G. Browne Goode, *Catalogue of the Collection to Illustrate the Animal Resources and the Fisheries of the United States*, Smithsonian, 1876, p. 58.
17 Nick Karas, *Brook Trout*, New York: Lyons & Burford, 1997, p. 206.
18 Louise Hall Tharp, *Adventurous Alliance: The Story of the Agassiz Family of Boston*, Boston: Little Brown, 1959, p. 335.
19 Capt. F.C. Barker, *Lake and Forest As I Have Known Them*, Boston: Lathrop, Lee, and Shephard, 1903, p. 132.
20 "Rangeley News," *Franklin Journal*, Farmington, Maine, March 11, 1884.
21 Shirrefs, p. 144.
22 Barker, p. 134.
23 Shirrefs, p. 90.
24 Lynne Harnden Lewandowski, interview with author, September 14, 2012.
25 Page, *Forest & Stream*, June 21, 1883.
26 Doug Hutchinson, *The Rumford Falls and Rangeley Lakes Railroad*, Dixfield, Maine: Partridge Lane Publications, 1990, p. 101.
27 *Mooselookmeguntic Fish*, Phillips, Maine: Phillips Phonograph, June 9, 1899.
28 Gary Priest, *The Gilded Age of Rangeley, Maine*, private printing, 2009, p. 211.
29 "Professor Agassiz Was Convinced," *Forest & Stream*, New York, June 24, 1905.
30 Aurelius S. Hinds II, interview with author, September 10, 2010.
31 Eleanor White, interview with author, June 10, 2013.
32 Priest, pp. 227–228.

CHAPTER 3

Forerunners

What brought young Herb Welch to Haines Landing in 1905 was a practice that had begun centuries ago: taxidermy. While taxidermy's precise origins are lost, Shakespeare's late-16th-century play *Romeo and Juliet* is one early source that mentions it:

> I do remember an apothecary...
> Meager were his looks,
> Sharp misery had worn him to the bones.
> And in his needy shop a tortoise hung,
> An alligator stuffed, and other skins
> Of ill-shaped fishes.
> Act 5, Scene 1

The first book to focus exclusively on taxidermy was published in 1787. The French monk L'Abbé Manesse's *Treatise Sur La Maniére d'Empailler et De Conserver Les Animaux, Les Pelleteries et Les Laines* indicates France had an early lead in taxidermy. But that would change. As the British Empire expanded, so did an influx of exotic species, along with a desire to preserve and study them. The English census of 1891 lists 369 Londoners as taxidermists, with another 500 employed in outlying towns.[1]

Despite having a smaller population, Scotland rivaled England with its taxidermy, centered in Aberdeen, Glasgow, Perth, Inverness, and Edinburgh. While studying medicine at the University of Edinburgh in 1826, Charles Darwin himself learned taxidermy under John Edmonstone, a freed black slave from Guyana.[2] Much of Scotland's success was a result of Queen Victoria (1837–1901) buying Balmoral Castle on the River Dee in 1852. The nobility flocked there to hunt. Scottish hunting focused on red deer—a far more difficult quarry than driven English grouse shoots. Landowners capitalized on Scotland's big game by emphasizing the need for deer stalking, which implied a greater degree of hunting prowess than mere hunting. True or not, the term did give its name to the deerstalker hat, which is best known today as the iconic hat worn by Sherlock Holmes.

Taxidermy was not limited to the British Isles, as even earlier work can be found in Germany, Italy, Sweden, Denmark, and the Netherlands. The Danish Hunting and Forestry Museum at Hørsholm contains a red deer from around 1690 that is thought to be the oldest mounted mammal in Scandinavia.[3] War horses were also a favorite subject, but they were not necessarily mounted by their fond owners. The Bavarian town of Ingolstadt still proudly exhibits a war horse shot from under Swedish King Gustavus Adolphus during his failed 1632 attack on their town. Conversely, the Museum of the Army in Brussels houses Archduke Albert of Bavaria's horse, which died in battle in 1600. Archduchess Isabella's horse, mounted sometime prior to 1635, presumably died a less bloody death.

One of the strangest early taxidermy specimens is a full-bodied crocodile dating from the 1530s, which still hangs from the ceiling of Saint Maria Annunziata at Ponte Nossa in Lombard, Italy.[4] Though not common, this is not the only example of ecclesiastical crocs overseeing the congregation. Given the Old Testament exhortation to "breakest the heads of dragons in the waters" and to put hooks in the jaws of the "great dragon that lieth in the midst of rivers," perhaps we should not be so surprised to find them in the rafters, given that the Hebrew word for *dragon* can also be translated as *crocodile*.[5]

These eighteenth- and nineteenth-century mounts owe their survival to the creation of arsenical soap. The soap was first invented by Jean-Baptiste Bécoeur (1718–1777), who took the formula to his grave. Eventually, however, the formula re-surfaced and arsenical soap became the preferred method for preserving birds and mammals. Despite years of experimentation with some 140 other preservatives, no other formula can protect against insect infestation and molds like arsenical soap.[6] While individual mixtures vary, the standard formula consists of 5 ounces of camphor, 2 pounds of white soap, 12 ounces of salt of tartar, 4 ounces of powdered chalk, and 2 pounds of powdered arsenic.[7] During the nineteenth century, arsenic was cheap and readily available by the pound at any corner store. Essentially undetectable, it was used so often as a poison by impatient offspring hoping to inherit wealth from older relatives that it became known as "the inheritors' powder." It was equally useful to wives with less than satisfactory husbands.

Too much has been made today of the dangers of arsenic although handling antique mounts with latex gloves will probably do no harm as fur and feathers contain keratin, which bonds to arsenic. Ongoing searches for an arsenic substitute have been underwhelming. Although useful against bacterial decay, borax does little to thwart insect damage. Now banned, DDT was a disaster in all applications. While considered safe for humans performing taxidermy, synthetic pyrethroids damage the DNA of the mount, making it useless for future DNA studies. Adapted from the food industry in the 1980s, the jury is still out on freeze drying as a defense against infestation.

An ecclesiastical croc overlooks the flock of Saint Maria Annunziata. MORRIS COLLECTION

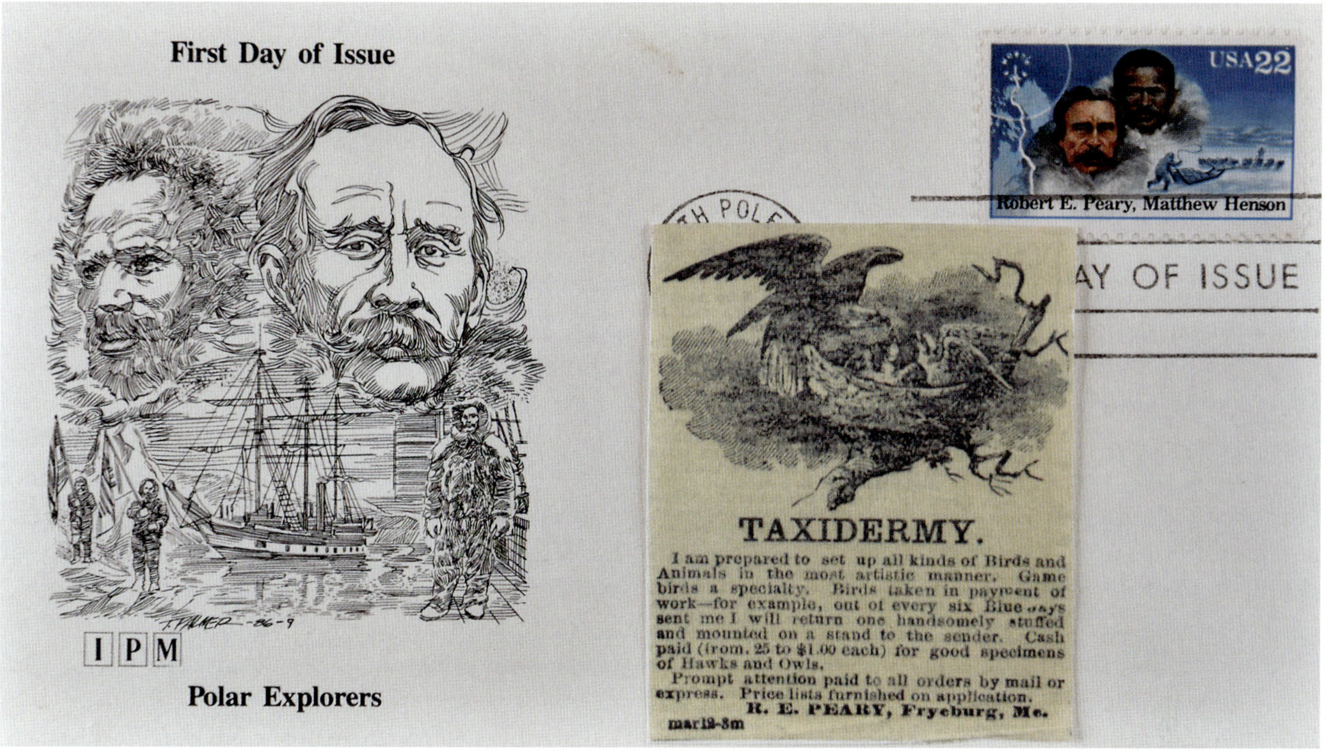

Taxidermy underwrote Peary's tuition at Bowdoin College. HILYARD COLLECTION

Taxidermy consists of preserving the skin of an animal and restructuring it into a lifelike form. The word itself derives from Greek: *taxis*, meaning to arrange, and *derma*, meaning skin. Taxidermy has its roots in the "cabinets of curiosities" created by the nobility and later adopted by a rising middle class. By the late 1700s, the Enlightenment had loosened the grip of organized religion and a scientific curiosity triggered by the age of exploration was in ascension. Eventually, those private cabinets overflowing with exotic specimens of flora and fauna led to the conception of natural history museums.

Spurred on by Darwin, who from 1831 to 1836 voyaged to both coasts of South America and the Galapagos Islands and in 1859 published *On the Origin of Species*, natural history museums became the focus of scientific study. Taxidermy and its preservation techniques were essential to this scientific shift. Darwin's own taxidermy skills allowed him to return from his voyage with his famous finches intact, and those finches proved instrumental in his theory of natural selection. While field notes have value, they often contain gaps, and returning thousands of miles for a source check is an unlikely option. A preserved mount or skin gives the naturalist something to study over time.

Practical photography was still far in the future. George Eastman would not introduce his Kodak camera until 1888 or his more affordable Brownie until 1901. Cameras required long exposure times, and animals are notoriously uncooperative. Not until after World War II would binoculars or accurately drawn field guides become affordable. Darwin did have access to John James Audubon's *Birds of America*, which he cited in *Origin of Species*, but most people back then would have found the book's $33 price tag daunting, considering that equals about $660 today. Although if they had bought a copy, their descendants might have thanked them: In 2010, Bloomberg Business News reported that a complete copy of *Birds of America* sold at Sotheby's for $11.2 million.

The effects of Darwin's radical new scientific ideas were felt far beyond England and Europe, with a similar scientific rebellion taking place in the New World. While many contributed to the freeing of science from theology, much of the credit for establishing science in America goes to Charles Willson Peale (1741–1827). Funded by the Philadelphia Philosophical Society, Peale initiated America's first significant archaeological dig in Orange County, New York in 1801. Five months later, he had successfully unearthed the reasonably intact skeleton of a mastodon, generating considerable excitement and national pride.[8] Later, in 1806, he documented the dig and all its complexities in an oil painting, *Exhuming the First American Mastodon*, currently displayed at the Maryland Historical Society in Baltimore.

Science aside, there were social ramifications to Peale's excavation as well. Since 1784, Thomas Jefferson had been at war with a French naturalist, the Comte de Buffon, who proposed the doctrine of Western degeneracy. This concept, embraced by much of Europe, proclaimed that from the Garden of Eden forward, all New World mammals had been smaller than their European counterparts and that they kept growing smaller daily. Soon, American dogs would cease to bark, and even American men were accused of having diminished virility in critical areas. That America had recently defeated England's military did not factor into Buffon's theory.

Reconstructed by Peale and sons, the mastodon (originally thought to be a mammoth) stood 11 feet high at the shoulder, 9 feet at the hips, and 17½ feet from tusk to tail.[9] Exhibited as the "9th Wonder of the World and the largest of terrestrial beings," it immeasurably helped Jefferson rebut Buffon's arguments. In 1806, Peale's mastodon crossed the Atlantic on something of a victory tour.

Peale is best known today for his portraiture, particularly his seventy canvases of George Washington,

Commemorating Peale by using his self-portrait, *The Artist in His Museum*.
HILYARD COLLECTION

Commemorating Washington by using paintings by Peale.
HILYARD COLLECTION

George Washington's pheasants, still with us some 230 years later. MUSEUM OF COMPARATIVE ZOOLOGY, HARVARD UNIVERSITY

under whom he served as a lieutenant in the Battle of Trenton, the Battle of Princeton, and at Valley Forge. Five of those Washington paintings and a self-portrait were commemorated as early U.S. postal stamps, which were reissued for the bicentennial in 1976. His artwork and that of his sons, Rembrandt, Raphael, Rubens, and Titian, continue to be prized by the nation's leading museums.

Peale, however, considered the pinnacle of his life's work to be his founding in 1784 of the nation's first museum to combine natural science and art. The Peale Museum, formally known as the Philadelphia Museum, lasted for fifty-one years and became the template for the National Portrait Gallery and the Smithsonian Institute in Washington, D.C. Early supporters of his museum included Washington, Jefferson, Madison, Hamilton, and Franklin. Portraits of them and others by Peale remain at the heart of the National Portrait Gallery.

At the core of the Peale Museum were taxidermy mounts from specimens obtained by the Lewis and Clark Expedition and other early expeditions into the American West. Peale's iconic painting *The Artist in His Museum* depicts many of these mounts housed in rows of glass cases, backed with water-colored images of the animal's natural habitat. Biographers describe Peale's taxidermy as "self-taught," and if so, he certainly taught himself well. Consider his following correspondence with George Washington:

> Washington to Peale, February 16, 1787. — You will receive by Stage the body of my Gold Pheasant, packed up in wool agreeable to your directions. He made his Exit yesterday, which enables me to comply with your request much sooner than I wished to do.
>
> Peale to Washington, February 27, 1787. — Your obliging favor of the Body of the Golden Pheasant, I have received in good condition... When you have the misfortune of losing the others, if the weather should be warm, be pleased to order the Bowels to be taken out and some pepper put into the Body, but no salt which would spoil the Feathers.
>
> Peale to Washington, March 31, 1787. — Your obliging favor of the 13th I received on the 28th. The Pepper I believe preserved the body from being thrown overboard. My Anticeptic Powders I hope will preserve the remains.[10]

Following a tangled journey, the Washington pheasants finally came to rest in 1914 at Harvard's Museum of Comparative Zoology. Having spent the previous fourteen years in an abandoned barn in Newtonville, Massachusetts, only then would Peale's taxidermy require restoration—a survival rate of some 127 years.

If taxidermy was the "what" that brought Herb Welch to Haines Landing, then the "who" was Walter Dewitt Hinds (1876–1928) of Portland, Maine. By the turn of the nineteenth century, taxidermy-fueled natural history museums were well established in America. Large houses, such as Ward's Natural Science Establishment in Rochester and the James L. Clark Studio of New York City, met the need for large habitat groups. Still in existence today, Ward's served as the training ground for the nation's premier taxidermists. These included Carl E. Ackley (1883–1887), who served as chief taxidermist at the American Museum of Natural History, and William Hornaday (1873–1881), who did the same for the Smithsonian.

Meanwhile, hundreds of other taxidermists across the country met the needs of local sportsmen. And not just sportsmen as Victorian England's vogue for pet taxidermy had spread to America as well. One such example was Walter D. Hinds, who in 1903 became the junior sales partner in the taxidermy firm of John A. Lord of Portland, Maine.[11] The entrepreneurial Hinds quickly moved on to establish his own taxidermy firm in 1904 at 642 Congress Street, Portland. The firm expanded rapidly, and eventually he moved his eighteen employees to the nearby 72–74–76 Pine Street property owned by his father, Aurelius Stone Hinds, an early pharmaceutical pioneer. Per the annually published *Maine Business Registers Yearbook*, except for his final two years at Plum Street, he remained at Pine Street until closing operations in 1918.

Rapidly, Hinds opened branches farther north in Maine at Haines Landing, the Belgrade Lakes, Oxbow, and Rangeley. He would soon expand into Canada with branches at Fredericton, New Brunswick, and Port-au-Basque in Newfoundland. To the

Poetic License

The most famous example of pet taxidermy may be Grip, the pet raven and traveling companion of Charles Dickens. Not just content to immortalize him in his novel *Barnaby Rudge*, Dickens preserved him as a mount as well.

When Dickens toured America in 1842, Grip was in the room for an Edgar Allan Poe interview. It was not necessarily a congenial session, as Poe, a literary critic as well as a poet, took issue with how Dickens had used Grip in *Barnaby Rudge*. Deciding that the best sermon was a good example, in 1845 Poe published "The Raven," the defining poem of his career. If *Barnaby Rudge* was not enough to turn Grip into a literary icon, "The Raven" surely was.

A century later, Colonel Richard Gimbel of Philadelphia and Mooselookmeguntic's Lytton Lodge bought Grip at an English auction, adding to his scholarly collection of all things Poe and Dickens. Gimbel donated Grip to the Free Library of Philadelphia, where he now resides in the rare book department. The rest of his comprehensive collection was bequeathed to Yale, where he had graduated with degrees in law and psychology and later taught as a professor of air science.[18] We don't know if Grip ever visited Lytton Lodge.

Both Dickens' writing and his raven have held up well. Dickens is in every library while Grip is perched in the rare book section of the Free Library of Philadelphia.
FREE LIBRARY OF PHILADELPHIA

The silver plaque reads: "Mounted by W.D. Hinds, Taxidermist, Portland, ME." It is the only known example of his work. RANGELEY SPORTING HERITAGE MUSEUM

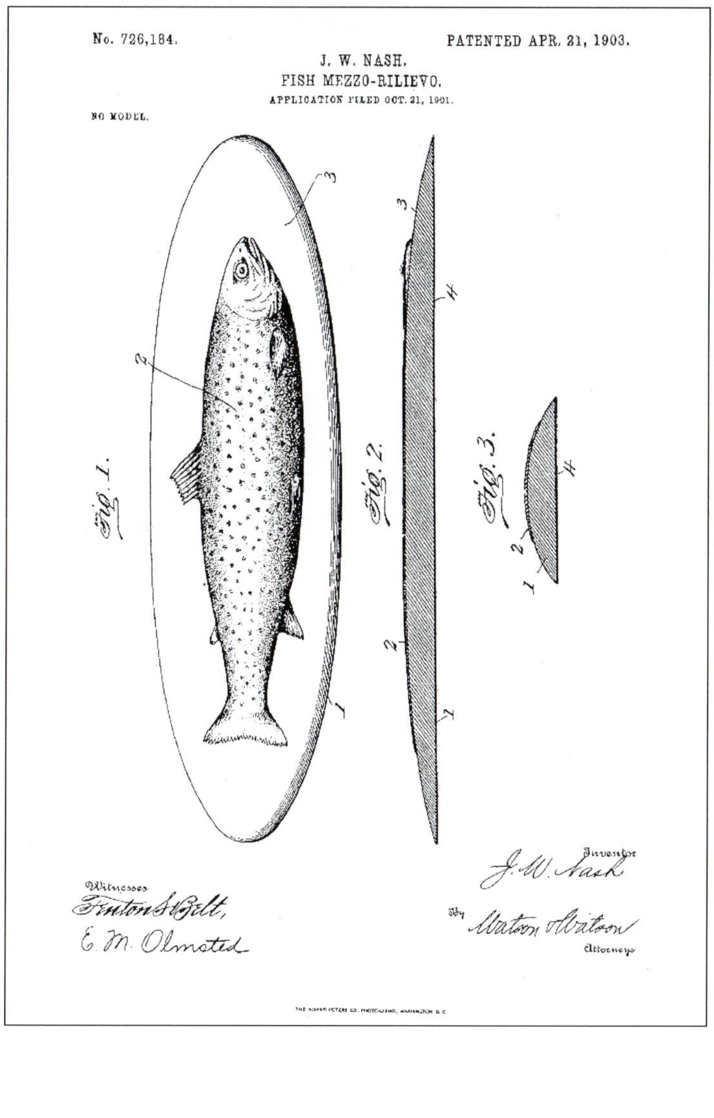

Using only one side of the fish, Nash's unique style resulted in two fish mounts from one fish.

A plaster mount by Nash of an Upper Dam brook trout weighing 11 pounds 2 ounces, caught by George Bearce in 1898.
RANGELEY SPORTING HERITAGE MUSEUM

A rare example of Nash's mezzo-rilievo style using both sides of the same salmon. Restored by Dave Footer of Lewiston, Maine.
CARLSON COLLECTION

Nash's enduring mezzo-rilievo style applied to a brook trout on a yellow birch medallion. The curvature of the back panel gives substance to the skin. Restored by Dave Footer of Lewiston, Maine.
CARLSON COLLECTION

south, he contracted with agents in Boston, New York City, and Palm Beach, Florida.

By 1906, "Fly Rod" Crosby was writing in the October 19th edition of *Maine Woods* that:

> Walter Hinds of Portland who with a party of 75 hunters made a trip to Newfoundland as soon as the season opened and had good luck... To see the amount of trout and salmon that are fast being shipped from his place at Haines Landing, each one done in wonderful good style, also tells their own story of fisherman's luck. Mr. Hinds has already a national reputation and has in his employ the best workmen in the country.

Establishing a taxidermy business at Haines Landing had its challenges. J. (John) Waldo Nash (1862–1919) of Norway, Maine, had preceded Hinds,

Hinds' shop in the foreground with Welch's in the background. The Welch trade sign is on display at the Rangeley Sporting Heritage Museum, but the Hinds trade sign was destroyed by fire in 1912. HILYARD COLLECTION

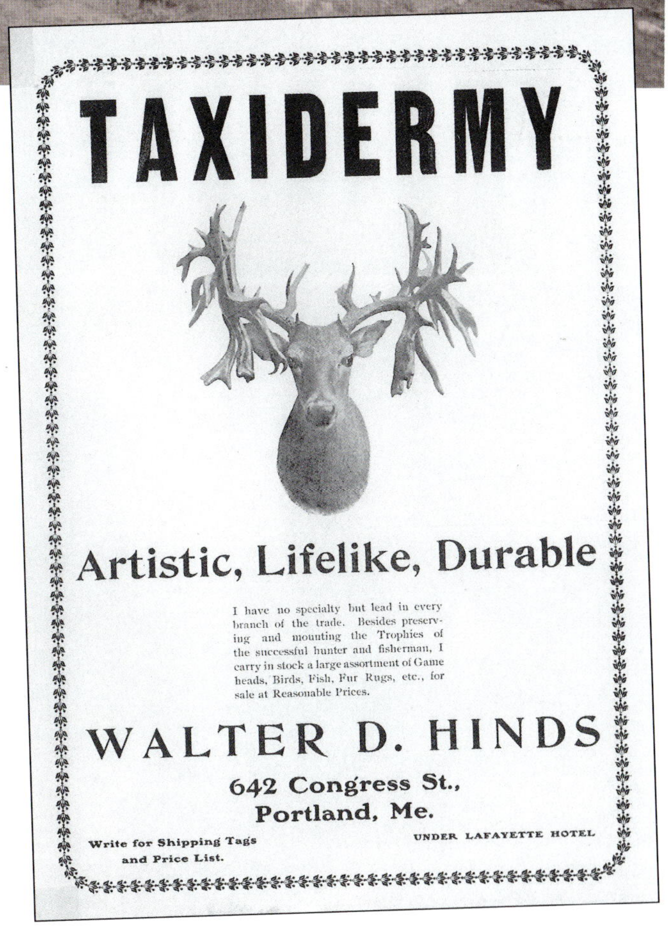

A full-page advertisement on the back cover of the *Maine Sportsman*, November 1904.

arriving there in 1900. Trained by Carroll Meade of Bridgton, Maine, and highly regarded as an internationally medaled taxidermist, Nash owed much of his success to his patented "fish mezzo-rilievo" style of fish mounting. With this method, crumbling plaster and broken fins were no longer a problem. Nash's technique used one side of the fish's skin glued to an oval, convex back panel, made of laminated or solid hardwood that was supplied by the Paris Manufacturing Company of South Paris, Maine.[12]

Nash did not limit himself to fish and large game: His personal bird collection consisted of some 300 specimens, most mounted by his talented wife, Alice Eastman Nash (1864–1945). Active in all aspects of the business, Alice specialized in birds and the landscape paintings found on Nash back panels.[13]

Upon J. Waldo Nash's death from a stroke in 1919, Alice Nash ably carried on the business until her retirement in the early 1940s, marking the end of Nash of Maine.

In 1905, Hinds had made Nash an offer that he could not refuse and Nash returned to his home base in Norway, Maine. Immediately, Hinds brought in his own staff, which included Herb Welch. When he could not eliminate his business rivals, Hinds competed with them. Despite the 1894 arrival of

Bernice Welch (seated) with her attendant, Dorothy Voorhees. ANDERSON COLLECTION

A Stalwart Lady

I also had a card from Lotie saying Mrs. Ordway said I was in bed, but so far, I have kept from going although some days I think I will give up and not try to fight my lameness, but that would not get me anywhere, so hang on, and am feeling better by doing so.

It's all my right hip – As long as I sit still, I am fine, but try to walk, it is another matter, but I think it will come along all right in time – It's the third time that the hip has balked me.

It's very hard for me to sit and have Dot and Herbert do all the work besides waiting on me, but I have had 28 years of it and don't feel so badly about it as long as I can get down stairs and wait on the desk and take care of the mail.

Bernice Welch writing to her
cousin Walter Batson Jr.
Aug 3, 1937

Maine's largest taxidermist, S.L. Crosby of Bangor, and the 1899 arrival of M. Abbott Frazar of Boston, Hinds opened a Rangeley branch in 1906 with the Frazar-trained Guy Pickel as manager. These competitors would have seemed like a challenge, but by 1911, there was no Rangeley advertising presence for either Crosby or Frazar.

Like his mentor, Herb Welch chafed at managerial restrictions. In the June 10, 1909, edition of the *Maine Woods and Sportsman* (the *Maine Woods* and *Maine Sportsman* having merged in February of that year), C.E. Pendleton noted:

> Continuing on, we soon came to Haines Landing. Here we found carpenters busy putting the finishing touches onto the taxidermist bungalow of Herbert L. Welch and the enlargement of Walter D. Hinds' store. We called at both places and saw an 8½-lb. salmon that was caught at Rangeley the day before and several other fish to be mounted by Mr. Welch who is said to be the best in Maine on that kind of work. At Mr. Hinds' we saw more fine specimens of moose and deer than it has been my privilege for sometime to see, besides many articles of fancy work done by the Indians and white people.

Herb's November 27, 1909, marriage in Columbia Falls, Maine, to Bernice Ida Batson (1880–1947) of Addison, Maine, was fortuitous. Having recently graduated from the Mary E. Beal's School of Shorthand, Bernice combined her business acumen with Herb's guiding and taxidermy skills, and together they successfully ran a business for some forty-five years.[14]

Some have suggested that Bernice was the moon to Herb's sun, pale and cold compared to his warmth and radiance. But many of those observations were made later in her life when she was in chronic orthopedic pain requiring constant nursing assistance until her November 1947 death and burial in Portland's Evergreen Cemetery.

Herb lost little time announcing his independence from Hinds. He placed ads in the 1909 *Maine Woods and Sportsman* and in the *New England Magazine*, where he was first listed in their 1907 directory of Maine Guides. Meanwhile, in Rangeley, Guy Pickel also ran his business independently from Hinds until his death in 1926. Like Alice Nash, Pickel's wife, Arbeth, soldiered on until a fire closed the Main Street business in the 1960s. But another assistant of Hinds referenced in "Fly Rod" Crosby's Madison Square Garden report did not fare as well as Pickel and Welch.

Born in 1881 on the Caughanwaga reservation in Québec, Tom Canadian first met Walter Hinds on a New Brunswick moose hunt. While he occasionally earned a mention in the contemporary sporting press, much of what we know is found in a 2004 Canadian publication, *Men of the Autumn Woods*, by Gerry R. Parker. Impressed by Canadian's guiding and taxidermy skills, Hinds hired him as head guide for his wilderness sporting camp at Ox Bow Lake in Aroostook County, Maine. Tom would take Walter's financial guidance seriously, invest wisely, and enter the insurance business in Portland, Maine. Personable as well as talented, in 1904 he married Aida McDonald, a Portland socialite. They wintered in Miami, Florida, where Canadian pursued his real estate interests, apparently quite successfully. In 1925, he announced to the Fredericton, New Brunswick, media that he was about to close on a Miami real estate deal worth $100,000. But the next we hear of him is a dark headline in the March 21, 1932, edition of the *Fredericton Gleaner*:

> Tom Canadian found shot dead in Miami Florida
>
> Mr. Canadian, aged 51 years, widely known as a sportsman and hunting guide, was found shot to death on a sidewalk in Miami on March 20, 1932. Although police ruled his death as self-inflicted, his widow, Aida Canadian, said he had no financial or health worries and she could give no motive for suicide.

There is no evidence that Hinds saw his assistants' independent spirits as a sign of betrayal. In the case of Welch, their competitive relationship seemed to be mutually beneficial. Judging by their respective letterheads and advertising materials, it seems the two divided their labor, with Hinds specializing in big game while across the street Welch focused on fish and birds.

Another sign of their good relationship was the founding of the Hillside Gun Club at Haines Landing in 1908. In its August 8th issue, the *Sporting Life* announced Walter Hinds as president and Herbert Welch as vice president. The following year, it noted: "The Hillside Gun Club of Haines Landing, Rangeley Lakes, Maine is distributing very artistic posters announcing the club's second registered

Nov 21, 1922 PORTLAND EVENING EXPRESS & ADVERTISER TUESDAY

Walter D. Hinds and John Canadian Shoot Hollis Gorge Rapids in Frail Canoe of Birch Bark as Another Thrilling Feature in Nine-Reel Picture

Top—John Canadian and Walter D. Hinds.

Below — Walter D. Hinds and John Canadian shooting rapids of Hollis Gorge.

Walter D. Hinds, son of the famous toilet cream manufacturer, hunter, trapshooter, and all-around sportsman, and his Indian guide of many years' service, John Canadian, on Friday shot the rapids at Hollis Gorge in a frail birch bark canoe.

The trip is believed to be one that has never been made before by a white man. If it was made by an Indian before white men had set foot on these shores, the story has vanished into the mists of antiquity. Hinds and his redskin guide are the first men that are known to have achieved the feat, and the two intrepid sportsmen did it to appease that modern Moloch, the movies.

Their daring deed will be perpetuated in the nine-reel James Oliver Curwood thriller, Jacqueline, soon to be released by Pine Tree Pictures, Inc., the motion picture company headed by Hon. Frederick W. Hinckley and Ex-Gov. Cart E. Milliken.

This Maine-made picture, said to be the biggest ever made by an independent company, with the most expensive cast ever assembled by an independent motion picture concern, contains exciting scenes in abundance. The forest fire scenes pictured at Sebago Lake, Two Lights and South Casco at a cost of $26,000, the daring leap of a famous Chinese character actor from a 50-foot cliff at Sebago, and an airplane rescue are among them, but the climax of them all was the shooting of the Hollis Gorge rapids.

Needless to say, Mr. Hinds volunteered to perform this service free of charge. Experienced woodsmen who are equipped to guide a canoe through that seething mass of foam are not to be easily recruited from among the ranks of Thespians, and when the time came for some one of the cast to volunteer for the work, none was

The ill-fated Tom Canadian (left) with his mentor, Walter D. Hinds (right). *PORTLAND EVENING EXPRESS*

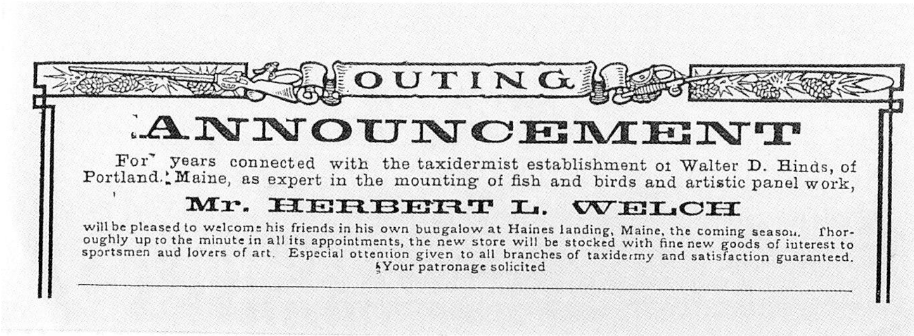

OUTING

ANNOUNCEMENT

For years connected with the taxidermist establishment of Walter D. Hinds, of Portland, Maine, as expert in the mounting of fish and birds and artistic panel work,

Mr. HERBERT L. WELCH

will be pleased to welcome his friends in his own bungalow at Haines landing, Maine, the coming season. Thoroughly up to the minute in all its appointments, the new store will be stocked with fine new goods of interest to sportsmen and lovers of art. Especial ottention given to all branches of taxidermy and satisfaction guaranteed. Your patronage solicited

Amicably and elegantly, Herb announced his change in status. In the May 1909 issue of *New England Magazine* (upper) and in the July 1909 issue of *Maine Woods and Sportsman* (lower). HILYARD COLLECTION

THE ARTISTIC MOUNTING OF FISH.

Mr. Welch has made the mounting and painting of fish a life-study. All work guaranteed. Shipping tags and directions for preparing fish for shipment on request. Prices consistent with the quality of the work.

HERBERT L. WELCH, Haines Landing, Maine.

tournament on June 1, 2 and 3. The full details can be obtained from Walter D. Hinds, 72 Pine Street, Portland, ME." If that poster was the work of Herb Welch, it would be a holy grail for any collector of Rangeley ephemera, as one has yet to surface.

Regardless of the artist, the poster must have worked, because John Philip Sousa (1854–1932) could be found shooting at Hillside in June and July of 1909 while staying at the Barker Hotel on Mooselookmeguntic. Sousa is best known as America's "March King," composing several famous patriotic marches, but he also had a lesser-known passion for trap shooting, Over the course of his lifetime, he shot over some 35,000 clays, with averages ranging from 75 to 90 percent, while his shotgun collection rivalled the world's best.

In 1916, Sousa was elected the first president of the American Amateur Trapshooting Association.[15] That same year, the Ithaca Gun Company of New York created a 12-gauge trap gun that was inlaid with 24-carat gold and engraved with field scenes of birds, dogs, and its signature mermaid. Called the Sousa Grade, the gun cost $1,000. Rarely found in today's collectible market, one was last seen at a

2007 auction going for a price of $31,050. In 1985, Sousa was inducted into the Trapshooting Hall of Fame in Vandalia, Ohio.

Even before incorporation as the Hillside Gun Club, the informal Oquossoc Gun Club was no stranger to celebrity shooting. Annie Oakley had stopped on her 1905 Maine tour, sponsored by the Union Metallic Cartridge Company of Bridgeport, Connecticut. The *Maine Woods* would report on August 30:

> She also hit bullseyes while shooting over her shoulder and taking aim by the reflection in a highly polished steel case knife. Steel disks, varying from one-eighth to half an inch in diameter were thrown into the air and plugged with the 38–55, 30–30, and 303 U.M.C. cartridges. The holes made were as clean as it had been made with a drill.

Sousa: March King and Marksman

It is interesting to chat with those who have come here to shoot with the Mooselookmeguntic Gun Club. One of the noted amateurs seen on the traps was the celebrated Band Master, John Philip Sousa, who with his wife is the guest of Mr. and Mrs. R.L. Spotts and has one of the cabins at the Barker.

This is the first time in three years that the famous band leader has been seen at the Maine traps, his last appearance being on the traps of the Portland Gun Club, where he shot his $350 gun made in Europe... During the past winter Mr. Sousa shot in Europe killing the chamois in the Alps and various European birds found in the Alps...

Mrs. Sousa is always among the women who daily watch the shoot and she is a most charming lady, interested and enthusiastic over her husband's shooting as when he stands before his celebrated brass band with baton in hand.

Fly Rod's Note Book
Maine Woods and Sportsman
June 13, 1912

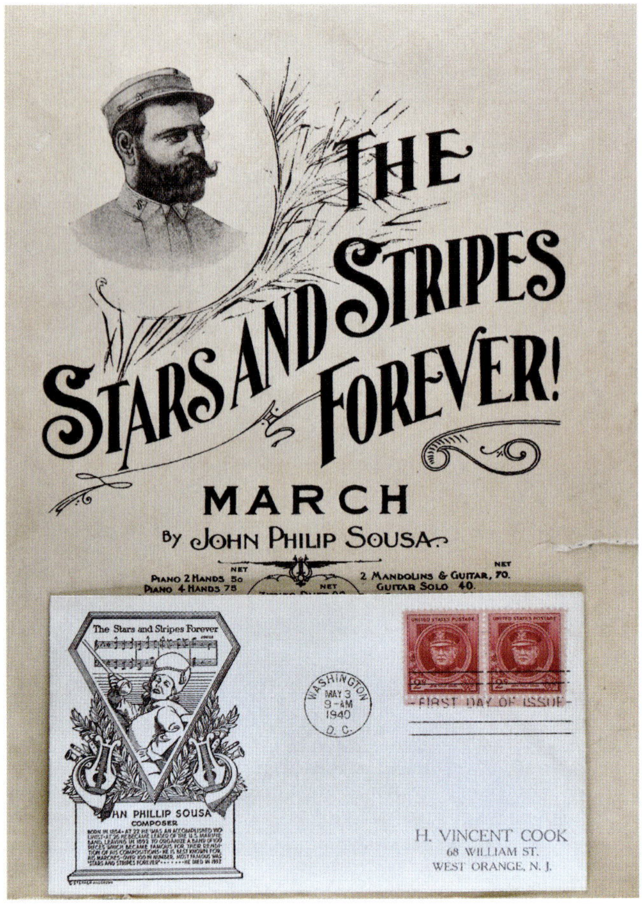

A First Day U.S. postal cover of Sousa on his iconic "Stars and Stripes Forever" sheet music. HILYARD COLLECTION

According to legend, during this tour "Fly Rod" Crosby shot against Annie Oakley and won, when they were both staying as guests at Marsquamosy Lodge on Rangeley Lake. However, our search of regional and sporting newspapers of the time turned up no mention of the two friends competing. Perhaps that's just as well. While "Fly Rod" was a capable hunter, she never had the skill to perform for European royalty as Oakley did.

After the Oakley demonstration, a shoot between club members credited Hinds with a score of thirty-eight out of fifty clays. Box scores reported in *Sporting Life* routinely mentioned Hinds and Welch, both competent shooters, but with Hinds usually edging out Welch.

In 1909, the Hillside became the Mooselookmeguntic Gun Club, with Hinds relinquishing the presidency to Ralph L. Spotts of New York City and his rockbound Camp Doraljo, found where the Cupsuptic flows into Mooselookmeguntic. Like many entrepreneurs, Hinds had more of a passion for the

Mounting the killer whale for a travelling circus required a coordinated effort by the Hinds team. Herb is on the left wearing a bowler. RANGELEY SPORTING HERITAGE MUSEUM

big picture than for day-to-day minutiae. Some of his big ideas included: acting as eastern agent for the New York City Madison Square Garden shows, demanding a New York City jury trial as a precedent-setting case for his crime of selling mounted snowy owls, and being filmed shooting dangerous rapids in a birchbark canoe. Hinds may have been a risk-taker, but he was not foolhardy. Following his nighttime seaplane crash into the Florida Everglades, he abandoned aircraft.[16]

Another example of his intrepid nature was found in a 1911 *New York Sun* interview that has him returning from four weeks in Nova Scotia and three weeks in the Maine woods before:

> Down to Mexico I am going to collect Mexican partridge which are known in some quarters as fool quail. They are sold in Mexico City alive, and the skin is worth $3. That is the only bird, so far as I can learn, whose eggs have never been found.
>
> I shall go to British East Africa another year and start in after some of that business over there. By the way, that Roosevelt stuff is still lying in the Smithsonian Institution unmounted. I understand they haven't enough money to fix it.

While Hinds was preparing for the future, his remaining competition at Haines Landing lay dying. Frail from birth, Daniel Ellsworth Heywood (1869–1911) passed away at forty-two from tuberculosis. Despite his frailty, Heywood's advertising reveals that he summered as a Parmachene guide and wintered in Rangeley as a taxidermist. His obituary notes that he had a studio at Haines Landing but does not mention where or when.[17] Heywood was a pioneer in night photography, and night image post cards occasionally surface stating "Pub. by D.E. Heywood, Haines Landing, Me." In later life, the *Maine Woods* and *Maine Sportsman* published his articles on the state of the Everglades and Floridian fauna. Given his fragile health and that he was living in Rangeley, it seems unlikely that Heywood had much of a presence at Haines Landing.

On June 21, 1912, the *Portland Evening Express and Advertiser* led with bold headlines:

Many taxidermist shops fell to fire, as early taxidermy required volatile chemicals and combustible material.
PENOBSCOT MARINE MUSEUM

A studio shot of J. Waldo Nash by Minnie Libby, known as the "Dean of Maine women photographers." Posing as a rough rider, Captain Nash of the Norway Company D Regiment served in the Spanish-American War.
PAUL COTE COLLECTION

> SPORTING CAMPS OF PORTLAND MEN BURN AT HAINES LANDING
>
> Five Persons Overcome by Smoke in Trying to Save Places of W.D. Hinds and Herbert L. Welch
>
> Loss $8,000.
>
> (Special to the *Express-Advertiser*) – Fire which started from the fireplace in the camp of Walter D. Hinds of Portland, destroyed the camp and taxidermal establishment conducted by Mr. Hinds, also the camp of Buckskin, the well known Indian guide, and damaged the taxidermal establishment of Herbert L. Welch and the cottage of Gardner Hinkley. The total loss is estimated at $8,000, Mr. Hinds' loss being $6,000.

Surveying the damage, Hinds decided not to rebuild at Haines Landing and sold his remaining stock and land to Welch, who had not been much affected by the fire. Act V was about to begin, with Welch playing a key role for forty-five years on Mooselookmeguntic Lake and far beyond.

ENDNOTES

1 P.A. Morris, *A History of Taxidermy: Art, Science, and Bad Taste*, Ascot, UK: MPM Publishing, 2010, p. 156.
2 Walter Karp, *Charles Darwin and the Origin of Species*, New York: Harper & Row, 1968, p. 22.
3 Morris, p. 21.
4 Morris, p. 14.
5 Psalm 74 v. 13; Ezekiel 29 v. 3–4.
6 Morris, p. 34.
7 Morris, p. 28.
8 Lynn Barber, The Heyday of Natural History *(1820–1870)*, Gordan City, New York: Doubleday, 1980, pp. 155–156.
9 Rembrandt Peale, *Disquistion on the Mammoth, or, Great American Incognitum, and Extinct, Immense, Carniverous Animal whose Fossil Remains have been found in North America*, London, 1803, pp. 60–61, reprinted in Keir B. Sterling, ed., *Selected Works in 19th Century North American Paleontology*, New York: Arno Press, 1974.
10 Elizabeth and Max Hall, *About the Exhibits*, Cambridge: Harvard Museum of Comparative Zoology, 1964, pp. 41–42.
11 "Trade Notes," *Maine Woods*, Phillips, Maine, January 16, 1903.
12 Henry R. Martin, letter to author, March 13, 2011.
13 "'Nash of Maine' and His Art," *Lewiston Daily Sun*, Lewiston, Maine, August 22, 1914.
14 Margaret Anderson, letter to author, July 21, 2010.
15 Paul E. Bierly, *John Phillip Sousa, American Phenomenon*, Ohio: Integrity Press, 1973, p. 224.
16 "Obituary of Walter D. Hinds," *Portland Press Herald*, Portland, Maine, January 5, 1928, p. 1.
17 "Obituary of Daniel E. Heywood," *Maine Woods and Sportsman*, Phillips, Maine, August 10, 1911.
18 "The Gimbel Story," *The Rangeley Highlander*, Rangeley, Maine, July 13, 1960.

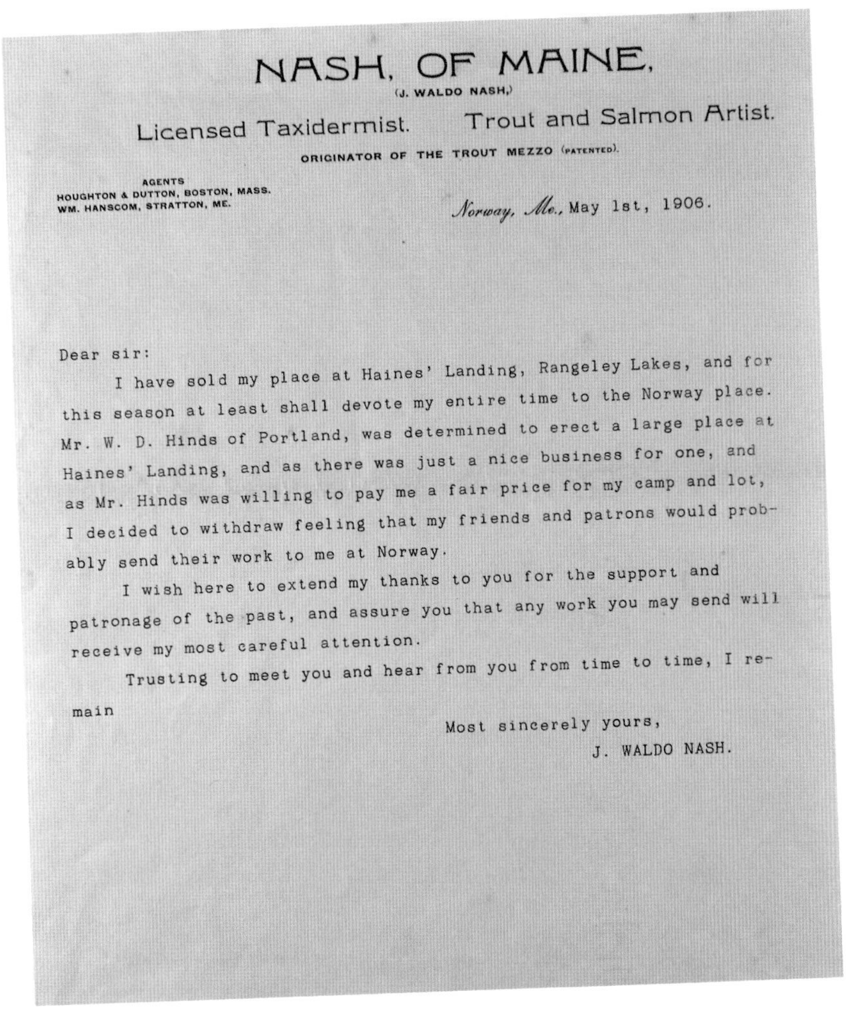

NASH, OF MAINE.
(J. WALDO NASH,)
Licensed Taxidermist. Trout and Salmon Artist.
ORIGINATOR OF THE TROUT MEZZO (PATENTED).

AGENTS
HOUGHTON & DUTTON, BOSTON, MASS.
WM. HANSCOM, STRATTON, ME.

Norway, Me., May 1st, 1906.

Dear sir:

I have sold my place at Haines' Landing, Rangeley Lakes, and for this season at least shall devote my entire time to the Norway place. Mr. W. D. Hinds of Portland, was determined to erect a large place at Haines' Landing, and as there was just a nice business for one, and as Mr. Hinds was willing to pay me a fair price for my camp and lot, I decided to withdraw feeling that my friends and patrons would probably send their work to me at Norway.

I wish here to extend my thanks to you for the support and patronage of the past, and assure you that any work you may send will receive my most careful attention.

Trusting to meet you and hear from you from time to time, I remain

Most sincerely yours,
J. WALDO NASH.

Doubtless an unhappy man.
CARLSON COLLECTION

HERBERT L. WELCH
COMPLETE OUTFITTER
HIGH GRADE SPORTING GOODS - EXPERT IN FISH MOUNTING
IN THE HEART OF THE RANGELEY LAKES
HAINES LANDING, MAINE
HERBERT L. WELCH
High Grade Sporting Goods
Mooselookmeguntic, Maine
P. O. OQUOSSOC, MAINE
PROPER EQUIPMENT AND ADVICE AT THE START MEANS BETTER SUCCESS
HERBERT L. WELCH
HIGH GRADE SPORTING GOODS
EXPERT IN FISH MOUNTING
HAINES LANDING, MAINE.
MOUNTED BY HERBERT L. WELCH HAINES LANDING RANGELEY LAKES MAINE
FROM
HERBERT L. WELCH
Taxidermist
HAINES LANDING,
Pattern:
Originated by:
Leslie Hilyard
Rangeley Trust Company.
52-210
FIDELITY
SECURITY
RANGELEY, MAINE
Rangeley, Me

CHAPTER 4

Mastery

Six years had quickly passed since 1905 when Herb Welch first stood on Haines Landing, surveying the mountains ringing Mooselookmeguntic Lake. In that time, the business landscape had changed irrevocably, leaving him as a solitary taxidermist at center stage.

A Welch painting of the Welch store at Haines Landing. The store was on the ground floor with the Welches' living quarters above. FOOTER COLLECTION

While other taxidermists of the era were generalists, Herb became a specialist in the art of fish mounting. With Hinds moving on, Welch was now free to mount big game, adding significantly to his income. However, he had little interest in this process, and judging from his shop invoices, he sourced the bulk of this work out to Carl A. Garris of Portland, Maine.

The fact that the writers have been able to study ninety-seven Welch fish mounts, some mounted over a century ago, can be attributed to Welch's use of wooden forms beneath the skin. Roughed out by a bandsaw and hand-finished from white pine, those forms provided a solid foundation impervious to the shrinking and crumbling that plagued the traditional plaster of Paris and clay mounts. Herb took the additional step of sealing the forms and coating them with white zinc paint to prevent moisture absorption that would cause swelling and splitting of the skin, thereby increasing the longevity of the mounts. It had the added benefit of creating a smooth painting surface, particularly important in the trout family, as trout have no discernable scales.

Herb never claimed to have originated this technique. In *Guide to Taxidermy*, published in 1908, the father and son team of Charles and Chester Reed of Worcester, Massachusetts, laid claim to have first used this innovation as early as 1885. But they failed to recognize the risk of claiming to be first. Since

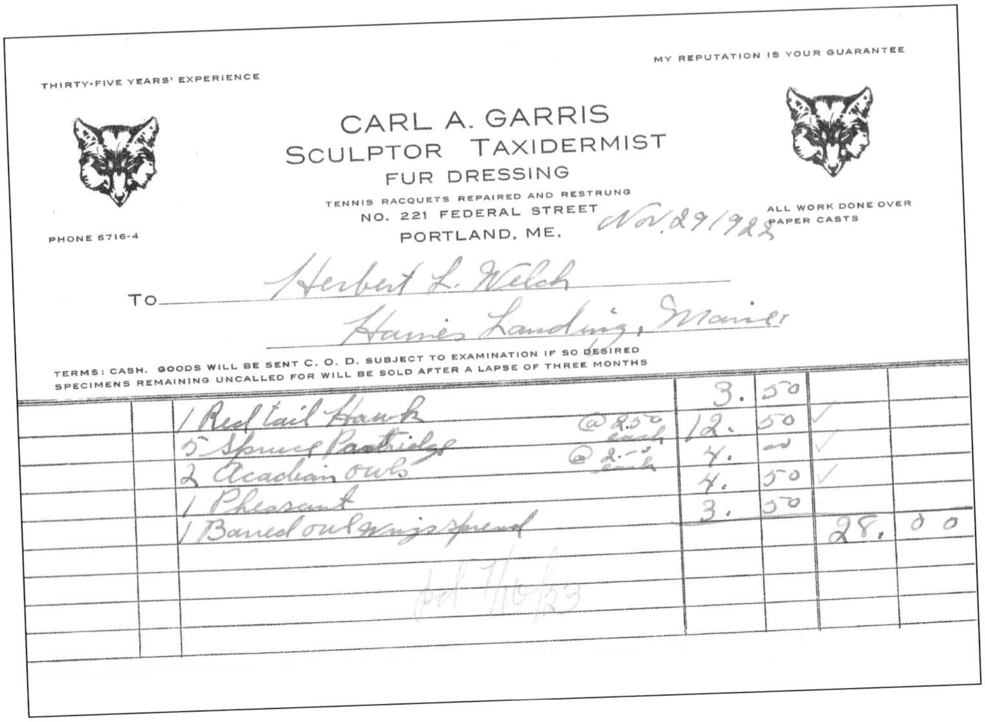

THIRTY-FIVE YEARS' EXPERIENCE

MY REPUTATION IS YOUR GUARANTEE

CARL A. GARRIS
SCULPTOR TAXIDERMIST
FUR DRESSING
TENNIS RACQUETS REPAIRED AND RESTRUNG
NO. 221 FEDERAL STREET
PORTLAND, ME.

PHONE 6716-4

ALL WORK DONE OVER PAPER CASTS

Nov. 29/1922

TO Herbert L. Welch
Haines Landing, Maine

TERMS: CASH. GOODS WILL BE SENT C. O. D. SUBJECT TO EXAMINATION IF SO DESIRED
SPECIMENS REMAINING UNCALLED FOR WILL BE SOLD AFTER A LAPSE OF THREE MONTHS

1 Red tail Hawk		3.50	
5 Spruce Partridge	@ 2.50 each	12.50	
2 Acadian Owls	@ 2.— each	4.—	
1 Pheasant		4.50	
1 Barred owl wings spread		3.50	28.00

Anything with fur or feathers was subbed out to Carl A. Garris by Herb. Four of these five species now require protection by law.

1781, Italy's University of Pavia in Lombardy has exhibited a dolphin skin mounted over a wooden body.[1] Like it or not, pretty much everything we Americans do in the sporting realm hearkens back to the Old World.

While today a serpentine style is considered the hallmark of Welch mounts, it was not always so. Herb was an artist whose painting and sculpting skills informed his taxidermy over time. While most of his taxidermy was attached to open back panels, some were displayed under protective glass bubbles. Although Welch used bird's-eye maple back panels most frequently, he chose to enhance some mounts with oil paintings of sylvan waterways. Many of these panels were signed and dated, giving an approximate timeline for his evolution as a taxidermist.

As late as 1919, Herb was still mounting fish either in a rigid, straight-line style or a slightly U-shaped curvature. But by the 1924 preservation of the Carrie Stevens trophy brook trout, Herb had abandoned these old techniques for a flowing, serpentine style that put the fish in motion. This sense of motion breathed life into his mounts and came to define the Welch style.

Preservation techniques aside, what separates the good from the great in fish taxidermy is the ability to paint. Unlike mounting mammals or birds, where fur and feathers can hide a multitude of flaws, an exposed fish skin, soaked in salt for ages, requires an artist's brush to look alive. While some taxidermists preferred the airbrush technique patented in 1876 by Francis E. Stanley (a cousin of H.O. Stanley), Herb rejected it in favor of his oil paints, Russian sable brushes, and easel.

Herb's skill as a painter may not always be evident to contemporary viewers. While his painting was always in harmony with a fish's home waters, the final coat of varnish that he applied (except on trout bellies) eventually yellowed and darkened. However, a competent restorer can help those original colors glow again.

Other more technical features exist that can help identify a Welch mount.[2] Prior to the 1940s, when light wire office staples became available, Welch used blued carpet tacks to attach the back of the skin to the wooden form. He also used a tack to hold down the pectoral fin, which was cut off by most other taxidermists. The rumor that Herb sewed the slit skin with a unique stitching pattern is just that, a rumor.

Always (or at least we have not seen otherwise yet), Herb glued the tail to the back panel to prevent it from breaking. Always, he cut the skin through from head to tail. Always, the fish's mouth was open, revealing a molded tongue of Herb's making. If the fisher had not supplied a fly, Herb would often insert a red-and-white streamer or bucktail.

A front view of a trout dated 1919, demonstrating Welch's early straight-line style of mounting. LIBBY COLLECTION

A head-on view of Welch's straight-line style. LIBBY COLLECTION

Front view of Carrie Steven's brook trout, dated 1924. This mount demonstrates Welch's later serpentine style, which would become his hallmark. This fish placed second in the 1924 *Field & Stream* contest and launched Carrie's career as a streamer tier. RANGELEY SPORTING HERITAGE MUSEUM

A head-on view of Welch's serpentine style. To disciples of Stevens, the streamer raises fascinating questions. Typically, the mounted fly is the fly that did the damage. Could this be the elusive Shang's-Go-Getum whose pattern remains a mystery? RANGELEY SPORTING HERITAGE MUSEUM

Meticulously, Herb cleaned out the brain cavity, ridding it of troublesome oils. To restore the head to form, he packed it with clay. He then used purified white beeswax (obtained from candle companies) to recreate the inner lining of the mouth. To tone down the brilliant white, he mixed a pinch of lampblack into the beeswax and used it to reshape the gills and gill cover. Beeswax had to be used sparingly, as any excess would melt in the summer heat of a wilderness cabin. Using pins that were removed after drying was completed, Herb carefully positioned the fragile fins.

Once attached to the wooden form, Herb sealed the fish skin by hand, painting it with artists oils and varnish, hiding the fact that the skin may have spent months soaking in salt brine. Unlike other taxidermists, who used Borax to treat skins, Herb preferred a super-saturated saline solution that he deemed sufficiently salted when it could float a large potato.

While Herb's clients had no choice in how their trophies were mounted, they certainly did in its presentation. Depending on how much a client was willing to pay, fish could be ordered in a variety of ways, ranging from a simple oval wooden panel to an elaborate glass bubble enclosure with a painted landscape background.

Provided by the Lang Carving Company of Beecher Falls, Vermont, wooden ovals ranged in size from 9 to 49 inches long and from 8 to 22 inches wide. The choice of woods included: walnut, mahogany, chestnut, curly birch, bird's-eye maple, and oak in quarter-sawn, Mission, and Flemish styles. Lang also supplied custom 4- to 5-inch wide beaded mahogany and walnut frames, which were needed to secure the glass bubbles used on trophy mounts and carvings. In later years, John C.W. Straub of Williamsport, Pennsylvania, and the Beal Furniture Store and the New England Cabinet Company of Portland, Maine, supplied comparable product.

On the reverse of the oval panels, red circular stickers can be sometimes found saying:

MOUNTED BY
HERBERT L. WELCH
HAINES LANDING
RANGELEY LAKES
MAINE

Boyhood Memories of Herb

In 1937, my grandfather, Captain F.C. Barker, died and my parents took over his Barker Hotel. This hotel was located about three quarters of a mile from Haines Landing where Herb's store sat. Since I worked several years for my parents, before acquiring the hotel myself, I spent summers near Herb, and we became good friends. Herb called Larry Hinds and me his "boys." Larry's family had a large summer cottage on "our" lake.

On one memorable afternoon, Dot and Herb and my father and I went in Dad's motorboat to Bemis to fly-fish. It was late September and many large brook trout were gathered at the mouth of Bemis Stream. We obtained two Rangeley boats from Bemis Camps and rowed out into the stream channel.

No other fisherman appeared, as there was no road to Bemis after the cessation of rail service following that disastrous 1936 flood. Herb used a spent-wing dry fly, fished wet. The fly had wide white wings and a brown body. That afternoon, the four of us landed twenty-two large brook trout. We released all but one, a 4-pounder that my Dad caught. Herb wanted one fish to mount for the Barker Hotel as a gift from him. I still have that mounting...

One year my parents wished to give me a new fly rod, so they purchased a Thomas bamboo rod at Herb's store. I still have that rod...

Once in a while I would stop at Herb's store and watch him remove a fish skin from his taxidermy brine barrel with a wooden stick, smooth it gently on the wooden form that he had carved for the fish, and pin the skin in place for drying. Herb advocated toilet paper soaked with varnish for repairing damaged fins. His long curving fingers and thumbs provided the expert touch required to finish the mounting.

Fred B. Harnden
Rangeley, Maine
2002

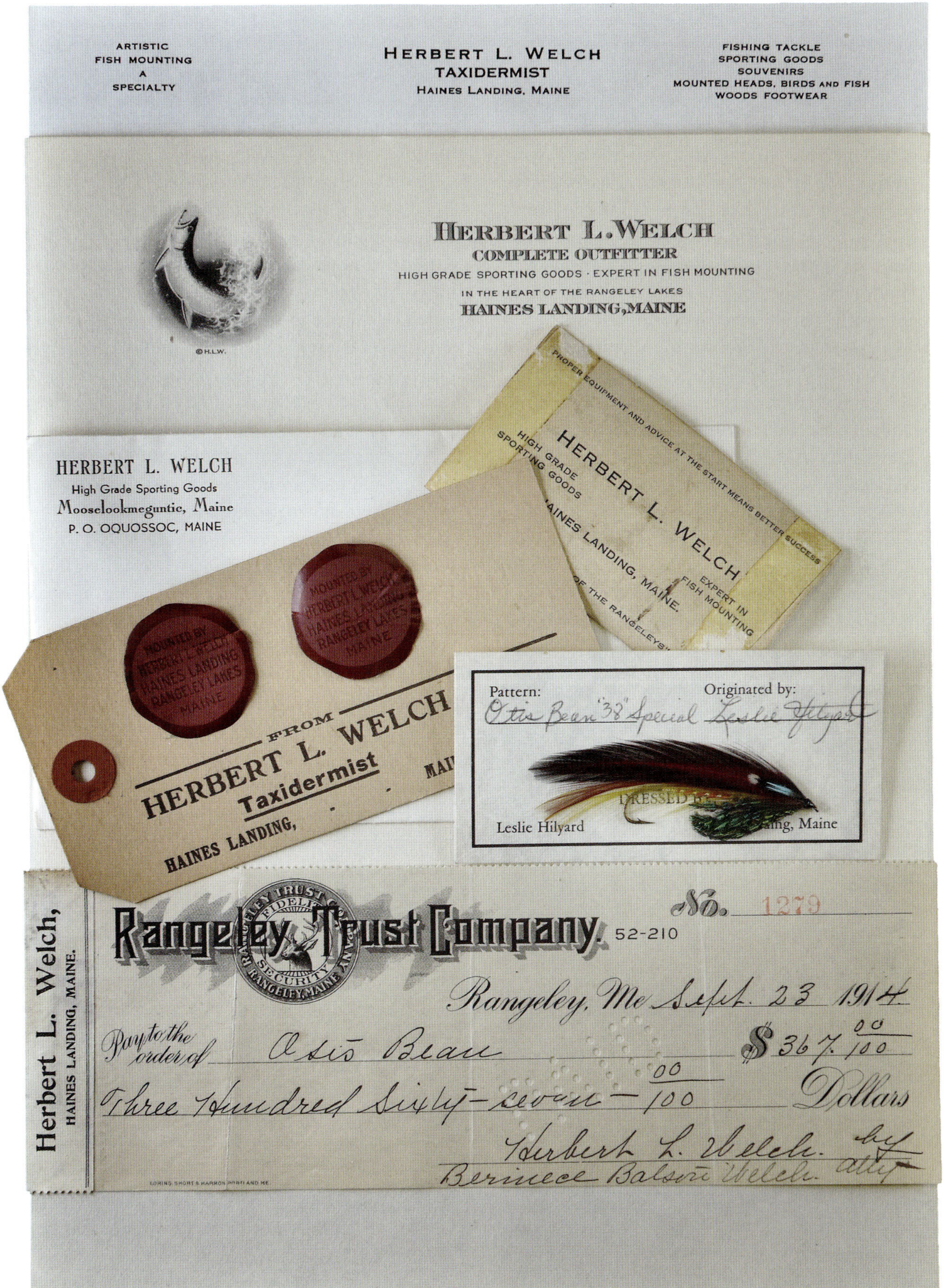

Various papers used in the Welch business. The Otis Bean .38 Special was originated and tied by Leslie K. Hilyard.
HILYARD COLLECTION

However, Herb did not use stickers for long, as they are notorious for falling off or, worse, being transferred to a lesser work.

While English taxidermists preferred five-sided, glass-paneled cases, often with bowed fronts, Americans tended to prefer the convex glass bubble. Patented by Joseph Storck of Boston in 1882, it apparently did not catch on, and so it was "re-patented" by H.L. Rand of Worcester, Massachusetts, in 1889.[3,4] Back then, it was not unusual for similar patents to be issued, as the patent office was a loosely organized agency overseen by the Secretaries of State and War and the Attorney General's office. Perhaps Rand's approach caught on instead of Storck's because Rand assigned half the rights to Charles K. Reed, who promoted it heavily in his *Guide to Taxidermy* and in his taxidermy business.

Provided by the Oriel Glass Company of St. Louis, Missouri, the oval convex glass bubbles were custom molded in a variety of sizes. Judging from the Welch shop invoices, there were three sizes: 18 x 26 inches, 20 × 35 inches, and 22 x 28 inches. Although these elegant glass bubbles offered protection, they were

Herb Welch at the easel, breathing life into his trophy mounts. RANGELEY SPORTING HERITAGE MUSEUM

a double-edged sword. If left in direct sunlight, they turned into an oven, drying out fragile fins and causing colors to fade dramatically. The glass bubbles were fragile, and their heavy weight made them difficult to transport and display.

The arrival of plexiglass in the 1970s mitigated some of these issues, but this new material had its own problems. Plexiglass often required additional expensive hours of fine sanding, since cutting a single bubble from a batch of bubbles could spray fine particles over the surface, where they bonded via static electricity. Often, no amount of care with emery cloths and buffing creams could remove the haze of particles that collected on some bubbles, rendering them useless.[5]

Another option for panels involved harvesting white birch bark from fallen trees. Aside from a few cooperative sawmills, no supplier existed for this product, but gathering it was well worth the effort. Laying the bark on a thin panel and then lacing its borders with sweetgrass created a stunning contrast, particularly for the shimmering brook trout.

Herb was not interested in childish debates about the glories of one fish species over another. If it swam, he would mount it. For example, his records reveal that he mounted white perch, brown trout, brook trout, lake trout, rainbow trout, smallmouth bass, and tuna tails for Julian Crandall of the Ashaway Line Company. In terms of sheer size, Herb's most impressive display was an orca he mounted for a traveling circus, which was so large that it required a team effort.

No one will ever know precisely how many mounted fish bear the Welch signature. His records that would have answered that question have long since been lost. Apparently for billing purposes, Herb kept 3 x 5 cards that noted the species, price, panel choice, and name of the owner, with a corresponding identification number. That number would match a lead tag attached to the wooden fish form. In the absence of a tag, Herb would sometimes write the number on the form itself or sometimes on the back panel. The highest lead tag number we know of is 806, which led us to believe he had a run of 1,000 tags made. This does little good, because we learned that when Herb reached his maximum number, he simply started over.[6] This left us to wonder: How many times?

An example of Herb combining his painterly skills with carved brook trout. Signed "Herb Welch, 1945" by its creator, lower left. VOORHEES COLLECTION

While the number of Welch mounts is unknown, we do know how much they cost in 1952:[7]

2 pounds or less = $25.00
2–5 pounds = $35.00
5–7 pounds = $45.00
7–10 pounds = $60.00
over 10 pounds = $60.00 + $5 for each additional pound

While there are no records of the cost of a glass-enclosed fish with a painted back panel, we can be reasonably certain that it did not come cheap. Price was based on weight rather than length, and for good reason. While anyone could observe the length of a submitted fish, its weight had to be reported. This proved an incredible temptation for many fishers, and any fragile egos who exaggerated to fatten the size of their trophies would also be fattening Welch's wallet.

The year 1946 was not the best time for young Dave Footer and his aging Model A to challenge the Height of Land, a narrow and panic-inducing approach to Rangeley. Only recently, had the road been cut through converging mountain ranges, thanks to a New Deal program. Meanwhile, driving spring rains and fog rising off Mooselookmeguntic Lake were severely reducing visibility. Footer's fishing companion, Johnny Gielarowski, began nervously suggesting that maybe they should turn back, if they could find a place to do it without hitting an oncoming logging truck or broadsiding a moose. But this was a problem, as civil engineers had not considered the possibility that a driver might want to turn and go in the opposite direction. Attempting to turn in low light on a narrow roadbed ran

Thanks to Welch, a stringer of fish frozen in time. RANGELEY SPORTING HERITAGE MUSEUM

An exquisite example of Herb putting a brook trout in context. Signed lower left "Herb Welch." PHILBRICK COLLECTION

Dave Footer commenting on the writer's aged mounts. HILYARD COLLECTION

the risk of a visit to the deep roadside ditches that were dug to minimize springtime washouts. Driving straight ahead was pretty much the only option.

But this was no matter to Footer. Ever since he had started fishing, Dave had heard of the legendary Rangeley Lakes. Armed with a tank of gas and $3 in his pocket, he was determined to finish his journey. When he and Gielarowski arrived in Rangeley soaking wet, their original plan to sleep overnight in the Model A now seemed less attractive. Although they had not budgeted for it, they decided to solve the problem of drying out by two hours of theater going.

Greeted the next day by the early morning sun, they went in search of fishing recommendations and were pointed toward Mooselookmeguntic. Searching for a boat rental, they landed at Bald Mountain Camps where no boats were available. But this turned out to be fortuitous. While Johnny was on the phone calling other camps, Dave roamed about the main lodge and had an epiphany:

> I was kind of looking around, and right next to the phone booth was this beautiful mounted trout. Oh, it was about three or four pounds. It was just magnificent to look at. I had been mounting some birds and small animals, but just a couple of fish and, so gee, I just looked at that fish and thought, "Oh, boy! If I could only be able to mount a fish that would look that good some day." So that was the first time that I ever saw a Herb Welch mounting.[8]

Mesmerized by the Welch brook trout, Dave returned to Lewiston and continued his studies in taxidermy, focusing more on fish. A shy sixteen-year-old, he had not even asked who the creator of that mount had been.

The Northwestern School of Taxidermy claimed to have 250,000 students, most of whom had grown up beguiled by its ads promising fame and fortune, but unlike most of those students, Dave completed all the supplied coursework. Equally important, he discovered the fine arts and added drawing and painting to his repertoire.

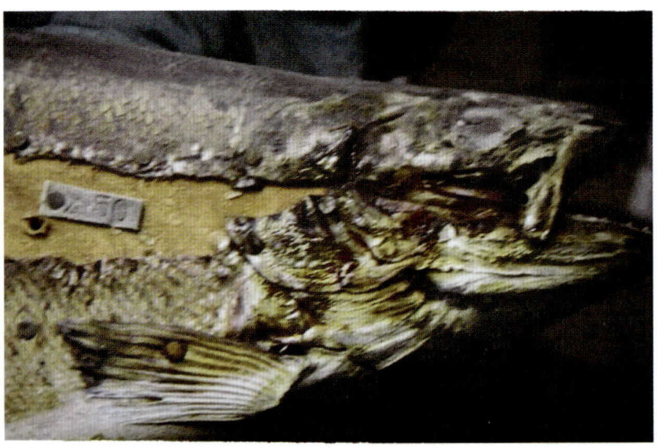

Herb's work behind the scenes. Unlike many Welch mounts, this salmon retains its lead tag. Thus far, the use of lead tags appears to be unique to Welch. JULIE FOOTER

Although enchanted by the arts, Dave knew he needed a day job and trained in masonry under the guidance of his father. However, he never abandoned taxidermy. He eventually married his high school sweetheart, Pauline Rita Olivier, and she would prove invaluable in his career, not unlike the wives of Nash, Pickel, and Welch. How she did this while also giving birth to seven children (Jane, Veronica, John, Julie, Dorothy, James, and Joseph) still mystifies.

As he approached eighty, Herb Welch was a man of two minds. For decades, he had been receiving accolades for his taxidermy work, and more orders kept pouring in. Internationally, his demonstration casting had made him a renowned fixture on the sportsman show circuit. Generations had grown up in awe of his ability to cast over 100 feet and his ability to write his name with his backcast, all while he and Chief Needebah bantered on stage about his misspelling his first name. He had traveled North America, fishing the great waters and holding records for trophy bonefish in the salt. Herb had also done well financially, thanks in part to Bernice's intelligent investments. Yet, no one who lives that long is without regrets.

Like many, Herb had dreamed of leaving a legacy behind for his children, but that had never been an option. Of all the children that Herb mentored—and there were many—none had been his own. Sadly, an early miscarriage, which required subsequent dilation and curettage, meant that Bernice had been unable to bear children.

Herb's recent attempts to train aspiring taxidermists had been a dismal failure. The candidates were more interested in pushing product out the door than in mastering the foundation work and artistry required of a Welch mount. Consequently, Herb took any new fish he received and shipped them to Fred C.N. Parke, who had a leading taxidermy house in Bangor, Maine, with branches from Alberta, Canada, down the east coast to Key West, Florida. Because of these failures, when Herb first heard of a twenty-year-old taxidermist from Lewiston, he was not enthused. Still, he told the

Discovering Enduring Love

When Dave and I first met Herb and Dot Welch back in 1952, I was star struck. After all, I was a very young girl and they were such famous people. But it didn't take long to realize that I was nowhere near as starstruck with them as Dot was with Herb.

Dave and Herb would be off in there owe little cocoon with a fish and I would be sitting upstairs above the store with Dot. From the very beginning, she was bubbling over with excitement and joy, telling me how absolutely wonderful it was that she married Herb Welch. And she didn't tell me this once, but time and time again on different visits. Different words, but always the same endearing tone.

Now, this was pretty amazing to me because I was only 18, and I could not imagine that people their age could still be that excited about being married. She was over 50 and Herb was in his 70s and, by then, they had been married, maybe, two or three years. She never said it openly, but I got the distinct feeling that she had loved him from afar for a very long time, but on Herb's part, it wasn't happening. But now she was finally married to him. She felt this marriage was made in heaven. I can tell you that much for sure.

As a young girl, it was wonderful for me to see such love between two people who not only lived together but worked together, just as Dave and I are doing.

Pauline Footer
Lewiston Maine, 2002

Herb and Dorothy in late life. RONALD TURMENNE

Herb's final photograph taken on May 9, 1960. RANGELEY SPORTING HERITAGE MUSEUM

Dorothy Welch preparing a salmon for shipment to Dave Footer for mounting. RANGELEY SPORTING HERITAGE MUSEUM

messenger that young Dave Footer should feel free to call anyway.

Their first meeting in October 1952 had a less-than-auspicious beginning, with Herb announcing that he was no longer looking to train anyone, and that as his health was declining, he just wanted to "be done with the whole business." But his tone changed after he saw a Footer mount on a painted panel. Soon he was regaling Dave with stories of his early years, like the one about a freight car full of dead seagulls that had arrived at Oquossoc, destined to become window displays for an East Coast department store chain. (Not such a good idea—dead seagulls and steel freight cars do not mix well in August heat.) Impressed by Dave's ability to paint, Herb asked him to visit again and suggested specific assignments in the meantime. Immediately, Dave abandoned plaster forms for wood and proved adept at grasping the subtleties of the Welch style. More trips followed, kept brief due to Herb's failing health.

By 1958, Herb had canceled his arrangement with Parke, and he was shipping prepared skins to Dave for 20 percent of retail. Since Herb shipped out both the Parke and Footer mounts under his own name,

From Acolyte to Master

Herb:"You give up on deer heads yet?"
Dave: "Why would I do that? They bring in a lot of money."
Herb: "You will. One day you'll be mounting a trout and a deer hair will get under the skin, and when you're done, it'll show up like a skunk in the fog."

As told to the writer by Dave Footer, 2002

Herb gave me a lot more than advice. He gave me his bandsaw used to rough out fish forms and his sander adapted from a bucksaw that got into tight spots on the form. Actually, it's the sander that fine tunes the forms and helps get that serpentine shape that is fundamental. Also gave me his airbrush that never saw much use. He preferred to hand paint fish and so do I. He gave me the mould that he made for making fish tongues. And a lot of paintings that I prize. Particularly, the one of Whitehead Cliff out in Portland Harbor. Most of all, he gave me confidence. He gave me courage.

any claims to "the last of the Welch mounts" should be regarded with suspicion.

In February 1960, Dave and his wife, Polly, visited Herb and Dorothy at their winter home in Moorestown, New Jersey. It was a memorable week, as Herb's health had rebounded and he was able to introduce them and their work to nearby sporting venues. They spent long and pleasant evenings together, with Dave drawing and Herb offering critique and instructing him on anatomy. The two laid plans for the coming season at Haines Landing. But in early May, Herb's health took another downward turn, and on May 19th of 1960, he breathed his last, leaving the sporting world in mourning—none more so than the young Footers.

ENDNOTES

1 Morris, p. 19.
2 David and Pauline Footer, taped interview with author, September 21, 2001.
3 United States Patent Office, Joseph Storck, Boston, patent no. 258,821, May 30, 1882.
4 United States Patent Office, Herbert L. Rand, Worcester, Massachusetts, patent no. 405,678, June 18, 1899.
5 Julie Ann Footer, interview with author, January 30, 2015.
6 David Footer, interview with author, November 29, 2011.
7 David and Pauline Footer, taped interview with author, March 16, 2002.
8 Ibid.

CHAPTER 5

Portrayals

At the age of 8, Herb figured that someday he would be a great artist, and he started on his career. Stopping by a waterfall, he sketched a painting, and if one went into his studio at Haines Landing today, they would find that very sketch proudly framed and displayed.

THE *RANGELEY RECORD*, MIDWINTER, 1947

While the prices Herb Welch achieved for his art may astonish us (some went for $250, roughly the equivalent of $2,800 today), the fact that he was actively painting should not. Throughout his long career, whenever Herb gave an interview, he rarely failed to mention his passion for art.

Following the Welch family's arrival in Pittsfield, Herb enrolled in art classes instructed by Della Dewey Pratt (1862–1946) of nearby Clinton. Born into privilege, Pratt grew up in the Massachusetts Berkshires and studied under Andros, a painterly name that has faded from sight. Primarily known for her landscapes, Pratt painted prolifically and taught art in both academic and private settings.[1]

Again, the family moved, but Herb kept pursuing his passion for art. He is listed in the Portland city directories from 1897 to 1904 as a crayon artist with a Congress Street studio. Still practiced today, crayon art was all the rage at the turn of the twentieth century, with four competing studios on Congress Street alone. While crayon art had long been practiced in Europe, innovations by the American company Binney & Smith (which is better known today as Crayola) resulted in less expensive, better quality, and easier-to-handle crayons. Their Crayolas had the added advantage of being non-toxic.

In 1906, the city directory no longer listed Herb as an artist. Instead, it listed him as a taxidermist in the employ of Walter D. Hinds. Herb would remain a taxidermist throughout his life, as every subsequent directory and census record would show. By no means, however, did Herb abandon art, as verified by a steady output of paintings that date as early as 1904.

Herb had to forego any additional formal art training while he went about establishing his business, but by 1920, it appears that he felt that academic urge again. Archival records from 1921 find him studying at the prestigious Art Students League of New York. Organized in 1875 "for the purpose of establishing and maintaining an Academic School

Della Dewey Pratt, Herb's first art instructor. Although directly descended from Netherland royalty on her paternal side, she rarely spoke of it. CLINTON HISTORICAL SOCIETY

1921 – B.B. Bryan, NYC – Fire Picture – $100.
1922 – E.E. Bigelow, Worcester, Mass. – Trout & Woodland – $150.
1923 – Louise Hirschon, New Rochelle, NY – Ross Pond – $75.
1924 – Mrs. F.T. Wheeler, Palinville, Conn. – Path In Woods – $150.
1925 – B.B. Bryan, NYC – Large painting – $250.
1926 – Mrs. G.A. Hobart, Paterson, NJ – Sunset Over Hobart Ridge – $150.

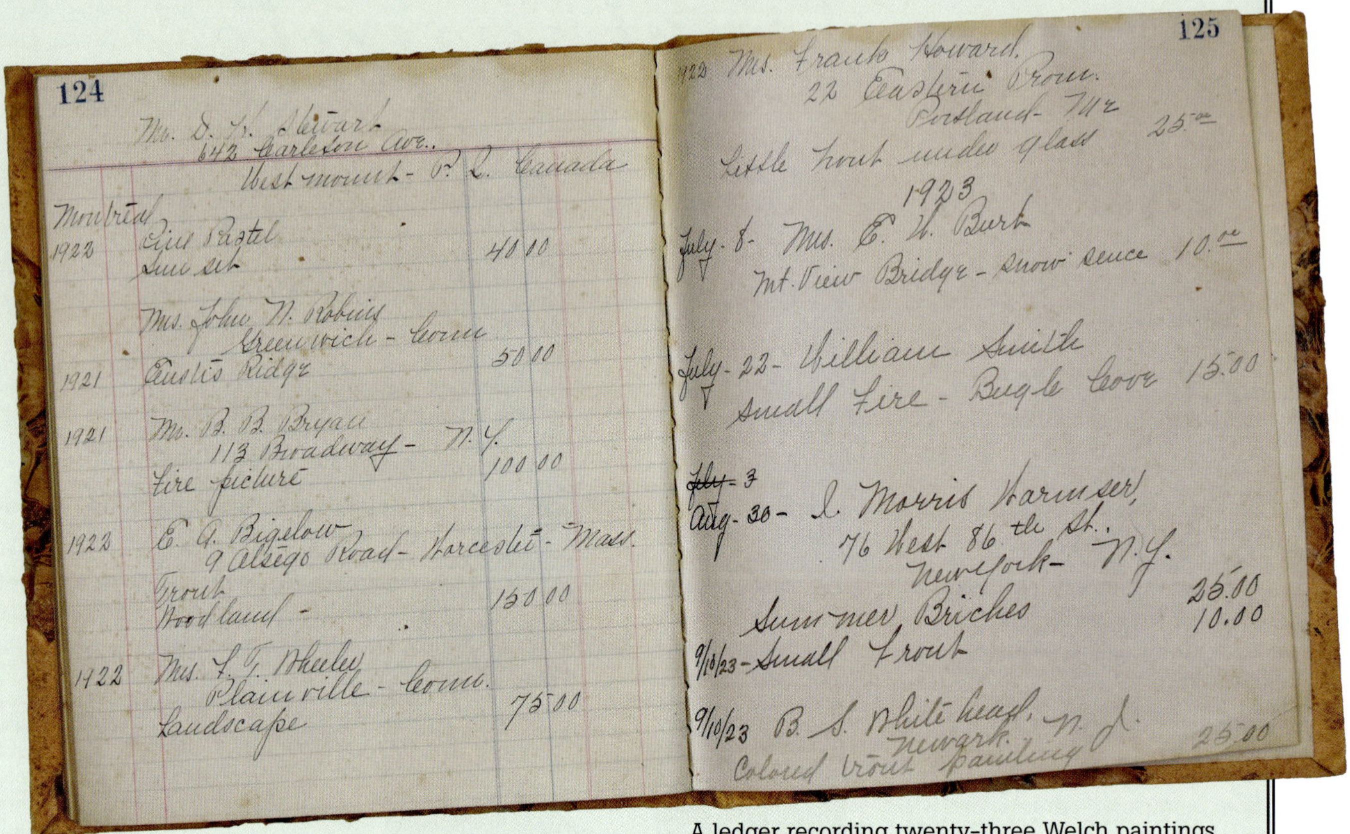

A ledger recording twenty-three Welch paintings, buyers, and prices. VOORHEES COLLECTION

of Art which should give a thorough course of study in Drawing, Painting, and Sculpture," its mission still continues today.[2]

At age 43, Herb was far from a provincial rustic. Still, even for him, it must have been heady times studying under Guy Pene du Bois, an American realist artist whose work remains just as relevant today. Despite the often profit-driven fickleness of the art world, du Bois has endured and is housed in the nation's leading museums. As recently as 2013, his painting *The Crowd* commanded $602,500 at a Sotheby's auction—a far cry from the $13 Herb paid to take his thirty-day course in March 1921.

Further formal training would require an Atlantic crossing. On January 15, 1927, Herb and Bernice boarded the ocean liner SS *Paris* in New York City bound for Havre, then Paris. In a first-class cabin, of course.[3] While at the Art Students League, Herb had developed an interest in the sculpture of Mahonri Young (1877–1957), a charismatic artist who many considered to be America's premier sculptor of the day. One of the highlights of Young's career was the 1950 unveiling of a 5-foot 11-inch marble statue of his grandfather, Brigham Young, at the National Statuary Hall in Washington, D.C.[4] Herb always gravitated toward the best and so was willing to go all the way to Paris to learn bronze casting from the master.

And learn Herb did, as demonstrated by his 1927 bronze of two entwined leaping trout, *On the Rise*.[5]

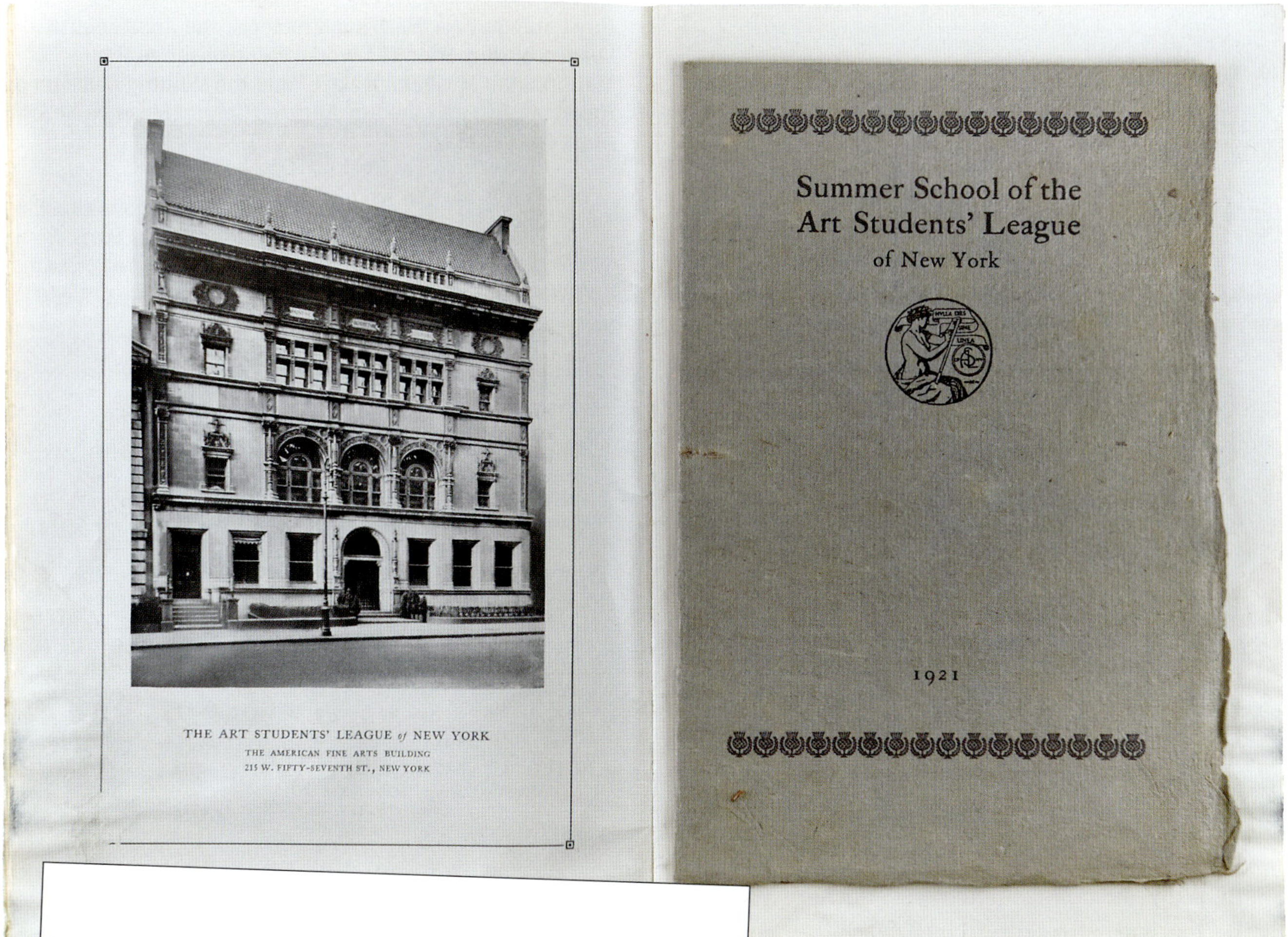

The Art Students League of New York, founded in reaction to the dominant National Academy of Design, which was seen as too conservative and old guard, and their catalog. HILYARD COLLECTION

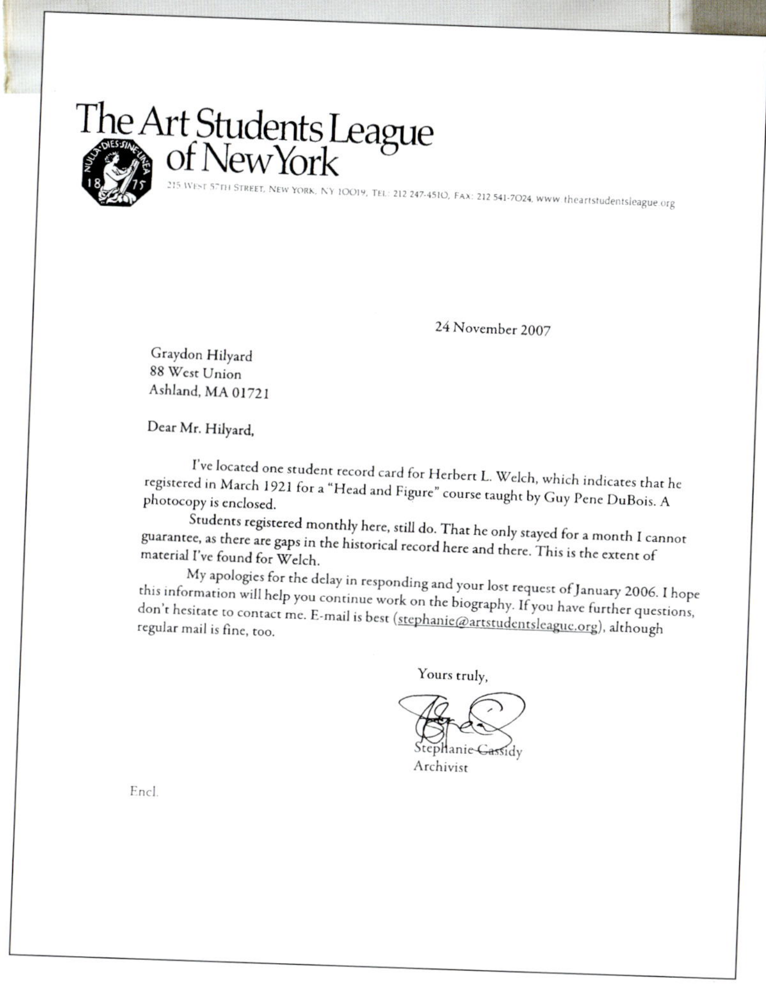
The Art Students League of New York
215 West 57th Street, New York, NY 10019, Tel: 212 247-4510, Fax: 212 541-7024, www.theartstudentsleague.org

24 November 2007

Graydon Hilyard
88 West Union
Ashland, MA 01721

Dear Mr. Hilyard,

I've located one student record card for Herbert L. Welch, which indicates that he registered in March 1921 for a "Head and Figure" course taught by Guy Pene DuBois. A photocopy is enclosed.

Students registered monthly here, still do. That he only stayed for a month I cannot guarantee, as there are gaps in the historical record here and there. This is the extent of material I've found for Welch.

My apologies for the delay in responding and your lost request of January 2006. I hope this information will help you continue work on the biography. If you have further questions, don't hesitate to contact me. E-mail is best (stephanie@artstudentsleague.org), although regular mail is fine, too.

Yours truly,

Stephanie Cassidy
Archivist

Encl.

Founded in 1875, the Art Students League of New York was a major force in the shifting of the world's art capital from Paris to New York City. HILYARD COLLECTION

Currently, one cast of this bronze rests on a mantle overlooking Mooselookmeguntic Lake, while another resides at Eisenhower's Gettysburg Farm adjacent to the battlefield where 51,000 died. The initial casting included seven bronzes, but the fates of the other five are unknown. Following the postwar arrival of polymer resins, a recasting of two was undertaken with Herb's permission, and one such reproduction is displayed at the Rangeley Sporting Heritage Museum in Oquossoc.

Guy Pene du Bois, Herb's instructor at the Art Students League of New York. His works can be seen at the Metropolitan Museum of New York, the Whiting Museum of American Art, and the Los Angeles County Museum of Art. KRAUSHAAR GALLERIES

Paris bound. Under ideal conditions, an Atlantic crossing by the SS *Paris* would take 14.4 days at sea. HILYARD COLLECTION

This sculpture contributed to yet another of the myths surrounding Herb. Despite the rumors, Herb never exhibited in the Louvre—it would have been quite impossible in his lifetime because, among other things, an artist must be dead to qualify for the Louvre. Neither is he in the Smithsonian, as some claim on the Internet. There was, however, chatter at the time that his bronze would be exhibited at the 1928 Paris Salon, a world-renowned art exhibition that was founded in 1673 and that, along with the École des Beaux-Arts and the independent ateliers, made up the Paris art world. Established in 1648, the École was considered the best in the world and required rigorous entrance examinations.

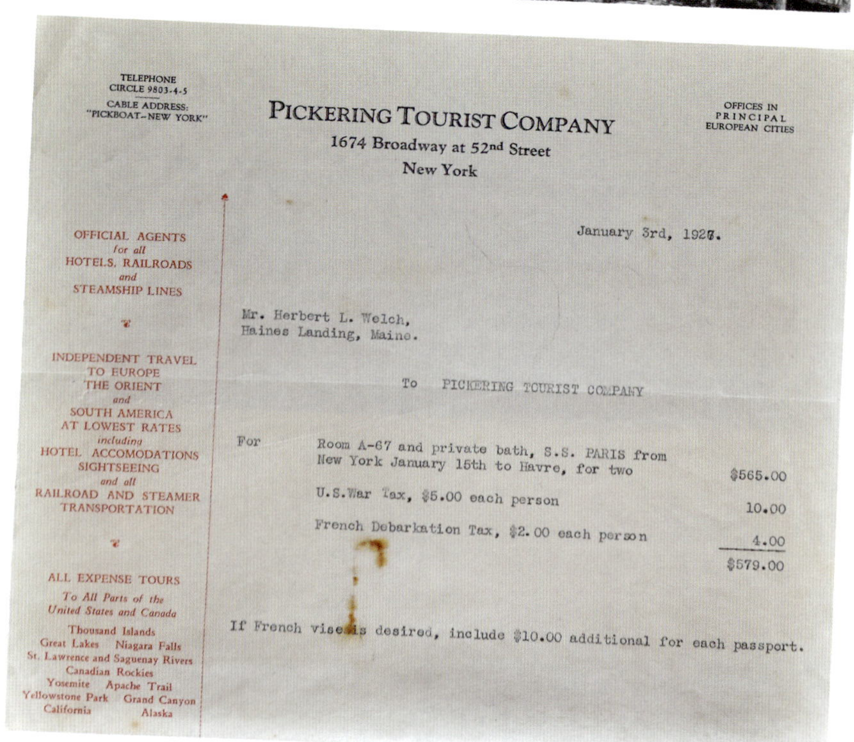

TELEPHONE
CIRCLE 9803-4-5
CABLE ADDRESS:
"PICKBOAT-NEW YORK"

PICKERING TOURIST COMPANY
1674 Broadway at 52nd Street
New York

OFFICES IN
PRINCIPAL
EUROPEAN CITIES

OFFICIAL AGENTS
for all
HOTELS, RAILROADS
and
STEAMSHIP LINES

INDEPENDENT TRAVEL
TO EUROPE
THE ORIENT
and
SOUTH AMERICA
AT LOWEST RATES
including
HOTEL ACCOMODATIONS
SIGHTSEEING
and all
RAILROAD AND STEAMER
TRANSPORTATION

ALL EXPENSE TOURS
To All Parts of the
United States and Canada
Thousand Islands
Great Lakes Niagara Falls
St. Lawrence and Saguenay Rivers
Canadian Rockies
Yosemite Apache Trail
Yellowstone Park Grand Canyon
California Alaska

January 3rd, 1928.

Mr. Herbert L. Welch,
Haines Landing, Maine.

To PICKERING TOURIST COMPANY

For	Room A-67 and private bath, S.S. PARIS from New York January 15th to Havre, for two	$565.00
	U.S.War Tax, $5.00 each person	10.00
	French Debarkation Tax, $2.00 each person	4.00
		$579.00

If French vise is desired, include $10.00 additional for each passport.

The ateliers were small, independent art schools that focused on a specialty and were anchored by a recognized master. In Herb's case, that master was sculptor Mahonri Young. Annually, these ateliers submitted the best

Restoring the Long Ago

I first started visiting Herb's domain in the summer of 2012. Early on, I saw in a dark corner of the back shed an odd plastic-shrouded presence. I thought I detected a profile. Later, I asked Jefferson about it, and he pulled back the plastic. Beneath was a recognizable, but largely ruined, face of an old Indian in a war bonnet. The oil-based clay, while still pliable, was deeply cracked. The jaw was entirely detached. Whatever details there had been in the feathers were long gone. I asked Jefferson why Herbie had never finished it. He guessed it was a late project. He also said that he had asked numerous artists to restore it, but they had all found it too spooky. We brought it out to Herb's workbench, where it was probably created, and I saw it in the light for the first time.

At supper, I was still haunted by its unfinished state. I decided to have at it that very night. Although I had never worked with clay before and the task required extensive reconstruction, as well as detailing, somehow my hands knew what to do, as if Herbie had accompanied me into the wee hours until it was done.

Talon van Howten
Albuquerque, New Mexico
2014

Much would be lost without restoration talent. RANGELEY SPORTING HERITAGE MUSEUM

of their students' work for jury review in hopes of being accepted into the Salon. Acceptance reflected well on them and offered a gateway to a student's acceptance in the École des Beaux-Arts.

One suspects that the myth about Herb in the Louvre arose from the fact that the Louvre holds all the records of the Salon. Having friends in Paris, we thought this would be a simple matter to research. Not quite. We would need friends elsewhere, like oh, say, Australia. Apparently the University of Canberra was the most convenient place the Louvre could find to store Salon records. (It should be noted that banging on doors has not gone out of style, as institutions often do not respond well to email.) But the search was all for naught, as our friend in Australia found no mention of a Herbert L. Welch in the annual listing of exhibitors.

Mahonri Young (1877–1957) was a sculptor whose work remains world-renowned. Born a Mormon, he did not limit himself to Mormon themes. BRIGHAM YOUNG UNIVERSITY

Views of Welch's bronze *On the Rise*, one of two known to exist. MILLER COLLECTION

Herb would do no other bronze work, only occasionally modeling in clay. This seems to bear out the family lore that Herb was a naturally restless spirit. Having mastered a given task, he often quickly moved on to the next one. This attitude is reflected in his advice to a young Dave Footer: "Always be open to the new. To be static is to go backwards."[6]

How far the Welches wandered from Paris during their ten-week stay is unclear. If they wrote letters home, none have survived, so it is pictures that offer us the best glimpse of what they saw.

Although Herb's study in Paris emphasized bronze casting, he never forgot painting and sketching, as demonstrated by his sketchbooks and notepads.

A study piece for *On the Rise*. Artists and sculptors often work out their ideas on paper before executing in an expensive medium. RANGELEY SPORTING HERITAGE MUSEUM

Parisian street scenes, skylines, café life, basilicas, and a church identified as Fontaine Rose are all recorded by his line drawings and pastels. Rural imagery of farmers, domed haystacks, herds of cows, flocks of sheep, and a hawk in flight appear, as well. A small oil on board of the chateau of Henry IV places him firmly at Saint-Germain, on the outskirts of Paris. Postcards that could not conceivably be sent through the mail hint of a visit to the Musée de Luxembourg. One of these, by Commére, would later serve as a study piece for Herb, as he took part in a long tradition of learning by copying from the masters. Notes in his sketchbook margins indicated an interest in Corot, Courbet, and Millet, all of whom were in the Louvre. These artists came from the school of Realism, which mirrored everyday life and death and overtook the more sublimely focused Romantic school in the 1850s.

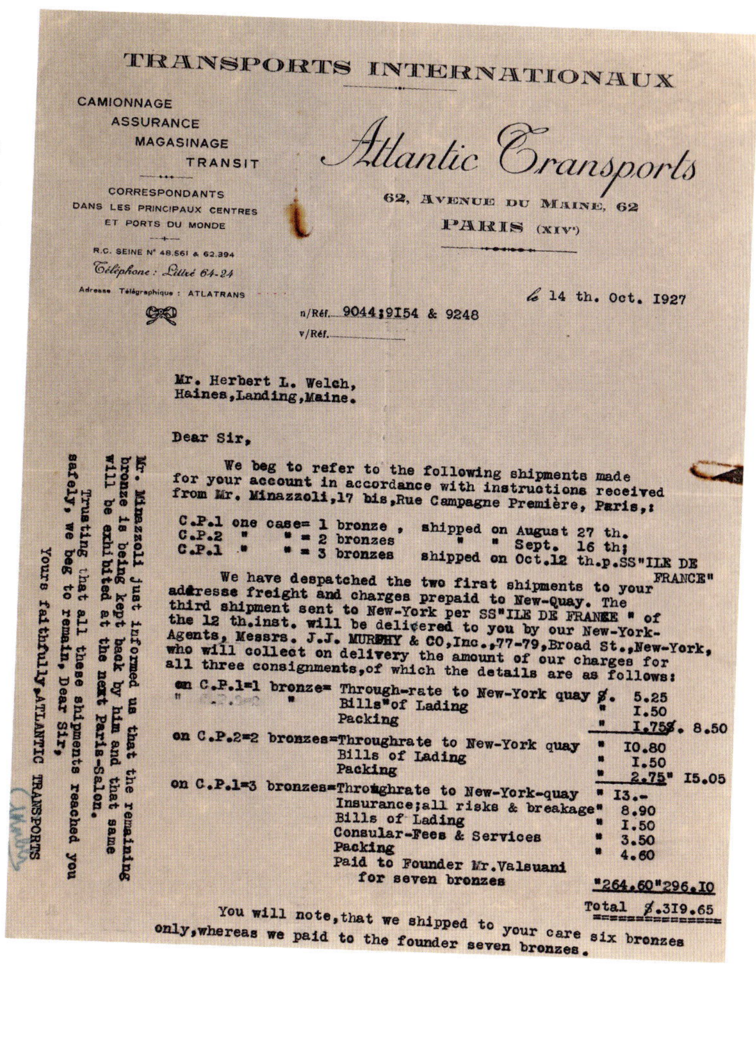

TRANSPORTS INTERNATIONAUX

CAMIONNAGE
ASSURANCE
MAGASINAGE
TRANSIT

CORRESPONDANTS DANS LES PRINCIPAUX CENTRES ET PORTS DU MONDE

R.C. SEINE N° 48.561 & 62.394
Téléphone : Littré 64-24
Adresse Télégraphique : ATLATRANS

Atlantic Transports
62, Avenue du Maine, 62
PARIS (XIVe)

le 14 th. Oct. I927

n/Réf. 9044;9I54 & 9248
v/Réf.

Mr. Herbert L. Welch,
Haines,Landing,Maine.

Dear Sir,

We beg to refer to the following shipments made for your account in accordance with instructions received from Mr. Minazzoli,17 bis,Rue Campagne Première, Paris,:

C.P.1 one case= 1 bronze , shipped on August 27 th.
C.P.2 " " = 2 bronzes " " Sept. 16 th;
C.P.1 " " = 3 bronzes shipped on Oct.12 th.p.SS"ILE DE FRANCE"

We have despatched the two first shipments to your adresse freight and charges prepaid to New-Quay. The third shipment sent to New-York per SS"ILE DE FRANCE " of the 12 th.inst. will be delivered to you by our New-York-Agents, Messrs. J.J. MURPHY & CO,Inc.,77-79,Broad St.,New-York, who will collect on delivery the amount of our charges for all three consignments,of which the details are as follows:

on C.P.1=1 bronze= Through-rate to New-York quay $. 5.25
Bills of Lading " I.50
Packing " I.75 $. 8.50
on C.P.2=2 bronzes=Throughrate to New-York quay " I0.80
Bills of Lading " I.50
Packing " 2.75" I5.05
on C.P.1=3 bronzes=Throughrate to New-York-quay " I3.-
Insurance;all risks & breakage" 8.90
Bills of Lading " I.50
Consular-Fees & Services " 3.50
Packing " 4.60
Paid to Founder Mr.Valsuani for seven bronzes "264.60"296.I0
Total $.3I9.65

You will note,that we shipped to your care six bronzes only,whereas we paid to the founder seven bronzes.

Mr. Minazzoli just informed us that the remaining bronze is being kept back by him and that same will be exhibited at the next Paris-Salon.

Trusting that all these shipments reached you safely, we beg to remain, Dear Sir,

Yours faithfully,ATLANTIC TRANSPORTS

A ship's manifest for the Welch bronzes. VOORHEES

While it is not known if Herb and Bernice journeyed as far as Zürich, where Courbet's 1871 masterpiece *The Trout* still hangs at the Kunsthaus, it certainly would have been of interest. As a taxidermist, Herb would have appreciated the realism of the dying brown trout spilling blood through a severed gill. As a painter, he would have been intrigued by Courbet's self-portrait, concealed within the painting, and his signature reading "*Courbet in vinculis faciebut*." Perhaps, Herb recalled enough of his schoolboy studies to translate that Latin as "Made by Courbet in chains," since Courbet had created the painting while in jail for political reasons.[7]

Another intriguing detail from Herb's notebook is the address "84 Rue d'Agges, end of the street on right, two flights up—no. 6." Perhaps the atelier where he studied, perhaps their apartment, or perhaps a nightlife party location?

On March 30, 1927, the Welches boarded the SS *Majestic* sailing from Cherbourg to New York City. But Paris would not be the end of the Welch's travels. In August of 1929, we find them packing art supplies and bamboo and heading westward over the Canadian Rockies. Judging from hotel statements, they boarded the Canadian Pacific Railroad in Montréal, bound for Vancouver. After a brief stay, they moved offshore to Victoria on Vancouver Island. There, Herb distinguished himself by landing a 54-pound Chinook salmon, which qualified him for membership in the prestigious Tyee Club of British Columbia, headquartered on the Campbell River.

Following a three-day stay back on the Vancouver mainland, they crossed the border to the Hotel Winthrop in Tacoma, Washington, then on to Portland, Oregon, where they arrived at the Multnomah Hotel on September 20th. A week later, they purchased railroad tickets for a month-long journey ending in Buffalo, New York. Since Herb's sketchbooks contain Western landscape themes, it seems likely he visited the Southwest as well. Certainly, that would explain his imposing painting of the Bright Angel Trail, located in the Grand Canyon National Park. Arguably his best work, it compares favorably with works by the masters of the Hudson River School.

However, Herb may have also gotten this Western inspiration from a variety of other sources, including Dorothy Knight Voorhees (1890–1964). Originally from Moorestown, New Jersey, she migrated to Hollywood, where she established herself painting background scenery for early motion pictures. Returning east, she arrived in Rangeley with plans to open a tearoom, but they were never realized. Instead, she was hired as a nursing assistant for the Welches and many years later on December 16, 1947, became Herb's second wife.[8]

There are some in the art world who will never accept a painting associated with taxidermy or sporting themes as fine art. At best, any such work will be denigrated as folk art. Any object with even a hint of useful purpose has a hard time gaining status in that rarified world. Nonetheless, any measured review of Herb's flat art will reveal his painterly skills, which included a keen sense of perspective and knowledge of anatomy, enough to elevate him into the realm of fine art despite his association with taxidermy.

Herb's work was never bombastic. Although he would have been familiar with Cubism and the emerging school of Abstract Expressionism, these styles held no interest for him. He felt no need to express his inner landscape. Our review of some

A young Dorothy Voorhees. VOORHEES

Five carved brook trout against the backdrop of a painted shelf mushroom. Per family lore, a call from Herb was needed to keep the owner from being cited for illegal possession of undersize trout by a skeptical game warden. CARVILLE COLLECTION

seventy-five pieces of his work bespeaks a man who was at ease with the external world and took it as he found it.

Undoubtedly, leaping brook trout sold well, but most of his work that we observed consists of landscapes and the female nude, with many of those nudes woven into landscape settings. An interior photograph of his home reveals one wall with twenty paintings: twelve landscapes, two horse portraits, two nudes, one seascape, one cityscape, one still life, and one leaping brook trout. Perhaps surprisingly, Herb showed no interest in the school of sporting art, a style of art that dated back to the eighteenth century and was characterized by the presence of a hunter-fisher in a landscape setting. This led us to wonder if Herb harbored mixed feelings toward blood sports as he aged.

A late-life image of Herb surveying his work. RONALD TURMENNE

The Art of Friendship

There is a bit of a story involved in how we came to own Herb's most famous bronze. My wife, Sallie Porter Faset Miller, and her folks were all longtime friends and customers of Herb when I married into the family. Now Herb had this large and beautiful painting of a trout (now hanging in the Rangeley Library), which sat on an easel in the center of the store. Everyone that came in was awed by it. Many tried to buy it, but Herb always said, "It's not finished yet." The truth was that Herb was so attached to this painting that he did not want to sell it. Herb told me that he never signed a painting until he sold it, and the only reason this painting was not finished was that he had not signed it.

Anyway, every time Sallie dropped in to see Herb she would make him promise to will the painting to her, as she liked the painting so much. Sallie's comments were in jest and both of them would have a good laugh with many wisecracks going back and forth between them.

When Herb died in 1960, Dot called Sally and told us she knew that Herb had promised the painting to us (there was nothing in writing and I really thought it was all in jest). She went on to explain that she would prefer the painting hang in the lobby of the Rangeley Bank where everyone could enjoy it. Sally and I immediately understood and agreed with her feelings, as this was a painting that had affected so many people over the years.

Dot went on to say that it would not be fair unless we had something of Herb's, and would we like the bronze of the leaping trout that had sat on his workbench for so long. We quickly agreed, as this piece had so much attachment for me in particular.

Years ago, I had been evaluating two brand-new materials used in the electronic field. I was so impressed with them that I showed them to Herb, who also got excited. We agreed to use Herb's bronze leaping trout as a model to see if I could:

1. Make a mold using this new silicon material, which was so rubbery and so stretchy that I could remove the mold from the original even though there were severe undercuts.
2. Cast a duplicate of the bronze in this new material called epoxy despite the original's severe undercuts and textures.

This I did, even to duplicating the color and weight. This is now a commonplace process and is called cold casting. During this time, Herb and I got to know each other well, another reason why I was so pleased to have the bronze. How much better to have the original work of art than a plastic one.

Wesley A. Miller Sr.
Naples, Florida
2005

Herb appears to have been curiously ambivalent about the sale of art. On the one hand, he was not adverse to sales, as his sporting goods store also functioned as a gallery. Ever the showman, he often made a major production out of signing his work in the presence of the buyer. Yet, when Robert Vose approached Herb to exhibit at the prominent Vose Galleries of Boston, Herb appears to have wavered.[9] Curious too, a reference Vose makes to the "little waterfall" already on exhibit. If this were the oft-mentioned waterfall done at age eight that hung in his store for years, it would seem a strange choice for the Boston market. And yet, there is no sign of this "little waterfall" in the Welch estate archives.

Our 2002 conversation with the Vose Galleries management determined that they had no record of any contractual agreement with Herb. They did, however, note that in 1963 they sold an oil on masonite of the Rangeley Cascades, signed H.L. Welch "40" (the year) to a Boston auction house for the sum of $8. Since no Welch paintings have come to auction in recent memory, it's difficult to assign a

Some of the Welch signature styles. To avoid a disproportional signature, artists often use monograms on small works.
HILYARD COLLECTION

dollar value to them. While many of Welch's paintings are signed and sometimes dated, smaller paintings often were not. It's possible than any unsigned large paintings may have entered the market after his death. To add to this confusion, there was also a contemporary and very competent painter named Herb Welch in the Midwest.

Over the years, Herb signed his work in a variety of ways. While it is worthwhile to be able to recognize these, collectors should remember the art world axiom that the artwork authenticates the signature and not vice versa. Accurately forging a painting requires talent, but not so for a signature forgery. As with any collecting endeavor, it is wise to do some studying before opening the checkbook. For those interested in seeing some authentic Welch art, the Rangeley Sporting Heritage Museum holds a significant collection.

Title: Unknown (date unknown). Footer Collection
Medium: Oil on canvas
Size: 12 x 8.75

This is a painting of the 1921 Bemis fire, which Herb fought. The fire burned over 2,000 acres and came close to destroying Herb's store. It is not easy to capture horror on such an intimate scale, but Herb accomplished that here. The work never sold—perhaps just creating it was cathartic for Herb.

JOHN SWAN, KENNEBAGO LAKE, MAINE

Title: Unknown (date unknown). Rangeley Sporting Heritage Museum
Medium: Charcoal on paper
Size: 12 x 16

This is a study of a posed male model, no doubt done in 1921 when Herb attended the Art Students League of New York. It is a well-composed likeness—striking. Perhaps, subconsciously, Herb inserted a bit of his own likeness into the painting.

JOHN SWAN, KENNEBAGO LAKE, MAINE

Title: Unknown (1929). Rangeley Public Library
Medium: Oil on canvas
Size: 28 x 40

This painting of the Bright Angel Trail in the Grand Canyon is one of Herb's most imposing paintings and also, arguably, one of his best. The color palette and bold brush strokes both reveal a French influence: Herb carefully studied the Impressionists when he was in Paris. Prior to this, for the most part, his work was more restrained, using smooth glazes and careful rendering. Notice how in the upper right hand corner, an image seems to peer down from the rock formation.

JOHN SWAN, KENNEBAGO LAKE, MAINE

Title: Unknown (1940). Knapp Collection
Medium: Oil on masonite
Size: 28 x 40

The cascades were a popular tourist attraction in early Rangeley. You can visit the exact location of this painting, although reaching it is risky at high water. This painting features rich, earthy, dark tones, contrasting with the lighter pastels of the water running through the middle. The masonite adds an interesting woven texture to the work. This is another solid piece by an artist who had already established his style by this point in his career. JOHN SWAN, KENNEBAGO LAKE, MAINE

Title: Unknown (date unknown). Footer Collection
Medium: Oil on canvas
Size: 28 x 22

Depicting Whitehead Cliff in Portland Harbor, this is one of Herb's few seascapes. It is an early work, as it shows no obvious French influence. Instead, it recalls a popular style used by many artists who painted New England seascapes. JOHN SWAN, KENNEBAGO LAKE, MAINE

Title: Unknown (date unknown).
Rangeley Sporting Heritage Museum
Medium: Oil on board
Size: 8.25 x 5.75

With its heavy paint and bold brush strokes, this small winterscape shows a strong French influence. It also has a dreamlike quality reminiscent of the American Impressionists working at the time. A finely executed piece, it ranks among Herb's best work. JOHN SWAN, KENNEBAGO LAKE, MAINE

Title: Unknown (date unknown).
Rangeley Sporting Heritage Museum
Medium: Oil on canvas
Size: 12 x 18

Probably executed around the age of eighteen, this self-potrait is Herb's attempt at honest self-reflection. At this point, Herb had not yet been influenced by any of the art movements of the day. Portraiture brings challenges and self-portraiture even more so, as our self-image often differs from how others see us. JOHN SWAN, KENNEBAGO LAKE, MAINE

Title: *The Golden Rain* (date unknown). James Stone Collection
Medium: Oil on Canvas
Size: 24 x 14

Like all artists, Herb learned by copying from the masters. This image is by Commère and was exhibited in the Palais des Beaux Arts in Paris. Herb's copy is a virtual clone of the Parisian postcard image that he used as a model. JOHN SWAN, KENNEBAGO LAKE, MAINE

Title: Unknown (date unknown). James Stone Collection
Medium: Oil on canvas
Size: 23 x 18

In this well-executed, if highly romanticized image, Herb appears to be interpreting the myth of Jason and the Argonauts. All shipwrecked sailors should be so lucky! We do know that Herb studied the classics in high school, giving further credence to this theory. JOHN SWAN, KENNEBAGO LAKE, MAINE

Title: Unknown (1904). Eleanor White Collection
Medium: Pencil on paper
Size: 30 x 20

The early date on this painting is confirmed by Herb's lack of confidence in his lines. At this point, he was still working out his own style. Nonetheless, the image is striking and is an impressive document of Herb's early work. JOHN SWAN, KENNEBAGO LAKE, MAINE

Title: Unknown (date unknown). Rangeley Sporting Heritage Museum
Medium: Mixed materials on paper
Size: 14 x 16

The leaping salmon image is executed in the gouache style, using India ink and Chinese white. While the salmon is well drawn, the water in particular is effervescent, making for a dramatic effect. Herb probably created this image specifically to use as his second letterhead, as the black-and-white format could easily be reproduced.
JOHN SWAN, KENNEBAGO LAKE, MAINE

Title: Unknown (date unknown). Jefferson Voorhees Collection
Medium: Carving on pine
Size: 28 x 18

Although the trout is at the center, Herb's treatment of the water dominates this painting. Instead of brush strokes, he used tool marks, which demonstrates an understanding and reverence for the wood. Using oils, Herb's coloring of the tool marks is both understated and pronounced. A tour de force, particularly as it is carved from one piece of wood. JOHN SWAN, KENNEBAGO LAKE, MAINE

Title: Unknown (date unknown). Footer Collection
Medium: Oil on canvas
Size: 40.5 x 27.5

Taking poetic license, Herb puts this brook trout into a romanticized setting to show off his skill at painting water. JOHN SWAN, KENNEBAGO LAKE, MAINE

Title: Unknown (date unknown).
James Stone Collection
Medium: Oil on canvas
Size: 25 x 14

Another of Herb's highly stylized nudes, cresting a wave. In terms of technical skill, this is the best of Herb's nudes that we have seen. As for its inspiration, we have no clue. JOHN SWAN, KENNEBAGO LAKE, MAINE

Title: Unknown (date unknown).
Hilyard Collection
Medium: Oil on canvas
Size: 18 x 24

Here, Herb presents a confounding mixture of Egyptian imagery and a rising or falling angel. Typically, depictions of angels have their wings attached to their backs, but Herb's angel has her wings flowing from her arms. It is safe to say this provocative work probably was not commissioned by the local church. JOHN SWAN, KENNEBAGO LAKE, MAINE

Title: Unknown (date unknown).
James Stone Collection
Medium: Oil on canvas
Size: 18 x 24

Another well-executed example of Herb's nudes. His composition here is exemplary, although it again raises the question of who acted as a model. JOHN SWAN, KENNEBAGO LAKE, MAINE

Title: Unknown (date unknown).
Rangeley Sporting Heritage Museum
Medium: Charcoal on paper
Size: 8 x 14

This work is based on a copy of a classical statue, either Greek or Roman, which is a standard training exercise that teaches students about shade and form. This work, like Herb's other studies, demonstrates a masterful grasp of anatomy. JOHN SWAN, KENNEBAGO LAKE, MAINE

Title: Unknown (date unknown). Rangeley Sporting Heritage Museum
Medium: Charcoal on paper
Size: 14 x 8

This recumbent nude is another life study that Herb painted as an art student, probably at the Art Students League of New York in 1921. JOHN SWAN, KENNEBAGO LAKE, MAINE

Title: Unknown (1932). Rangeley Public Library
Medium: Oil on canvas
Size: 32 x 26

In this painting, we see Herb placing his iconic brook trout in a dangerous, dramatic setting. You almost expect Poseidon himself to step from the water. Herb's confident use of color exhibits a mature style, with a technique both accomplished and painterly. This magnificent piece is a great reason to visit the Rangeley library, where it hangs today. JOHN SWAN, KENNEBAGO LAKE, MAINE

Title: Unknown (date unknown). Rangeley Sporting Heritage Museum
Medium: Watercolor on paper
Size: 8 x 6

This illustration of a lunar moth reflects Herb's interest in all phases of nature. Here, he demonstrates a light and delicate touch. JOHN SWAN, KENNEBAGO LAKE, MAINE

Title: Unknown (1908). Palmer Collection
Medium: Watercolor on paper
Size: 6 x 10

This accurate rendition of hanging game birds again demonstrates a light touch. Depictions of sporting life date back to antiquity and are popular across a range of cultures. JOHN SWAN, KENNEBAGO LAKE, MAINE

Title: Unknown (1943). Rangeley Sporting Heritage Museum
Medium: Pastel on paper
Size: 11 x 29

This is a well-executed brook trout painting, a staple of sporting art. Herb probably made good money selling his brook trout paintings to the summer folk. His use of the scrolled birch bark lends this work a certain elegance. JOHN SWAN, KENNEBAGO LAKE, MAINE

Title: A *Bonney Point View* (date unknown). Rangeley Sporting Heritage Museum
Medium: Oil on canvas
Size: 16 x 12

This ethereal summer landscape is among Herb's best work. It captures a hazy day and shows Herb's fine, impressionistic touch with the brush. Bonney Point is on Rangeley Lake, which means the view may have been a commission. If so, the owners were most fortunate. JOHN SWAN, KENNEBAGO LAKE, MAINE

Title: Unknown (date unknown). Beisler Collection
Medium: Watercolor on paper
Size: 8 x 12

In this enchanting watercolor, Herb demonstrates his ability to walk the fine line between affection and sentimentality. JOHN SWAN, KENNEBAGO LAKE, MAINE

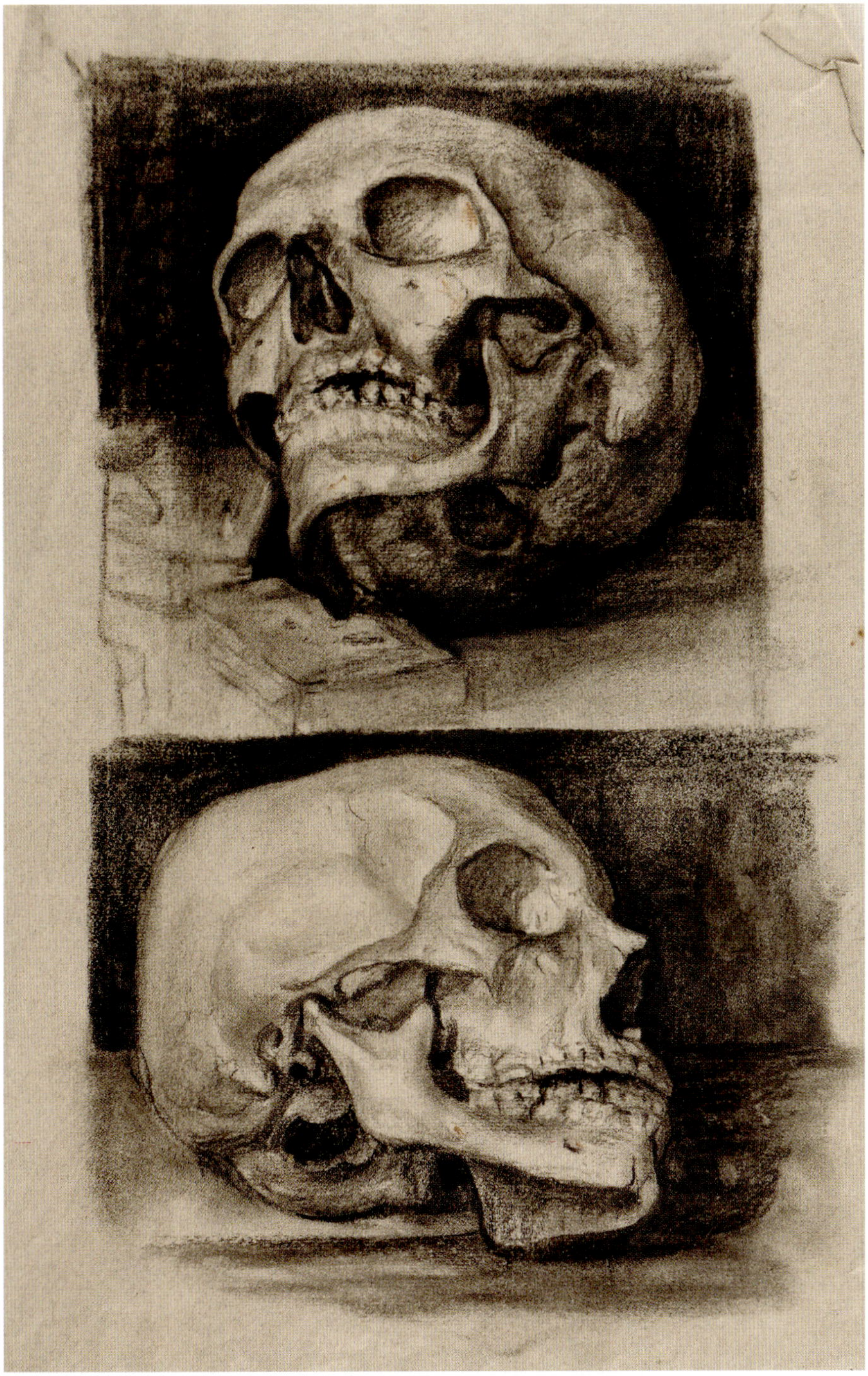

Title: Unknown (date unknown). Rangeley Sporting Heritage Museum
Medium: Charcoal on paper
Size: 8 x 14

Another example of art school studies, this time focusing on the underlying anatomy—one of the most fundamental skills any artist must master. JOHN SWAN, KENNEBAGO LAKE, MAINE

ENDNOTES

1 "Obituary of Della Dewey Pratt," January 11, 1946, newspaper source unknown.
2 *The Art Students League of New York, Season 1920–1921 Catalog*, 215 West 57th Street, New York City.
3 "*Liste des Pasagers, Cie Gle Transatlantique French Line*," January 15, 1927.
4 Thomas E. Toone, *Mahonri Young: His Life and Art*, Salt Lake City: Signature Books, 1997, pp. 190–191.
5 Anne Simmons (Library of Congress reference librarian), correspondence with author, January 6, 2006.
6 David Footer, interview with author, September 24, 2008.
7 Stefano Zuffi, *One Thousand Years of Painting*, Milan: Mondadori Electra Spa, 2004, p. 255.
8 Jefferson Voorhees, interview with author, September 20, 2011.
9 Robert Vose to Herbert L. Welch, personal correspondence, November 30, 1946.

The Death of Otis Bean

By the 1920s, Herb's status as a champion grade fly caster was well established. But in 1923, Herb would find himself in the spotlight for another role: as a witness at a trial for the murder of Otis Bean.

A murder has a way of drawing attention—particularly in a closely knit community like Rangeley, with a population in the triple digits. Until the death of Otis Bean on October 6, 1922, there had never been a murder in the area, and there would not be another until 2016.

On October 9, 1922, the *Lewiston Daily Sun* reported: "When found he was laying on his back, his right hand ungloved and extended toward a .38 calibre Colt laying about a foot away. Near his head lay his hat under the mail sack. His body lay in a pool of blood." Having heard the shots, Herb and the victim's wife, Ethel, drove to the scene from across the street at the Welch home.

As with many small towns, the residents of Haines Landing preferred to blame the murder of Otis Bean on people from "away." After Herb identified the body, removed the gun, and consoled Ethel, it only took an hour for the local police to arrest two men: Norman Mowser of Methuen, Massachusetts, and Jeremiah Wheaton of Elmira, New York. Due to the quick work of an Oquossoc posse, the two men were jailed but never charged. Held without bail, they languished for four months until eventually the widow of Otis Bean was charged. Apparently the two men's only crime had been to walk 12 miles from Kennebago Lake in search of work and arrive at Haines Landing at the wrong time. Released, but held as material witnesses, they could not make the $1,000 bail and so were sent back to the county jail. At the trial's end, each received $44 from the state.

Even before the Bean trial started, all of the Maine, New Hampshire, Massachusetts, and New York papers had reporters on the scene crafting lurid headlines. A young widow slaying her philandering husband, combined with rumors of love triangles, certainly made for good copy. So while the judicial court focused on greed and jealousy as the motive, the court of public opinion focused on the more salacious details.

While Herb had been part of the community for twenty years, that did not grant him immunity from wagging tongues. In Maine, unless you were born on the kitchen table of a farmhouse that your grandfather built, you are from "away." Having given up on the original theory that robbery was the motive, on February 9, the state jailed Ethel Bean without bail on the charge of murder in the first degree. Next they impaneled a jury pool of forty-five men and four women. Of those women, none were chosen to serve. Then the state hinted broadly that the trial might be delayed for months while the prosecution searched for missing witnesses.

On February 12, the *Lewiston Daily Sun* reported that Ethel Bean was treated in her cell for influenza, spiking to a temperature of 102° while losing 10 pounds. On February 14, they reported that the widow had threatened suicide and was being guarded in her cell by her sister. The Farmington hotels were full and a crowd gathered daily in front of the Franklin County Court House to watch the case, where tickets were required for admission. With public opinion increasingly favoring the young widow, the state finally set a trial date of February 27, 1923.

The court proceedings included a grilling of Herb Welch, who had sold the murder weapon and been first on the scene. Even more interesting for the crowds was the testimony of Miss Elsie Stewart, described by the press as "The Queen of Pleasant Island," where Otis worked. Cross-examination by the defense could not shake her testimony that Otis Bean was in her company the greater part of the previous summer.

MRS. ETHEL R. BEAN CHARGED WITH MURDER OF HER HUSBAND ARRAIGNED FOR TRIAL TODAY

DAY MORNING, FEBRUARY 28, 1923 — PRICE THREE C

BEANS IN A FOUR HOUR MIDNIGHT BATTLE IS ALLEGED BY THE STAT

THE BEAN JURY

Foreman, George L. Taylor, married, Jay, granite worker.
E. D. Orr, 65, married, farmer
James A. Davis, 42, married, New Sharon
H. E. Mayo, Freeman, 61, farmer, married.
George E. Gould, Jay, 55, married, farmer.
Guy Currier, 30, Madrid, married
Fred O. Bemis, 45, Phillips, married.
Ernest V. Thompson, 28, Jay, farmer, married.
O. M. Conant, 42, Weld, farmer, married.
Harry Foster, 30, Wilton, married.
Donald Cheek, painter, Farmington, 32, married
C. F. Holden, 48, farmer, married, Wilton.

IN SUPPORT OF THEORY THAT SHE WAS JEALOUS OF HUSBAND'S CONDUCT

Auto Ride to Farmington Fair, Bean's Early Morning Visit to Camp Where Young Woman Was Employed as Maid, Were Mentioned in County Attorney's Opening

Alleged Mrs. Bean Had Not Been Living With Husband for Some Time Prior to the Shooting—That She Had Made Statements Construed as Threats Against His Life—Jury of 12 Men Completed at Morning Session—Court Room Crowded—Sensational Developments Expected

RANGELEY MAN MAY BECOME INVOLV

Haine's Landing, Feb. 27 There are persistent rumors here tonight that as the trial of Mrs. Ethel Bean for the murder of her husband Otis A. Bean, well known guide, progresses a man well known in the Rangeley region may become involved in the case. While no names are being mentioned and no one is willing to make any definite statement relating to any possible new turn the case may take, it would appear that any developments along this line, would come as no great surprise. It is understood that tracks made by a man's shoes, other than those of the victim were noticed near where the body was found. It is felt here that certain persons have been withholding information that may prove of great importance in fixing the responsibility for the crime.

MEN AND WOME

Reported That State W Depend Entirely Upo Circumstantial Evidence

Many Out of State Witness Including Experts—Both Ho tels at Farmington Crowded

Farmington, Feb. 27.—A murd case without a parallel in this Sta opens tomorrow when Mrs. Eth Bean, Rangeley, will be arraign

MRS. ETHEL BEAN
Whose trial for the Murder of he Husband Otis A. Bean, widely known Rangeley guide, Begins today.

charged with the murder of her hus band, Otis A. Bean, noted Maine guide at Haines Landing, Oct. 6 last. All indications point to a prolonged session with the outcome possibly hanging on the admissibility of certain evidence to be presented by the State.

He is said to have been aproached by two woodsmen who asked him to take them across the lake to Burrell's lumber camps. This he is said to have agreed to do on his return from Oquossoc, a mile from the landing. A few minutes later Robert Martin of Auburn, a guide happening along, heard three shots fired in succession, coming from the direction of a garage a short distance up the road across from Herbert Welche's store on the right between Oquossoc and the landing. His attention, attracted by a light near the garage, for it was quite dark, set to rout his first thought that someone was shooting skunks, the presence of which in that vicinity had been noted of late.

Going at once to investigate, he saw when a short distance from the garage the form of a man stretched in front of the unopened doors. Alone and excited he started toward Oquossoc without stopping to investigate further, but he had taken only a few steps when Herbert Welch came along in an automobile accompanied by his wife and Mrs. Bean, wife of the murdered man. Upon being informed that there was a dead man by the garage, Mr. Welch went to look for himself and by the aid of his flash light identified the prostrated form as that of Mr. Bean.

Examines Revolver

Attorney General calls on Sheriff Small to empty large Colt revolver, which Welch is asked to examine.

Court: "Take that outside if you are going to make any experiments."

The county attorney informed Justice Dunn that the shells in the chambers were empty but the judge notified the Sheriff not to unload it in the court room.

Welch says he can't identify the pistol as the one he sold Kimball, which weapon is alleged to have killed Bean.

Shaw starts to read serial number on revolver, when Pattangall inquires: "Who's going to testify?"

Witness has some difficulty comparing number on revolver with that on his bill of sale, but finally admits that they are the same.

Invited to Movies

"Who was at Mrs. Bean's house when you went there?"

"No one, but my wife came over later."

Talked with Mrs. Bean about her teeth, asked her to ride to Oquossoc when we went nightly for the mail. Says Mrs. Bean expected to go over with Otis (Mr. Bean.) but if Otis didn't call for her, she would go with him. Welch invited her to go to movies with him the following (Saturday) night, and she answered she would if Otis couldn't get off.

Welch brought revolver from ne Bean's body, he testifies, to h store where officers took it the ne day. On examing ground from gara to the body, Welch had noticed bloo spots, in various places. Also sa bullet mark on door, made by glancing shot. Flesh was noticed c the door, besides some blood stain Doesn't remember how many mark they were. Couldn't see lead but o one mark.

WITNESS DIDN'T KNOW WH REMOVED BODY

"Did you make any investigatio regarding the revolver?"

"Yes, I went down to the Kimba house".

"How did you get in."

"Took a key which was hangin outside.

Was aware where Kimball kep revolver and noticed it was gon when he looked for it.

"When did you see Mrs. Bean afte making investigation."

"Shortly after; she was upstairs i my house."

Witness says he first talked wit his wife, then went back to garage returning to his house he asked Mr Bean if Otis was right or left hand ed. She replied "He was right hand ed." To my question 'Did he have gun?"

She answered "No".

Welch's next move was to repor to Deputy Blodgett both going t the Kimball house. From there the went down to Otis' boat. Can't re member.

Judge Warns Welch

Judge warns witness he will ex ercise means in his power to mak witness speak louder, if he continue in an inaudible manner.

By March 1, things were not going well for the prosecution. While they had promised "surprise" witnesses, none could be found. Other witnesses changed their minds and didn't testify or simply disappeared. Under cross-examination, the county sheriff divulged that the county attorney had badgered the widow for five hours. Despite threats of immediate jailing unless she immediately confessed, Ethel Bean had not signed any confession.

On March 2, the *Lewiston Daily Sun* reported that there had been a late-night conference between the prosecution and the defense. On March 3, they led with the headline: "MRS. ETHEL BEAN IS FREED; SORRY SHE DIDN'T HAVE AN OPPORTUNITY TO BE HEARD." A motion of *nolle presequi* (Latin for "unwilling to pursue," referring to the prosecution's decision not to pursue charges) had been accepted by the defense, who never had to call a witness. The courtroom had erupted in loud applause. However, the motion was not the same as a not guilty verdict and gave the state the option of reopening the case at a later date.

The state never did.

The trial had ended in a dismissal and the widow walked, never to be heard from again. Still, for many, this dismissal was not a satisfactory way of determining guilt or innocence. As late as the 1980s, we were hearing whispers that Herb had been somehow "involved."

This trial is not going well. The damn judge is already threatening me. God help me if they put Bernice on the stand. After 15 years of marriage and no kids, she's already grumpy enough. Tongues are already wagging in Rangeley. Who knew a few harmless flirtations could snowball into this? Herb Welch, man about town—Christ. Well, maybe there was some truth to it, but there was no need to lock up the women just because I showed up.

Probably wouldn't put Bernice on the stand anyway, being my wife and all. Still, it would be good to hear her say in court that she was with me and the widow when Otis got himself shot.

God, what a mess he was. A shot to the head, one into the chest, maybe more. Blood all over the place. A .38 Colt will do that. Of course, it had to be done with a gun that I sold. Not that it meant anything. I sold a lot of guns. One more thing for tongues to wag about, though. That

Mrs. Bean Tells of Attempts to Make Her Sign Murder Confession---Widow Believes Slayer of Rangeley Guide Meant to Kill Someone Else.

MRS. ETHEL H. BEAN, FREED FROM THE CHARGE OF MURDERING HER HUSBAND

Details of the interview between Mrs. Ethel H. Bean, who was freed this week on a nol pros after being placed on trial for the murder of her husband, Otis A. Bean, and County Attorney Currier C. Holman of Franklin County, which took place in the office of George C. Wheeler of this City while the latter was absent in California, were revealed to the press for the first time yesterday by the discharged respondent.

Talking with a Sunday Telegram reporter, Mrs. Bean told how County Attorney Holman and Sheriff W. B. Small called upon her on New Year's Day shortly before lunch and asked her to come to an office on Exchange street for an interview. Luncheon was waiting, and she suggested that they talk with her at the home of her sister, Mrs. Frank E. Hollis, at which she has lived since the death of her husband. They were insistent that they could talk better without interruption in the downtown office, and she finally consented to go with them.

Grilled Many Hours.

The dramatic interview, Sheriff

(Continued on Section C, Page 11)

Lewiston *Daily Sun*

THE LEWISTON DAILY SUN

VOL. XXX. LEWISTON, ME., FRIDAY MORNING, FEBRUARY 9, 1923 PRICE THREE CENTS

122 ENTOMBED IN NEW MEXICO MINE; FEAR MANY KILLED

Two Bodies Removed Late Last Evening—Another Despatch Reports Finding of 100 Victims—Terrific Explosion Reported—Is Second Disaster That Has Occurred in the Dawson Mine Within Past 10 Years

12 PAPER MILLS BUSY MAKING GERMAN MONEY

NOW A QUESTION IF TURKISH OFFICERS CAN BE CONTROLLED

Allies Have Orders to Open Fire If Attacked by the Shore Batteries

LEWISTON GIRL SAVES THREE AS HER HOME IS BURNING; PARENTS OUT

Six Year Old Daughter of George Saranlopoulos, Dale Street, Proves Real Heroine—Father Was Accompanying His Wife to Local Hospital When Flames Totally Destroyed the Home and All Its Contents

BURNED TO DEATH ALONE IN COTTAGE

DROPS DEAD TRYING TO SAVE GIRL FROM FLAMES

MRS. BEAN ARRESTED FOR MURDER OF HER HUSBAND; WOODSMEN NOT INDICTED

Action of Franklin County Grand Jury Is a Sensation—Widow of Slain Man Takes Arrest Calmly—Not Likely to Be Tried at This Term—Insurance Policy and Domestic Troubles Possible Motives

FREED ON MURDER CHARGE

NORMAN MAWSON

JEREMIAH W. WHEATON

REPORTED THAT THE BEANS HAD SEPARATED

Mrs. Bean in Farmington Jail—Had Not Previously Figured in Case

Surprising Turn to the Apparently Baffling Murder of Franklin County Guide

DIRECT CHALLENGE TO RECTOR FROM BISHOP

Asks Dr. Grant to Utter in Clear Language Doubts of Deity

CATHOLIC TEACHERS TOLD TO "GET OUT"

Louisiana Superintendent Brings to Light Klan's Warning Letters

TEN LOSE LIVES WHEN TRAPPED IN A TORONTO GAS MAIN; 30 OVERCOME

STATE MUST PAY FOR FIRE SET BY MANIAC

Law Court Sustains $23,650

Girls Say They Were Forced To "Marry Men They Did Not Love"

HOUSE TO PASS DEBT SETTLEMENT TODAY

Measure May Be Side-tracked in Senate for the Shipping Legislation

$800,000 Damage Suit Instituted Against the House of David

YOUNG COUPLE FOUND DEAD IN AUTOMOBILE

Not Known If Lowell Pair Froze to Death or Suffocated From Fumes

Lewiston *Daily Sun*

and he managed to get himself shot practically in my front yard while I was with his wife.

All this is probably not going to do the business any good. Even the *New York Times* is covering it. This could sink my plans for getting on the show circuit. Might have to wait a while for all this to die down. Who knows how it's all going to end up? Never thought that Ethel would be jailed for murder, either. But there she is, sitting over there with her lawyers. God, it really hurts to see her looking so sad.

Didn't one of those lawyers used to be the attorney general? Wonder who's paying for that? Money sure didn't come from Otis. I'll probably get credit for that, too...

Courtroom Misgivings
March 1923

CHAPTER 6

Showman

As early as April 12, 1907, the *Boston Globe* was reporting from the 2nd Annual Mechanics Hall Sportsmen's Show that "the competition for accuracy and form in casting for live fish from a canoe had been won by H.L. Welch with a 100% rating." They also noted that his 105-foot distance cast was sufficient for second place, describing him as "H.L. Welch, the caster that has come forward so phenomenally during the tournament."

So, when the New England Sportsman and Camping Show was founded in 1927, Herb's status as a champion-grade fly caster was well established. Yet, when the Campbell and Fairbanks promoters tried to recruit him, Herb was hesitant. It took an intercession from George Stobie, the Maine Fish and Game Commissioner, before Herb would accept the role of demonstration fly caster.[1] But once Herb did, he never looked back, continuing until his retirement from the show circuit in 1950.

Despite Herb's ability to cast for distance and accuracy, you will not find his name in the definitive *History of the Sport of Casting* by Cliff Netherton. Competition tournament casting started in the United States during the 1860s. Since then, it has been regulated by a variety of organizations. Although the names of Leonard, Hawes, and Mills are legendary both as manufacturers and participants, in later years, the sport's governing organizations restricted participation to nonprofessionals only. Anyone making a living from the sport of fishing was excluded.

That Herb's casting was not sanctioned by a governing body made no difference on the show circuit, where thousands came daily to witness his skills in person. As impressive as his ability to routinely cast over 120 feet was, many were even more impressed by his ability to write his name with his backcast, one letter at a time. According to Joe Brooks in his *Complete Book of Fly Fishing*: "That famous fly caster, Herb Welch of Mooselookmeguntic, Maine could actually spell out his name in the air above him (but not the name of his home town!), without ever stopping his line or letting it touch the ground."

Mundane tests of accuracy, like dropping a dry fly into a floating ring at 60 feet, were too easy for Herb. Preferring more audacious displays, Herb once removed a cigar right from the mouth of Walter Brown, owner of the Boston Celtics and manager of the Boston Garden (where early sportsmen shows were sometimes held). Grinning at the stunned Walter, Herb reeled in 50 feet of line and returned the cigar with a "No Smoking Allowed" reminder.[2] Year after year, Herb returned as the lead act for demonstration fly casting in Boston, Hartford, New York

Herb Welch on the casting platform before thousands of enthralled spectators. In full regalia, Chief Needebah is seated on the left poolside.

Prior to the stage, Needebah worked for the Old Town Canoe Company. His solo tours featured lectures on Indian life, including dancing and singing followed by archery and fly-casting demonstrations. MCLAUGHLIN COLLECTION

City, Philadelphia, and Toronto, as well as at lesser known rural venues.

The same was true of his good friend Roland Eugene Nelson (1892–1954), who joined the Campbell-Fairbanks troupe in 1927, under the name Chief Needebah. Although Nelson was of Penobscot descent, the Chief was never a chief per tribal records. Using his profound knowledge of Eastern Abenaki traditions, he acted as the Penobscot Tribe librarian and lectured at the university level. Perhaps this is why some in the press referred to him as "the Indian with the Harvard accent."

Although most American indigenous populations were essentially exterminated by the late 1800s, the 1900s found much of American culture busy romanticizing them. One way for them to gain acceptance from the buying public was to claim to be a chief or a princess. The stage name Needebah, translated from the Abenaki, means "Great Friend."[3]

Of all the annoying fishing advice, one of the chief offenders is, "You should have been here yesterday." But perhaps in this case it is worthwhile to compare the sports shows of today to the shows of yesteryear.

If I close my eyes, even now, I can hear Herb telling me, "Your grandfather taught me how to fly cast, and now I'm going to teach you."

Of course, back then, I did not know that it was his son, Uncle Walter, who brought Herb to Haines Landing to manage his taxidermy shop there. Teach me he did, and to this day, I still fish with a Thomas rod that my parents bought from his shop for my eighteenth birthday.

When I was about ten, as we often did, our entire family took the train from Portland to Boston to attend the Sportsmen's Show at the old Mechanic's Hall. And of course there was Herb up on stage with Chief Needebah, wowing the crowd by writing his name with his fly line. No surprise there. Then he launched into how fly casting was not that hard and that, with proper instruction, even a child could do it.

"You there, young man," he said. "Yes, you. Come right up here." Now that was a surprise, as it was me that he was pointing at. So with a shove from my father, up I went. Fortunately, I was too overwhelmed at being up there on stage surrounded by thousands of people to let on that I knew him. Of course, I had no trouble following his step-by-step instructions, and I guess I did OK, as the crowd was cheering as I left the stage.

As we spent every summer at Mooselookmeguntic just down the road from Herb, he was always part of my life. During World War II, I served as a bombardier in the United States Air Force over Germany. When that was finally over, Herb was one of the first people to be visited.

One of my deepest regrets is that I was working in Arizona at the time of his death and could not attend his funeral. I am told that the Oquossoc Log Church was packed to overflowing with lines down the street.

I still visit, but Haines Landing and Mooselook have never been the same for me. Some things you just don't get over.

Aurelius S. Hinds II
Wilton, Maine

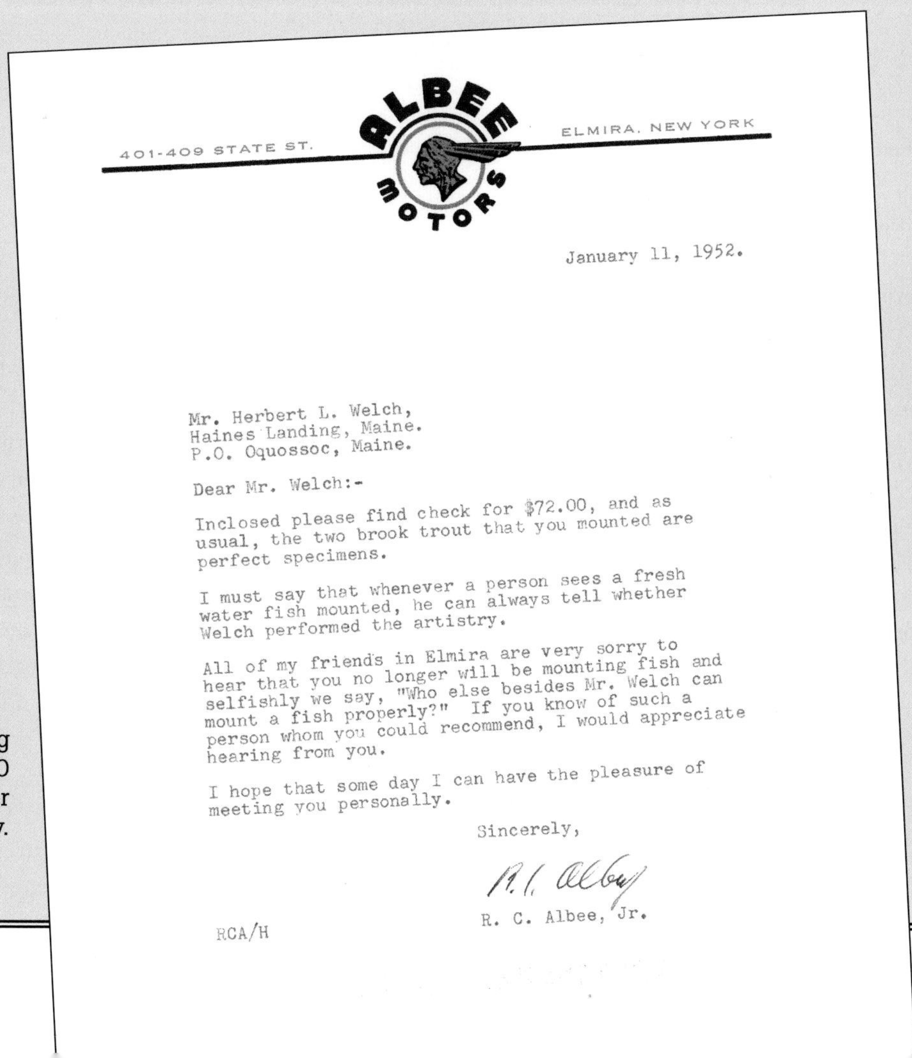

ALBEE MOTORS

401-409 STATE ST. ELMIRA, NEW YORK

January 11, 1952.

Mr. Herbert L. Welch,
Haines Landing, Maine.
P.O. Oquossoc, Maine.

Dear Mr. Welch:-

Inclosed please find check for $72.00, and as usual, the two brook trout that you mounted are perfect specimens.

I must say that whenever a person sees a fresh water fish mounted, he can always tell whether Welch performed the artistry.

All of my friends in Elmira are very sorry to hear that you no longer will be mounting fish and selfishly we say, "Who else besides Mr. Welch can mount a fish properly?" If you know of such a person whom you could recommend, I would appreciate hearing from you.

I hope that some day I can have the pleasure of meeting you personally.

Sincerely,

R. C. Albee

R. C. Albee, Jr.

RCA/H

A B-17 bombardier during WWII, Larry Hinds flew over 30 bombing missions over Nazi Germany.

Needebah's lectures on Indian affairs were broadcast worldwide by the Voice of America, a source of U.S. agitprop during the Cold War.
HILYARD COLLECTION

Having carved a record of twenty-three years as a master of ceremonies at Boston sportsman's shows, the Chief recalled how Chester I. Campbell, backer of the show at that time, asked him if he could construct an entire Indian village at the show. The "village" was successful enough to be retained a second year, but at the end of the second year, the operators told Needebah to take a couple of years off.

"I knew I had to sell myself or I was through," the theatrical Needebah had said. "I told the boss, 'Why don't you let me be master of ceremonies of this show? The audience doesn't know half of what's going on. If you let me direct their attention, they'll really enjoy the whole show.'"

The boss decided to try Chief Needebah out. The show opened on a Saturday, he recalled. On Wednesday, he said, Al Rau, Campbell's right-hand man, who had been observing Needebah's showmanship ability, yelled up from the spellbound audience, "Hey, Chief, tell them you're hired for next year!"

Interview, newspaper unknown, c. 1953.

Imagine Chief Needebah, in full tribal regalia, hushing a crowd of 20,000 with his captivating call of the wilderness loon to signal the start of the festivities. Then came the Parade of Champions, as Needebah introduced each performer and described their talents. For the next two hours, the Chief was the glue that kept the extravaganza together, while the crowd focused on casting tank events. While a 200-foot tank containing thousands of gallons of water was not absolutely necessary for casting demonstrations, it certainly was for log rolling, canoe wars, and Orin Benson's retrievers working on live ducks (presumably after the Olympic swimmers had performed).

Now, offstage, imagine a running trout stream with Herb netting the New York conservation commissioner's 18-inch rainbow trout and later sending it to Eleanor Roosevelt, whose husband, Franklin D. Roosevelt, was at that time governor of New York.[4] Imagine the nation's best decoy carvers competing for top-dog status. Imagine live bears, moose, and deer competing with their taxidermy counterparts. Imagine six live beavers working in a pond. Imagine husky sled dogs waiting for deer meat. Imagine a vampire bat that required a wine glass of fresh, warm blood daily. Imagine Maine Guides and Native Americans roaming aisles lined by hundreds of vendors, while gun shots rang out from the shooting gallery in the basement.[5]

Judging by a Campbell-Fairbanks offer sheet to Herb, no one worked their shows for the money alone. While $1,475 plus expenses was not too shabby for a month's work in 1948, Herb would have needed an additional source of income. That source, Welch's Sporting Goods, was itself a microcosm of a sportsmen show and would more than suffice. Launched in 1909 and expertly managed by his wife, Bernice, the store was an immediate success, as proven by checkbooks dating from 1911. Back

Patience Rewarded, Faith Restored

One of my favorite early rods was an Orvis bamboo 9-foot 3-piece that I bought from Herb Welch at Haines Landing. One year I took it up on the river, I can't remember the exact year, but it was when that Son of Sam thing was going on in New York City. We were up on the Restigouche and one of the correction officers needed to get back to Bangor in a hurry to fly to New York, so I gave him a ride down. Unbeknownst to me, someone had stolen the rod somewhere along the line, and when I got home, all I had was an empty case. I gave it up for lost and put the case in the back of the closet.

This past year [2001] a fellow called me and asked if I had ever lost a salmon rod. I said no, but then it dawned on me that yes, I had, back around 1980. "Well," he said. "There is a rod down here with your name engraved on it. It's a bamboo." I got out the case that had the serial number on it, and sure enough, it was mine.

I got it back after all these years, the first Orvis rod that I ever owned and bought from Herb Welch back in 1947. It still had the Ashaway silk line, number 9, on it that I had used for years. Just the fact that I had got it from Herb Welch meant so much to me, and when it was stolen I was heartbroken.

Stanley Bogdan
Nashua, New Hampshire
2007

then, spent checks were glued into bound ledgers, creating an ongoing expense account record. As the Welches paid for everything by check, their ledgers reveal much about the store history and their personal lifestyle.

By 1915, they had paid $2,500 to A.S. Hinds in order to buy the remaining stock and land from his son, Walter Hinds. That land would eventually be the site of the Welch store, but before that, Bernice's elaborate rose garden became a tourist attraction that merited its own signage and parking lot. Bernice, who held power of attorney for the business, managed a sound investment portfolio built using a variety of brokerage houses. Sadly, checks and invoices from as early as 1929 reveal that she suffered from chronic orthopedic issues involving her spine, pelvis, and knees that required multiple Boston hospitalizations.

As far as personal expenditures, we find that the Welches were shipping furniture from Paine's in Boston, and food from S.S. Pierce. Bernice favored jade and lapis jewelry and told time with a $200 diamond-studded watch from Carter's Jewelers in

A deerskin vest worn by Herb during casting demonstrations.
RANGELEY SPORTING HERITAGE MUSEUM

An interior view of Welch's Sporting Goods c. 1955. Note the brook trout painting referenced by John Swan on page 97 and by Wesley A. Miller Sr. on page 86. RONALD TURMENNE

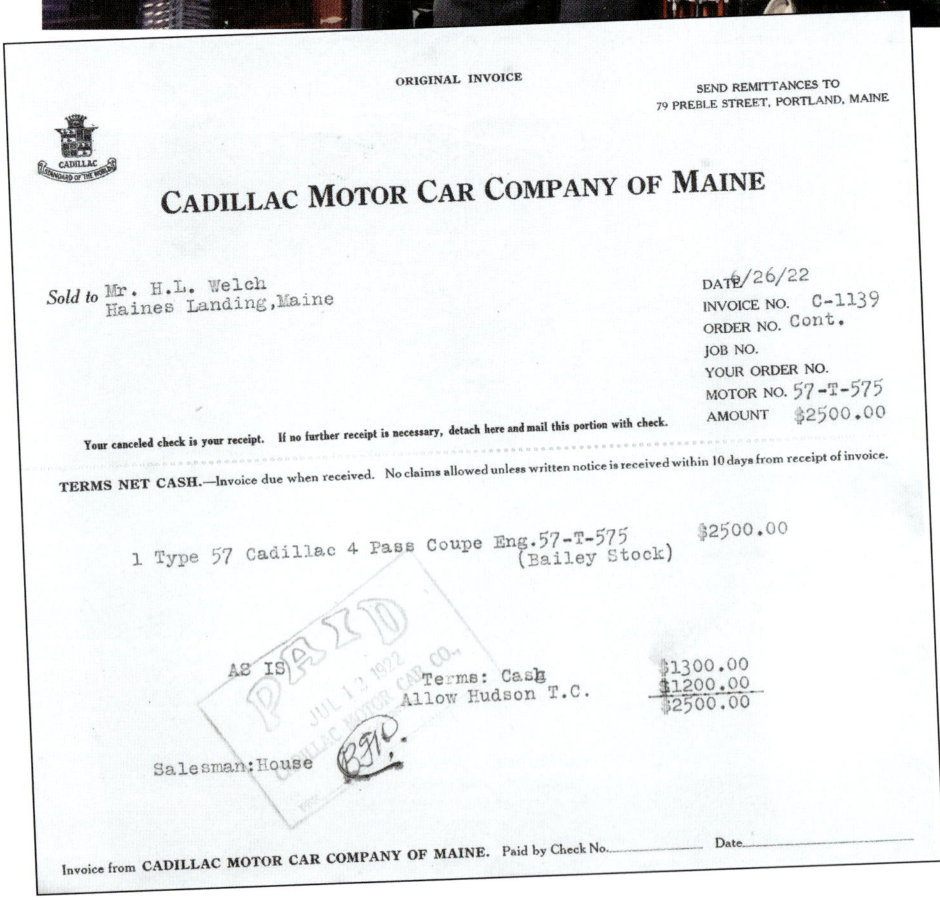

ORIGINAL INVOICE

SEND REMITTANCES TO
79 PREBLE STREET, PORTLAND, MAINE

CADILLAC MOTOR CAR COMPANY OF MAINE

Sold to Mr. H.L. Welch
Haines Landing, Maine

DATE 6/26/22
INVOICE NO. C-1139
ORDER NO. Cont.
JOB NO.
YOUR ORDER NO.
MOTOR NO. 57-T-575
AMOUNT $2500.00

Your canceled check is your receipt. If no further receipt is necessary, detach here and mail this portion with check.

TERMS NET CASH.—Invoice due when received. No claims allowed unless written notice is received within 10 days from receipt of invoice.

1 Type 57 Cadillac 4 Pass Coupe Eng. 57-T-575 (Bailey Stock) $2500.00

AS IS Terms: Cash $1300.00
Allow Hudson T.C. $1200.00
$2500.00

PAID JUL 12 1922 CADILLAC MOTOR CAR CO.

Salesman: House

Invoice from CADILLAC MOTOR CAR COMPANY OF MAINE. Paid by Check No.______ Date______

By 1922, Herb had upgraded from horses to a Hudson and on to a Cadillac.

FLY CASTING *Is Easy*

Herb Welch, artist, taxidermist, and fly fisherman gives a few casting hints to attractive Joan Cooper who responds by taking a sizeable New England land-locked salmon.

Photos by Col. Cooper, Joan's father

10

Many the child that called Herb "Uncle." When Miss Joan Cooper married, Herb received a wedding invitation. *HUNTING AND FISHING MAGAZINE*

Ted Williams, Red Sox slugger, casts a fly for Herb Welch at the Boston show last year. Herb will demonstrate this winter at Boston, New York, Toronto.

Herb as casting coach. The large spool held by Herb was used in competition casting to increase distance by minimizing resistance and line overlap. Ted Williams is on the left and Herb Welch on the right. *BOSTON RECORD-AMERICAN*

Portland. Herb favored wearing custom-made shirts from Abercrombie & Fitch while driving his Cadillac over Oquossoc's dirt roads.

While Irving Berlin may have been dreaming of a "White Christmas," many in Rangeley spent winter dreaming of Florida, and the Welches were no exception. As early as 1923, they began wintering in West Palm Beach and had bought land in Ormand, Florida. Judging from tax records, the land was never developed and was finally sold in 1940.

Aside from gratifying Herb's theatrical side, the sporting show circuit provided advertising exposure that money could not buy. According to the press, a week-long New York City show could attract a total gate of some 277,000 visitors, with Philadelphia and Toronto not far behind.

When not on stage bantering with Chief Needebah, Herb could be found in the Ashaway Line Company's booth hanging out with Lou Gehrig, if in New York, or Ted Williams, if in Boston. If you asked Welch, he was happy to extol the virtues of Rangeley Lakes fishing guided by Herb Welch and expound on the need to have the inevitable trophy fish mounted—by Herb Welch, of course.

While under Herb's care, you would never be left wanting. He was happy to provide: extra clothing by Pendleton and Woolrich; footwear by Bass and Russell; rods by Hardy, Leonard, Thomas, Edwards, Payne, Hawes, and Kingfisher; reels by vom Hofe, Pfleuger, and a young Bogdan; fly boxes by Wheatley and Perrine; fly lines by Ashaway; streamers by Stevens and Percy; and original art by Welch. All this and more seemed to magically appear from a one-level store that spanned a mere 40 x 20 feet.

If you had money left over, there were always the slot machines. Or at least there were slot machines until, as the *Rangeley Record* reported on August 20, 1937, "one of the most daring daylight robberies ever attempted in these parts occurred at about 11

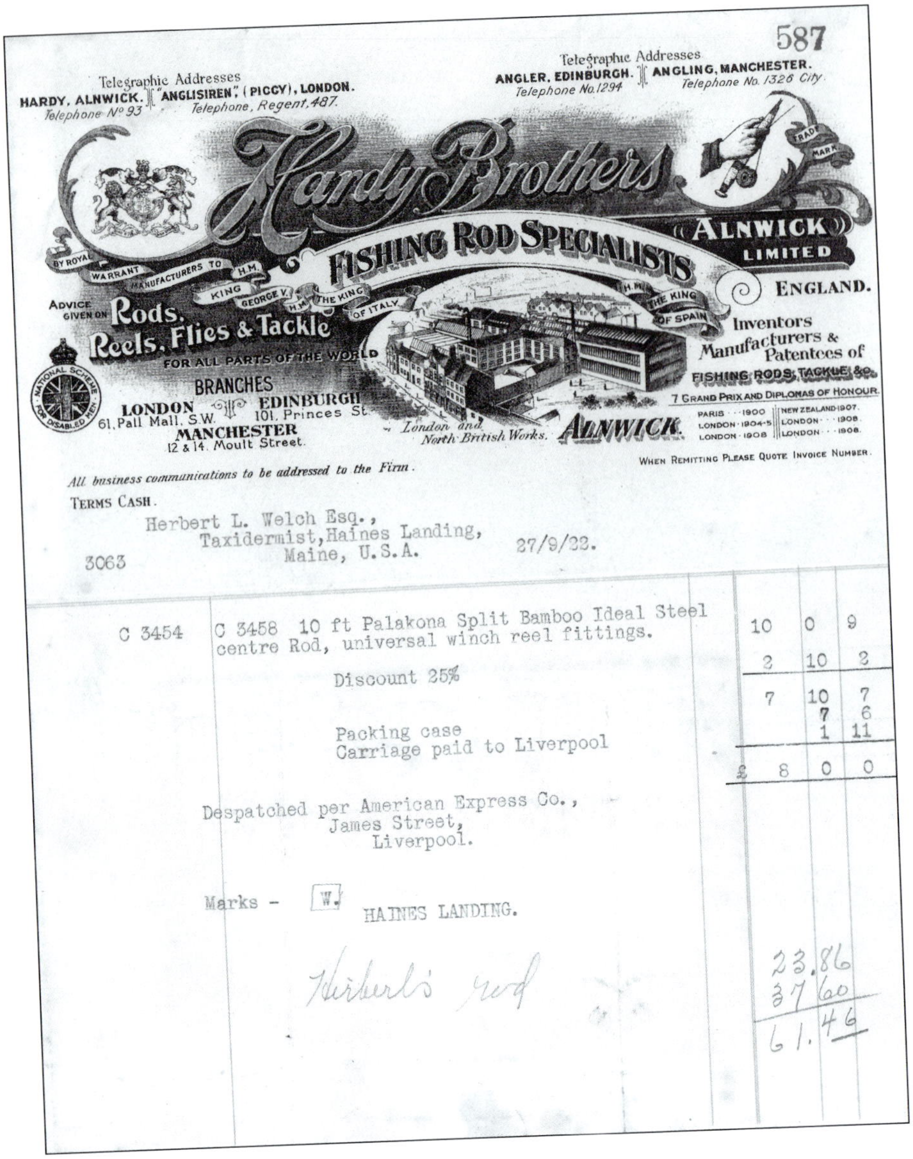

587

Telegraphic Addresses
HARDY, ALNWICK. ‖ "ANGLISIREN", (PICCY), LONDON.
Telephone Nº 93 · Telephone, Regent,487.

Telegraphic Addresses
ANGLER, EDINBURGH. ‖ ANGLING, MANCHESTER.
Telephone No.1294 · Telephone No. 1326 City.

Hardy Brothers
FISHING ROD SPECIALISTS
ALNWICK LIMITED
ENGLAND.

By Royal Warrant Manufacturers to H.M. King George V, H.M. the King of Italy, H.M. the King of Spain

Advice given on Rods, Reels, Flies & Tackle for all parts of the world

Inventors Manufacturers & Patentees of Fishing Rods, Tackle &c.

BRANCHES
LONDON 61, Pall Mall, S.W.
EDINBURGH 101, Princes St.
MANCHESTER 12 & 14, Moult Street.

London and North British Works. ALNWICK.

7 Grand Prix and Diplomas of Honour.
Paris ··· 1900 | New Zealand 1907.
London · 1904-5 | London ··· 1908.
London · 1908 | London ··· 1908.

When Remitting Please Quote Invoice Number.

All business communications to be addressed to the Firm.

Terms Cash.

Herbert L. Welch Esq.,
Taxidermist, Haines Landing,
Maine, U.S.A. 27/9/22.

3063

		£	s	d
C 3454	C 3458 10 ft Palakona Split Bamboo Ideal Steel centre Rod, universal winch reel fittings.	10	0	9
	Discount 25%	2	10	2
		7	10	7
	Packing case		7	6
	Carriage paid to Liverpool		1	11
		£ 8	0	0

Despatched per American Express Co.,
James Street,
Liverpool.

Marks – [W.] HAINES LANDING.

Herbert's rod

23.86
37.60
61.46

American rodmakers would soon dominate the world market, but no one has ever surpassed a Hardy Brothers' letterhead.

Invaluable advertising for Herb as Ashaway regularly distributed its fishing periodicals at no cost. Ashaway Line and Twine was founded in 1824 by Lester Crandall and remains in business still owned by the Crandall family of Ashaway, Rhode Island.
RANGELEY SPORTING HERITAGE MUSEUM

o'clock, Wednesday morning at the Welch Sporting Goods Store, when 3 young men stole the quarter slot machines… Officers searched fruitlessly throughout the day."

Not wanting to lose the revenue stream, Herb replaced the machines, but the *Rangeley Record* would report the following year that "Twenty state policeman swooped into the Rangeley Lakes and picked up 46 slot machines"—Herb's among them. Charged with "keeping a gambling house," he paid court costs of $7.15 and went home.

The Campbell-Fairbanks shows would not be Herb's sole means of advertising, however. Reflecting both his business savvy and his fondness for camaraderie, he held memberships in the Knights of Pythias, Knights Templar, Shriners, Odd Fellows, Masons, Rotary, Elks, Oquossoc Angling Association, and the Kennebago Tribe. It all leaves one wondering how he had time for anything else.

While Herb's mounts still line the walls of the reclusive Oquossoc Angling Association, which belatedly accepted him in 1951, it was the Kennebago Tribe that he held closer to his heart. This fraternal organization first banded together on March 20, 1917, under the leadership of Charles Zibeon Southard of Groton, Massachusetts. An engineer, Southard married into the prominent Dix family and moved with his wife, Rosa, from Brooklyn back to her ancestral home in Groton.[6] In another classic example of avocation overtaking vocation, Southard is remembered today for his three books published by E.P. Dutton of New York: *Trout Fly-fishing in America*,

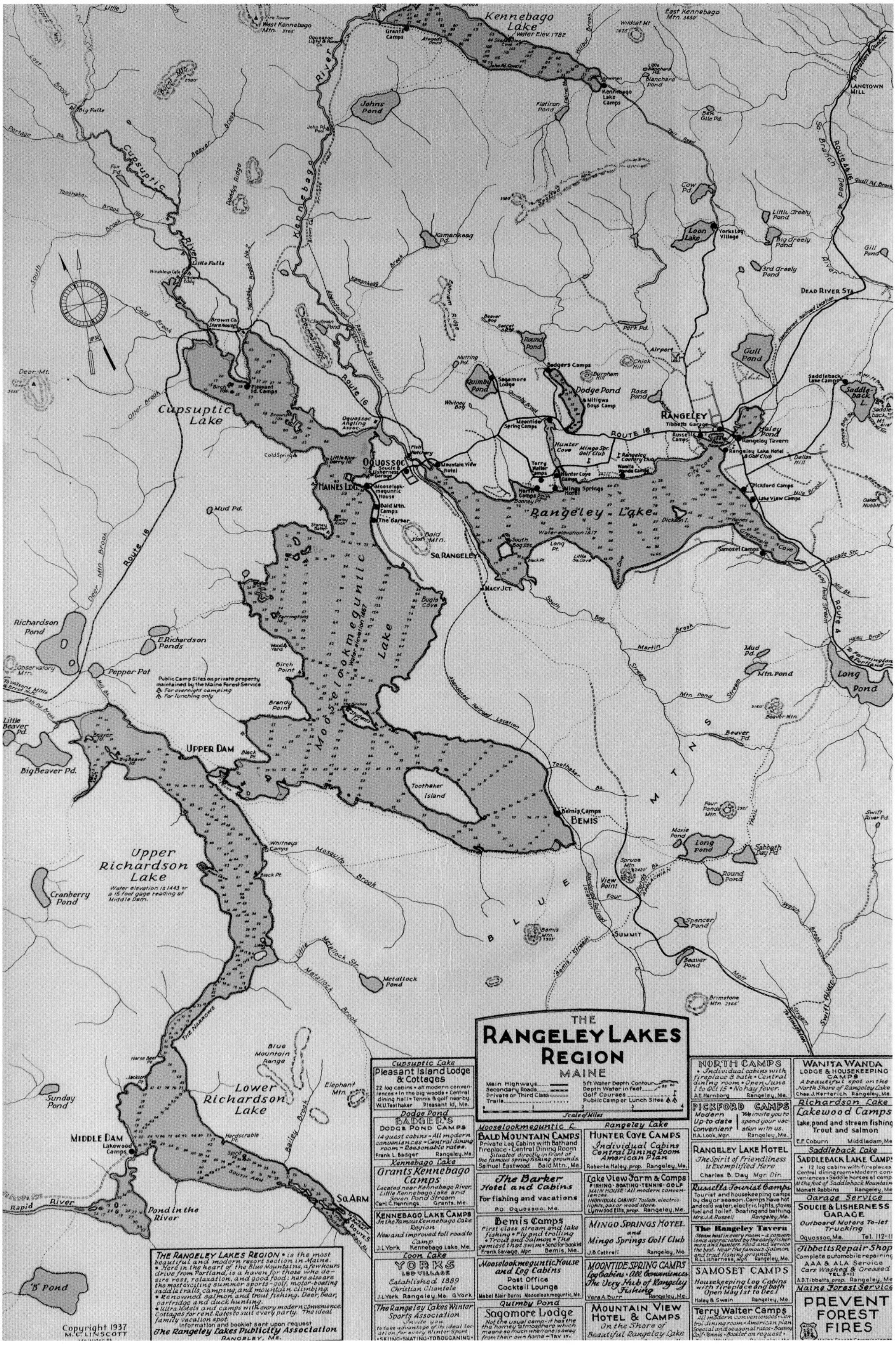

The Rangeley watershed served by Welch's Sporting Goods. All told, the Rangeley region contains 112 lakes and ponds. LINSCOTT

Kennebago Tribe members in full regalia.

RANGELEY SPORTING HERITAGE MUSEUM

KENNEBAGO TRIBE MEMBERS (clockwise, starting with Converse)

Henry E. Converse is Chief Sleeping Bear
Herbert L. Welch is Chief Black Hawk
James T. Roche is Chief High Bear
Leslie E. Latham is Chief Dustmaker
Edward M. Benson is Chief Kicking Bear
Theodore De Witt is Chief American Horse
Richard Wayne is Chief Red Cloud
Frank L. Bickmore is Chief Spotted Horse
Charles Zibeon Southard is Big Chief Zibeon
Edward Grant is Chief Sitting Bull
John W. Cook is Chief Eagle Elk
George Fiig Jr. is Chief White Buffalo
Durward M. Hyde is Chief Thunder Cloud
John B. Hunter is Chief Wolf Robe
D. L. Yingling is Chief Little Bird
Fred C. Kress is Chief Little Bear
Andrew F. Van Thun Jr. is Chief Turning Eagle
Henry K. Hooker is Chief Swift Dog

Each tribal member has been venerated by a tribute streamer reflecting his Kennebago persona.
All patterns originated and tied by Leslie K. Hilyard. HILYARD COLLECTION

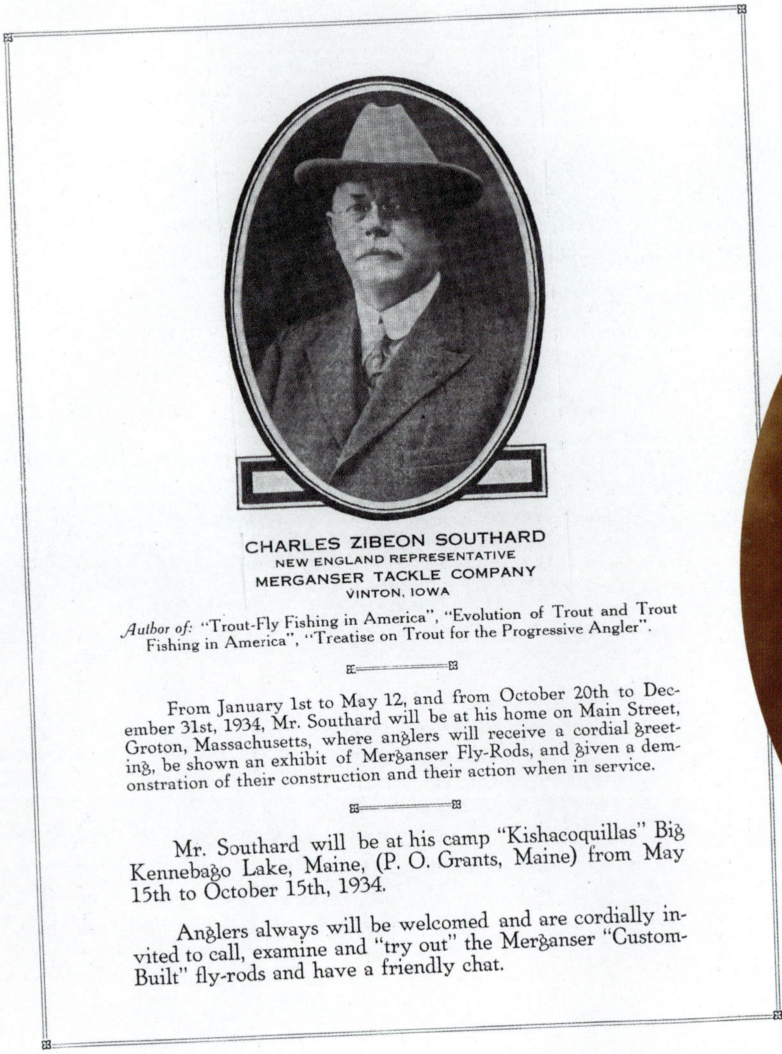

CHARLES ZIBEON SOUTHARD
NEW ENGLAND REPRESENTATIVE
MERGANSER TACKLE COMPANY
VINTON, IOWA

Author of: "Trout-Fly Fishing in America", "Evolution of Trout and Trout Fishing in America", "Treatise on Trout for the Progressive Angler".

From January 1st to May 12, and from October 20th to December 31st, 1934, Mr. Southard will be at his home on Main Street, Groton, Massachusetts, where anglers will receive a cordial greeting, be shown an exhibit of Merganser Fly-Rods, and given a demonstration of their construction and their action when in service.

Mr. Southard will be at his camp "Kishacoquillas" Big Kennebago Lake, Maine, (P. O. Grants, Maine) from May 15th to October 15th, 1934.

Anglers always will be welcomed and are cordially invited to call, examine and "try out" the Merganser "Custom-Built" fly-rods and have a friendly chat.

Southard was an early mentor to a young Herb Welch, publishing articles about him and promoting him in the Kennebago community.

Herb as Chief Black Hawk.
RANGELEY SPORTING HERITAGE MUSEUM

The Evolution of Trout and Trout Fishing in America, and *A Treatise on Trout for the Progressive Angler*.

Kennebago Tribe membership followed rules formally laid out in their constitution. Considering this constitution contains secret seals, signs, and even a secret handshake, much of it appears to have been written with tongue firmly in cheek. Membership was capped at twenty, but peaked at eighteen, consisting of sixteen affluent businessmen from Massachusetts, Connecticut, New York, and Pennsylvania. Inducted in 1918, Herbert L. Welch was Maine's second representative after Ed Grant, an early Kennebago pioneer and Southard mentor who held the rank of "Honorary Tribesman."

On induction, each member received ceremonial regalia consisting of a tribal blanket, a peace pipe, and a one-feather headdress with the headband embossed with an emblem of the sun, a star, and a quarter moon. Members wore this regalia at the Kennebago summer powwows and at the winter meetings held at Sherry's, a fashionable watering hole near Fifth Avenue in New York City.

Each member held the rank of Chief with the exception of their leader, "Big Chief Zibeon," who set himself apart with a three-feathered headdress. A peaceable band, this tribe had no war bonnets, bows and arrows, or fireside councils about waging war against bait fishers.

Each member adopted a tribal name to reflect his new persona. While some of the names have a manufactured quality, Herb selected the great Sauk warrior, Chief Black Hawk, as his namesake. The Kennebago

Kennebago Tribe Membership Requirements

1. An angler must have fished the Kennebago region for at least two years.
2. An angler must have caught and landed a trout or salmon, the actual weight of which was not less than 2½ pounds and with a fly-rod, which weighed not in excess of 5 ounces.
3. An angler shall be proposed by two Tribesmen to whom he shall be personally well known.
4. An angler shall be endorsed by two other Tribesmen whom he has met.
5. To become a Tribesmen of the Kennebago Tribe an applicant shall be unanimously elected by all members of the Tribe.
6. An applicant shall be elected only at one of the regular council meetings of the Tribe after his qualifications have been thoroughly considered.

The Ritual (To be used in initiation ceremonies)

The applicant for membership to the Kennebago Tribe is brought into the council meeting by two Tribesmen. The applicant is blindfolded and is placed standing facing the Big Chief.

The Two Tribesmen then take their respective places in the council circle.

Big Chief	Who is this man?
Big Scribe	He is an applicant for membership to the great Kennebago Tribe of angler-sportsmen.
Big Chief	Is he qualified to become one of us, O Big Scribe.
Big Scribe	We, your Tribesmen, believe he is, O Big Chief.
Big Chief	Unblindfold him, O Big Medicine Man, that he may better hear what I am about to say.

The applicant is unblindfolded by the Big Medicine Man, who again resumes his place in the council circle.

Tribe appears to have been short-lived, as the *Kennebago Tribe Scraps(book)* compiled by Durwood Hyde documents nothing after 1921.[7] The book contains numerous references to members' failing health. In all probability, the organization had disbanded by Southard's death in 1925. However, Herb's focus on the Kennebago fishery would never waver, and his guiding history finds him consistently on the Kennebago Lakes, Big and Little, and on the Kennebago River, only occasionally straying to Upper Dam and Bemis.

By the 1930s, the combination of Herb's irrepressible personality and advertising had given him national name recognition. *Field & Stream* magazine ran regular ads for Camel cigarettes with Herb touting the product as a cure for indigestion. Willys, the forerunner of Jeep, ran full-page ads of Herb, decked out in hip boots, reaching inaccessible waters thanks to their four-wheel-drive vehicles. *Hunting and Fishing Magazine* ran ads for Bass Outdoor Footwear, revealing that Herb "had worn Bass moccasins for ten months a year for practically forty years."

The Downtown Athletic Club of New York City emblazoned their 1938 journal cover with the same image of Herb that Aetna Insurance Company used for their 1940 calendar. Tackle manufacturers H.A. Whittemore of Boston and Julian Crandall's Ashaway

Just two of many magazine covers graced by Herb. By 1920, he no longer paid for advertising thanks to his celebrity. HILYARD COLLECTION

Today's Jeep evolved from Willys. All previous owners of the Jeep brand have long since gone bankrupt. HILYARD COLLECTION

A daily reminder of Herb during the month of March. HILYARD COLLECTION

Line of Ashaway, Rhode Island, frequently featured Herb on their catalog covers. Realizing the value of Herb's celebrity, Canada routinely issued him complimentary fishing licenses. When the state needed a photograph to symbolize fly-fishing in Maine for its Maine Sesquicentennial, 1820–1970, they used an image of Herb up to his knees in the Kennebago River, ten years after his crossing the River Jordan.

When Grantland Rice, the nation's premier early-twentieth-century sportswriter, wanted to create a film about fly-fishing, he arrived at Haines Landing in the 1930s with a camera crew. Rice's Sport-light Films featured regularly in America's movie houses, playing as a ten-minute "short" prior to the feature film, and were viewed by thousands coast to coast. Not surprisingly, Herb took Rice to the Kennebago River, where he put on a clinic, laying out lavish amounts of line at John's Pond pool and catching a large salmon that was ably netted by Rice. Returning to Haines Landing, Herb put on another clinic, demonstrating the basics of the taxidermy process.

When President Hoover arrived at the Kennebago Lake House, it was Herb who guided him on Kennebago Lake. The June 9, 1939, issue of the *Rangeley Record* noted that "President Herbert Hoover using a fly especially tied and named for him by the Rangeley region's champion fly caster, caught his limit in Kennebago Lake recently." A diplomat as well as a showman, Herb would later reminisce that Hoover "didn't have a great deal to say. He was a good fisherman, though. He never missed a rise. I didn't have to tell him a thing."[8]

Left to right: President Hoover, Herb Welch, and Maine's Governor Barrows on Kennebago Lake in 1939. Sadly, the pattern for the Hoover fly originated by Herb is among the missing. VOORHEES COLLECTION

When Osa Martin, the famed African explorer and documentary filmmaker, arrived at the Kennebago Lake House in 1941, again it was Herb who got the call. According to the *Boston Globe* report of June 28:

> She caught fish everyday at Kennebago starting off with 17 trout, all over a pound and a half, on her first day of fishing, when she kept 6 and released the rest. She learned a lot about flycasting from Herbie Welch, she learned a lot about flies from Bert Quimby.
>
> Osa would rather catch small fish in New England than big fish in Africa, where her record catch was a 73-pound catfish, which she might never have landed if two of her black boys hadn't jumped in and grabbed it by the gills... One reason she prefers New England fishing is the absence of snakes and crocodiles, her pet peeves.

When President Eisenhower arrived in Rangeley on his 1955 tour of New England, the Boston press had been reporting that Herb would guide him on Kennebago Lake as he had done with Hoover.[9] But it never came to pass. Although Herb's famous line to Ike was "I was going to guide you, but the damn Democrats wouldn't let me do it," the Secret Service was justifiably concerned by Herb's advanced seventy-five

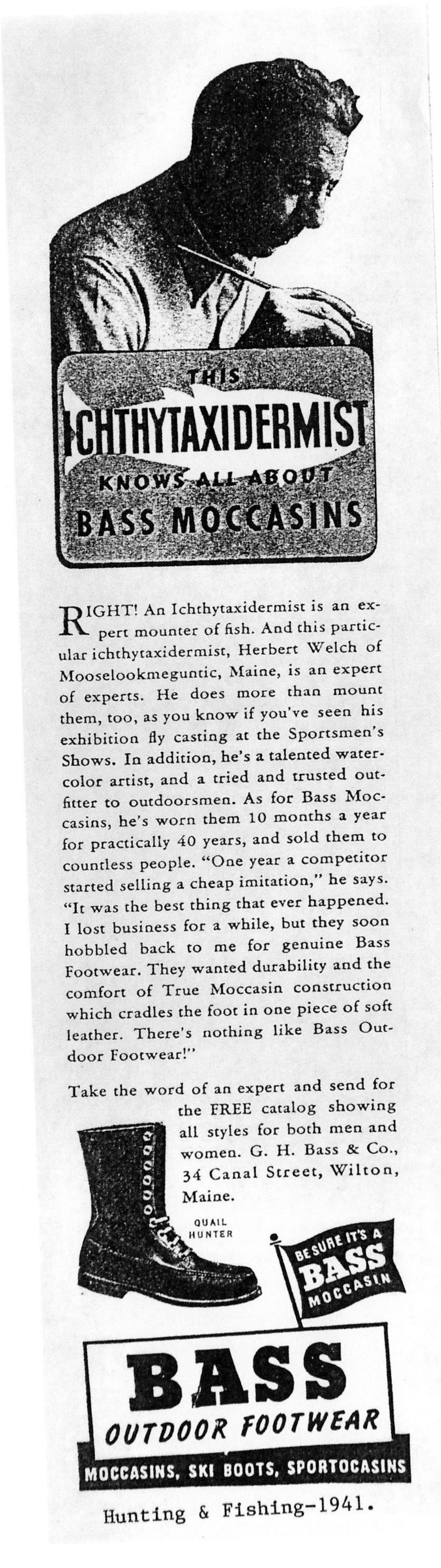

Given the nature of Maine winters, it is hard to imagine wearing moccasins ten months of the year. HUNTING AND FISHING MAGAZINE

years. They also deemed lake fishing too exposed and felt that river wading would be safer. Consequently, the Brown Paper Company of Berlin, New Hampshire, offered up their isolated Camp Caribou on Parmachenee Lake, which had access to the upper reaches of Maine's Magalloway River. A bronze plaque commemorating the event can be found at Little Boy Falls on the upper Magalloway.

More than 150 newspaper, radio, magazine, and television outlets covered the three-day event and breathlessly reported on every fish Ike caught.[10] What they did not report was Ike's fury when he learned that Maine had heavily stocked the waters and that his favorite dry fly, the House and Lot, was probably not the reason for his success.

FAMOUS EXPLORER TURNS TABLES

When Osa Johnson, famous explorer, writer, and lecturer, was at Kennebago Lake this week fishing, she turned the tables on the boys by taking their pictures on the dock. Left to right, Osa, Bert Quimby, Sam York, Herb Welch.

Revered by the safari community, the Johnson's many acheivements are memorialized by the Martin and Osa Johnson Safari Museum in Chanute, Kansas. *RANGELEY RECORD*

On the advice of his guide, Don Cameron, and much to the chagrin of the Secret Service, Ike abruptly abandoned the scheduled Magalloway itinerary and crashed through the woods to Rump Pond, where the fish were guaranteed to be wild. To this day, stories are told of the black-suited, black-fly-bitten, and half-crazed Secret Service agent who stumbled shoeless out of the woods three days later, babbling, "I got one bullet left, but I was saving it for myself."[11]

At age seventy-five, Herb was in decline, and he knew it. He had abandoned the rigors of the show circuit five years earlier, and five years later, he'd pass on the taxidermy torch to an able Dave Footer. Selling off his legendary sporting goods store would prove more difficult, however. Both Stan Bogdan and Dave Footer declined offers to purchase the store, as they could see that the Rangeley sun was setting. Those hotels that had once fueled the Welch business were now empty. During 1959, Herb managed to gradually sell off his dwindling stock and finally sell the building. It was moved across the street to its present location and opened as the White Fawn restaurant, a short-lived venture.

Declines often have their origins in the distant past, and that was certainly the case with the Rangeley Lakes. "Fly Rod" Crosby provided a hint of what was to come when she wrote in the June 16, 1905, issue of *Maine Woods*:

> To ride in a Stanley auto, with Frank E. Stanley the inventor at the wheel, the Franklin county boy we are all so proud of, has always been my desire, and last week it was my pleasure with Mrs. J.B. Marble to accept the invitation of Mr. and Mrs. Stanley and such a delightful ride we had!

By the late 1940s, the descendants of the Stanley Steamer were on a collision course with the

THE WHITE HOUSE
WASHINGTON

July 1, 1955

Dear Mr. Welch:

It was nice to meet you at Rangeley, and once again I want to thank you for the bronze figure that you gave me. Since it depicts one of my favorite sports, I am more than delighted to have it and grateful for your thought of me.

I was interested to know that you had at one time been a guide for President Hoover -- and of course delighted to see a life time Republican!

With best wishes,

Sincerely,

Dwight D. Eisenhower

Mr. Herb Welch
Haines Landing
Maine

The General Ike was originated by George Fletcher and tied by Leslie K. Hilyard. Disenchanted with teaching, George Fletcher arrived in Rangeley in 1945 and established Fletcher's Fly Shop. It remains in business, now known as the Rangeley Region Sports Shop. HILYARD COLLECTION

Rangeley's tourism. After World War II, the age of the automobile was in full gear, creating new travel options for tourists. Families no longer depended on trains to deliver them to hotels for the entire summer, and short visits to a variety of locales became the norm. Ironically, the Stanley who had pioneered Rangeley was a cousin of the Stanley whose car contributed to its decline.

In 1958, the Mooselookmeguntic House that had anchored Haines Landing since 1877 burned down. No phoenix would rise from the ashes: As a commercial entity, Haines Landing was dead. Upper Dam House would not have the dignity of cremation, instead being torn down in 1955. Nor would the Mountain View House or the Rangeley Lake House, both torn down in 1956. Of the twenty-seven resorts opened in the area prior to 1900, nineteen had either ceased to exist or been privatized. Those that remained were struggling. Even the landmark Barker Hotel, which had been exceptionally attentive to changing tastes, would close in 1966.

But rarely are declines caused by a single event, and in the case of the Rangeley Lakes, that decline involved more than just the postwar automobile boom. Again, we return to the distant past—the year 1904.

Alpine beauty aside, what had always sustained the Rangeley Lakes as a resort area was the exceedingly large brook trout. Their exceptional growth was fueled by the diminutive *Salvelinus oquossa*, better known as the blueback trout. From time immemorial, fishers have complained that the fishing was "going to hell in a handbasket." Rangeley was no exception, and in 1875 the solution was to introduce the landlocked salmon. Only later did it occur to the architects of this scheme that the salmon might need additional feed, and so they introduced smelt in 1891. By then, pursued by both trout and salmon, the bluebacks were wiped out.

Compounding the blueback's plight, Maine protective law for trout passed in 1869 offered no protection for the blueback of Oxford and Franklin counties.[12] Local settlers had heavily depended on the blueback as a winter food supply, and their demand for the continued right to slaughter the fish was granted. As the blueback was not considered a gamefish and was rarely taken by hook, officials probably thought little of this exemption.

But by 1874, the exemption was being challenged. The Maine Fish Commissioner's report for that year stated that "it was a great mistake to allow these beautiful fishes to be taken at all as it is to the blueback

The Mooselookmeguntic Hotel burned with flames which sometimes reached and estimated 200 feet in the air. The fire companies of Oquossoc and Rangeley confined the flames to the main building and an other structure immediately adjacent.

One of many Maine hotels that burned in the 1950s. The hotel was empty when the fire started, and how the bottled gas ignited remains a mystery. RANGELEY HIGHLANDER

Sea and River Fishing.

FISH IN SEASON IN NOVEMBER.

Black Bass, *Micropterus salmoides; M. nigricans.*
Mascalonge, *Esox nobilior.*
Pike or Pickerel, *Esox lucius.*
Yellow Perch, *Perca flavescens.*
Sea Bass, *Sciænops ocellatus.*
Striped Bass, *Roccus linneatus.*
White Perch, *Morone americana.*
Weakfish, *Cynoscion regalis.*
Bluefish, *Pomatomus saltatrix.*
Spanish Mackerel, *Cybium maculatum.*
Cero, *Cybium regale.*
Bonito, *Sarda pelamys.*
Kingfish, *Menticirrus nebulosus.*

FISH IN MARKET.—Fish in good quantity. Codfish very plenty and caught off Long Island. Bass, 18 to 20 cents a pound; smelts, 20 cents; bluefish, 15; salmon, frozen, 35; mackerel, 18 to 25; white perch, 15; Spanish mackerel, 35; green turtle, 18; terrapin, $15 a dozen; halibut, 18 cents a pound; haddock, 8 cents; codfish, 8 to 10; blackfish, 10 to 15; flounders, 10; lobsters, 10; sheeps head, 25; scollops, $1.50 per gallon; soft clams, 30 cents per 100; white fish, 18; pickerel, 18; salmon trout, 15; hard crabs, $3.50 a 100; blue-back trout, 50 cents a pound.

—The first of the Rangeley Lake blue-back trout have come to market from Maine, and will be as usual at Mr. E. G. Blackford's stall in Fulton Market. It may be remembered that these peculiar fish have the honor of being the single exception to the general rule in regard to the close season, as far as trout are concerned; and sometimes amusing incidents have occurred on the part of the officers of State associations for the protection of game, who through excess of zeal have interfered with the selling of the blue-back trout at this time of the year.

Forest & Stream, November 15, 1877.

Driven by public demand, commercial fishing often spells doom for fragile fisheries. FOREST & STREAM

Blueback trout mounted by Dave Footer—fuel for the legendary Rangeley brook trout. With the bluebacks' extirpation, the size of the brook trout rapidly diminished. HILYARD COLLECTION

that they attributed the great size of the Rangeley trout."[13] In 1899, a more comprehensive protective trout law was passed, but it came too late. By 1904, the bluebacks had largely disappeared, and the smelt were proving to be an inadequate replacement.[14]

No longer the dominant predator species, the brook trout found itself undernourished and under attack by the far more aggressive landlocked salmon. With this regal fish's rapidly diminishing size and numbers came a diminished interest in the Rangeleys.

Herb had often expressed his grave environmental concerns for both the Maine and Rangeley fisheries, as revealed in an undated *Atlantic Monthly* article, "Farewell to the North Woods Guide":

> There I talked with, among others, Herb Welch, champion fly-caster and creator of the streamer fly whose tackle store at Oquossoc has been a headquarters these past fifty years... He is bitter as are many guides over the results of pulpcutting... and power companies, the chief enemies of natural fishing conditions.
>
> "Take the salmon," said Herb Welch. "Whether he's Atlantic or landlocked, his instinct urges him to the sea. He starts down our streams and he runs smack into waters polluted by sulphite. He never reaches full maturity, and that's why big salmon become increasingly scarce. It ought to be possible to develop some substitute for sulphite which would not be harmful to fish. Here's the state of Maine, which has spent millions publicizing its attractions for sportsmen, throwing away a substantial source of revenue because the politicians down in Augusta won't stand up to the lumber companies."

What might have surprised Herb is that today's fly fishers can still occasionally attract 4- to 6-pound brook trout and landlocked salmon from the Kennebago, Mooselookmeguntic, and, farther downstream, the Rapid River.

Also surprising: that the elegant Bald Mountain Camps, founded in 1897, are still in operation. And that Lagomonte Lodge, built by his mentors in 1903, remains in pristine condition, as does Senator Frye's complex, as do all the cabins within Haines Landing territory. And that a visionary land trust now has permanent guardianship over 10,500 acres, ranging from Mooselookmeguntic's Stony Batter up the shoreline to Steep Bank Pool on his treasured Kennebago River. And that Herb himself was a major focus of a recently opened museum celebrating the Rangeley Lakes sporting heritage.

While Herb would have been gratified by his inclusion in the museum, he would have been even more pleased to learn that the museum's focus was twofold: to remind the community of what it had once been, and to encourage consideration for what it could again become—a harbor for trophy brook trout and the fishers that pursue them. Many who have studied the matter believe that the blueback trout alone contains the required nutrients to help the Rangeley brook trout regain their historic weight. So, if there is to be a Rangeley revival, it

Nightfall at Bald Mountain Camps hearkens back to a gilded age. MACLEOD

will be fundamentally linked to the return of the blueback trout.

Recovery will be difficult but not impossible. Mooselookmeguntic Lake is large, ranging over 17,000 acres with depths up to 124 feet. As smelt and bluebacks live in different thermoclines and spawn at different times, territorial disputes will be minimal, allowing the bluebacks to gain a foothold in their rightful waters.[15] Meanwhile, all species benefit from the present water conditions, which are much enhanced now that log drives are a thing of the distant past. While such a recovery effort could have unintended consequences, there are also consequences for standing idly by. One thing is certain: If there is to be a Rangeley revival, it will be linked to bluebacks, brook trout, and appropriate fishing legislation. Smelts, salmon, and slot limits have not done it. Community support for any fisheries restoration project is mandatory, as is state involvement. No matter how good the science, without the political will and community support, nothing can be started or sustained. Happily, a change in the Maine state leadership has brought a more open and enlightened approach to fishery management. What better way to honor a man of Herbert L. Welch's stature than to increase the risk of danger to any Black Ghost streamers found swimming in his Mooselookmeguntic and Kennebago waters?

Kennebago trout will rise
but only to a fly that swims like light.
For years these trout have memorized
the ghost of such a fly, the feathered lure
named for its maker, crack shot, fisherman,
Black Ghost, guide to those who could afford him.
And the wealthy clients' lonely wives,
who could blame them?
They say his moves were graceful, clean
as water flowing through the Steep Bank pool,
they say his hands could call back current
to the gills of fish he'd taken from the stream.
They say that he could slant a woman's thoughts
to water.
It may have been, with one, that she was only looking
for something in her life to mark off time,
but there are no markers to the Steep Bank pool.
A railroad bed, untracked, runs through the woods.
You know it only by its history,
swamp-lined in places where the story darkens.
They say she listened to the river,
they say it spoke her language,
they say she trusted it,
they say that its desires were her own.
Beyond this, nothing certain can be known:
they found her husband dead, the lamp
burning, shotgun loaded by the door,
the Black Ghost gone, the pool in flood
along its banks.
The widow told no secrets,
sold the camp, moved on downriver.
The Black Ghost came back home
when the floodwash fell
but would not say where he had been.
No one thought to ask the trout
hovering beneath the steep bank,
remembering how light swims.

Linda Warren
Princeton, Massachusetts

A testament to a life writ large.

Cosseboom vs. Welch

THE *RANGELEY RECORD*, JUNE 12, 1934
KENNEBAGO

A fly casting contest was staged at the Kennebago Lake House, last Tuesday, with John Casseboom, President of the One Hundred Footer club, and Herbert Welch, Haines Landing, tying for honors. Their casts were 124 feet and Mr. Welch gained for himself the position of tenth member in the organization. Another match will be held soon to determine the better man. Payson Tibbetts came second, casting 95 feet.

A testament to Herb's casting ability. RANGELEY SPORTING HERITAGE MUSEUM

ENDNOTES

1 Bill Riviere, "Down Memory Lane with Sportsmen's Show," *Boston Globe*, January 16, 1972.
2 Stan Bogdan, interview with author, August 14, 2004.
3 Nancy Lacompte, letter to the author, August 20, 2008.
4 Lincoln A. Werdent, "1000's at Opening Session of the National Sportsman Show," *New York Times*, February 19, 1939.
5 "Reptile Exhibit Proves Popular," *Boston Globe*, February 19, 1939.
6 Helen McCarthy Sawyer, *More People and Places of Groton*, Groton Massachusetts Historical Society, p. 87–88.
7 *Kennebago Tribe Scraps(book)*, compiled by Durwood M. Hyde, Johnstown, Pennsylvania, c. 1921.
8 Earl Banner, "Ike's Maine Fishing Guide Could Teach Him About Art, Too," *Boston Globe*, June 12, 1955, p. c-70.
9 Ibid.
10 "Our Guest, the President of the United States," *The Brown Bulletin*, p. 12.
11 Tom Rideout, interview with author, September 2, 2007.
12 William Converse Kendall, "The Rangeley Lakes, Maine, with Special Reference to the Habits of the Fishes, Fish Culture and Angling," Washington, DC, *Bulletin of the Bureau of Fisheries* 35(1915–16): 28.
13 Ibid.
14 Gerald P. Cooper, "A Biological Survey of the Rangeley Lakes, with Special Reference to the Trout and Salmon," Fish Survey Report No.3, Augusta Press, 1940, pp. 145–6.
15 Frederick W. Kirchesis, "Landlocked Charr in Maine," Report No. 80, Maine Inland Fisheries and Wildlife, 1985, p. 2.

PART II

TO THE TIERS

Pattern No.
Hook size 4
Made by
Mrs. Carrie G. Stevens
Upper Dam, Me.

CHAPTER 7

Creations and Innovations

For all of Herb Welch's achievements in the arena of taxidermy and the fine arts, he is best remembered today for his 1927 origination of the Black Ghost streamer. Some ninety years later, in an age dominated by size 22 tricos and nymphal shucks, it remains near the top of the streamer sales charts, challenged only by the Gray Ghost, created by Carrie Stevens around 1934.[1]

The year 1927 proved pivotal in establishing Welch's legacy, as it saw two landmark events: the debut of both the Black Ghost streamer and its originator on the Campbell-Fairbanks stage. Thousands of spectators saw Herb on the casting platform while thousands of Black Ghosts continue to be submerged as prey. Both events served to cement the Welch name in the sporting world: He would remain on the stage until his retirement in 1950, while the Black Ghost will endure so long as trout and salmon do.

Although Herb retired from the casting platform in 1950, he did not retire from casting. That same year, he wintered in Florida, laying out 85 feet of line in search of Islamorada bonefish. Perhaps mystified by the unorthodox offering of a streamer, the bonefish took, and its 12-pound 4-ounce weight established a record for bonefish on the fly that would last until 1952.[2] Not surprisingly, it was caught on a Thomas rod and a Hardy Cascapedia reel loaded with Ashaway line. Sadly, Herb did not give the streamer pattern that he used. It's equally sad that Herb's bonefish patterns, one named for the legendary bonefish guide Bonnie Smith, were never recorded.

Since saltwater fly-fishing was experiencing a renaissance, the Welch bonefish was reported by newspapers ranging from Miami to Maine. Even the *New York Times* weighed in, noting that after the Islamorada achievement Herb "moved up to Stuart and went out to the Gulf Stream with Captain John Whiticar. He came in with a 7 foot 8 inch sail which is to be mounted for his cabin on Mooselookmeguntic."[3] Who might have mounted the sailfish remains a mystery. While there are reports of the sailfish hanging in the Welch store, there are none for the bonefish, which seems strange, given what an achievement that fish was.

The complicated logistics of shipping a large sailfish to Oquossoc, combined with Herb's relative lack of experience with large saltwater species, would suggest that Herb probably used a local taxidermist. Given Herb's insistence on having the best, that would have meant Al Pfleuger Sr. of Hallandale, Florida. Well established since 1926, he had revolutionized saltwater taxidermy by patenting a process that used a hollow mold to fit the species size. According to his son, Al Pfleuger Jr., who sold the company to Shakespeare in 1960, their first move

All the Black Ghosts were tied by Herb Welch. HILYARD COLLECTION

The Black Ghost Endures

Dear Mr. Hilyard,

One of the more popular flies is the Black Ghost, developed by Herbert "Herb" Welch in 1927 with a "featherwing." The fly worked so well that different versions of the pattern were created: the Black Ghost original "featherwing," the "marabou wing" and the "bucktail wing" tied as a streamer fly, the Black Ghost tied on a salmon hook with variations for trolling, and the Black Ghost tandem fly with "featherwing" and "marabou wing."

Here at LL Bean I tie a variety of Black Ghosts. Two versions on a streamer hook, the original "featherwing" in a size 4, and a "marabou wing" in sizes 4, 6, 8, and 10. I also tie a "calftail wing" version on a salmon hook in sizes 6, 8, and 10. For trolling, I tie a Black Ghost tandem fly size 4 with a "featherwing." I tie an average of 1,300 Black Ghosts for LL Bean annually.

LL Bean also sells Black Ghosts online and streamer flies in the store tied by others. My best guess for those would be an average of 900 flies, of course it could be higher.

As of 2015, I'm going to say that LL Bean must sell an average of 2,200–2,500 Black Ghosts a year.

Sincerely,
Ellen Belyea
Maine Tied Flies
Poland, Maine

4-D THE MIAMI HERALD Tuesday, March 7, 1950

NEW BONEFISH RECORD is represented by this catch of Herb Welch, famous Maine fly casting expert. The big fish, which weighed 12 pounds, 4 ounces, took 20 minutes to bring to net. It's a potential world record for bonefish caught on fly tackle. For further details, see Allen Corson's column on Page 5-D.

A foursome fished that day: Herb was guided by Jimmy Albright, while Dorothy Welch was guided by Jimmy's wife, Frankee Albright. Julian Crandell, owner of Ashaway Line, was guided by Bill Smith and Mrs. Crandell by Bill's wife, Bonnie Smith. *MIAMI HERALD*

was to burn all the shop records in a bonfire. Their second move was to abruptly sell the company.[4] So much for tracking Herb's saltwater trophies.

In 1950, Herb patented a leader-tying vise, but despite back and forth over production costs between Stan Bogdan and the assignor, Ashaway Line, it never made it into production. However, the previous year, a Herb Welch–designed trolling spoon made and marketed by H.A. Whittemore Company of Boston was produced.

In retrospect, Herb's belief that he "invented the streamer fly back in 1901" was never needed to cement his place in fly-fishing history. Equally unnecessary was the apocryphal story that he invented the streamer hook. These misguided claims have been proven false in Andrew Herd's *The Fly* and Paul Schullery's *Fly-Fishing Secrets of the Ancients*, two eloquently written books on fly-fishing history.

The *De Natura Animalium* by the Roman historian Aelian (170–230 AD) notes how Macedonians

George Fletcher Reflects

That Black Ghost trolling streamer Herb tied up and gave me influenced me to the point where I hardly ever used a streamer fly in the Rangeley area other than some type of Black Ghost. It got to the point where I tied up Black Ghosts in sizes 4, 6, 8, 10, and even 12s using hair instead of feathers and finally using white marabou for wings. I used a small amount of marabou with a small amount of white bucktail to sort of hold the marabou close to the hook...

I literally sold bushels of the bucktail and white marabou Black Ghosts for mostly spring fishing on Quimby Pond...

You know I fished for Atlantic salmon for years with Ai Ballou and that had something to do with my using white marabou on Black Ghosts.

George Fletcher
Strong, Maine
October 18, 1993

Left to right: Bonnie Smith, Herb, and Frankee Albright, all legendary guides. The sisters took over their husbands' guiding business during WWII and never looked back. GEORGE W. PINDER

caught trout by "fastening crimson wool around the hook, and fix onto the wool two feathers which grow under a cock's wattle which in color are like wax," but this is not necessarily the definitive origin of streamers. Given the ancient time frame, discerning the streamer's true origins is unlikely. As for the assertion that Herb invented the streamer hook, we know that fishing with a hook dates to the Neolithic Age, some 10,000 years ago.[5] Somehow, it seems dubious that mankind waited patiently until 1901 for the arrival of a long-shanked hook capable of carrying elongated feathers. It may well be that Herb re-forged a salmon hook into a suitable format for streamers as we know them, but this would not have been the same thing as bringing a new type of hook into existence. As early as 1882, T.H. Bates of New York City, which evolved into the venerable William Mills & Son, was offering English-made extra-long-shank hooks.[6] As late as the 1940s, S. Allcock of Redditch was still using that vague terminology.

The key to a modern streamer hook is the extra-long shank, but this term is poorly defined. By the early 1800s, the industrial city of Redditch, England, had evolved from being the center of needle making to being the center of hook making, home to seventeen competing companies. Despite the arrival of the machine age, Redditch hook makers resisted standardization, in an apparent attempt to protect market share. Any of five different hook scales were in play, which meant that an S. Allcock hook size 1 was not necessarily identical to a Milward or a Bartleet hook size 1.

Curiously, manufacturers documented the hook gap, but not the shank length. Dr. Herd, citing Jack Hedden, theorizes that this absence reflects the blind-eye era, when fly tiers trimmed the shanks to suit their individual needs. If so, there was no point in giving shank measurements and the custom of not doing so was carried forward.[7] Given the fly-fishing

The stock photo of Herb casting was frequently used in advertising during the 1930s and 1940s.

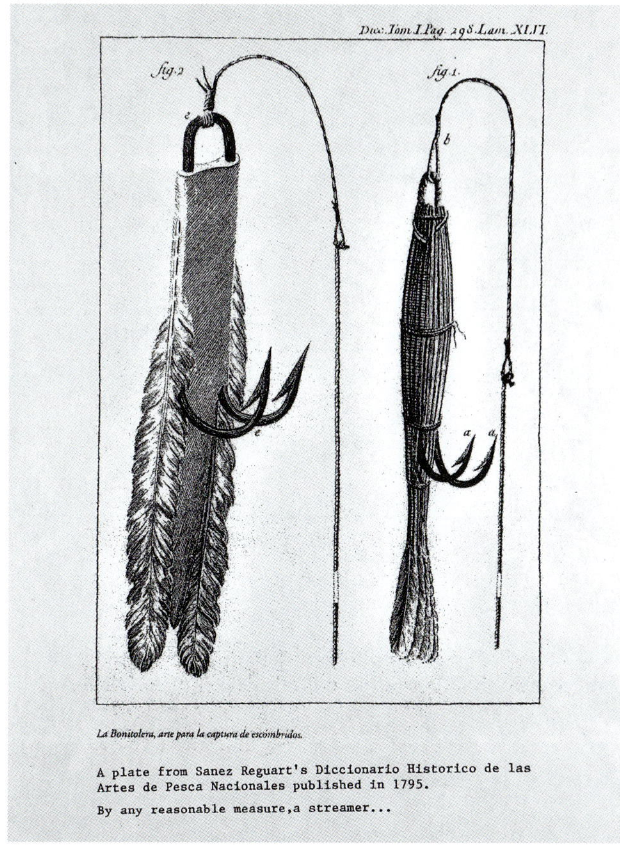

The *Reguart Diccionario,* written in 1795, documents the early existence of both streamers and doubles.
NEW YORK PUBLIC LIBRARY

community's resistance to change, this would make sense. No matter: If the answers to hook shank length cannot be uncovered in nineteenth-century catalogs, they can be found in seventeenth-century Jamestown, Virginia.

In a 2006 paper, "Subsistence Fishing at Jamestown, 1607–24," published by the Society for Post-Medieval Archaeology, Daniel Schmidt reports that over 170 fish hooks have been excavated at James Fort dating from 1607 to 1612:

> All but one are of iron, they vary considerably in size. Those that retain their terminal end are not pierced with a hole like modern hooks, but are flattened into a spade shape to allow for attachment of the line... [T]hey show evidence of barbs...
>
> Measurements were recorded from x-rays of 34 samples. Several of these are over 100mm long with some as large as 130mm, but there are also smaller examples only about 40mm in length...
>
> While the hooks vary in size, the gauge of the wire from which they are made is surprisingly regular, when measured in units of 0.1mm, most of the wires were found to be of 2.0, 2.5, 3.0, 4.0, 5.0, or 6.0mm thick. This suggests that the wire was drawn using standardized drawplates and was not merely the result of improvisation, it seems likely that it was produced professionally in England.

So, converting those metric measurements, hook shank lengths ranged from 1.57 inches to 5.11 inches. While the 130 mm (5.11 inches) hook was probably used for either sturgeon or cod, the 40 mm (1.7 inches) and the 50 mm (1.96 inches) would have been ideal for the modern streamer. Given these measurements, it seems clear that the origin of the streamer hook was not modern. That these myths exist despite clear evidence to the contrary suggests that sometimes origination credits are more a reflection of who has the loudest press than of reality.

FISHING AT JAMESTOWN 85

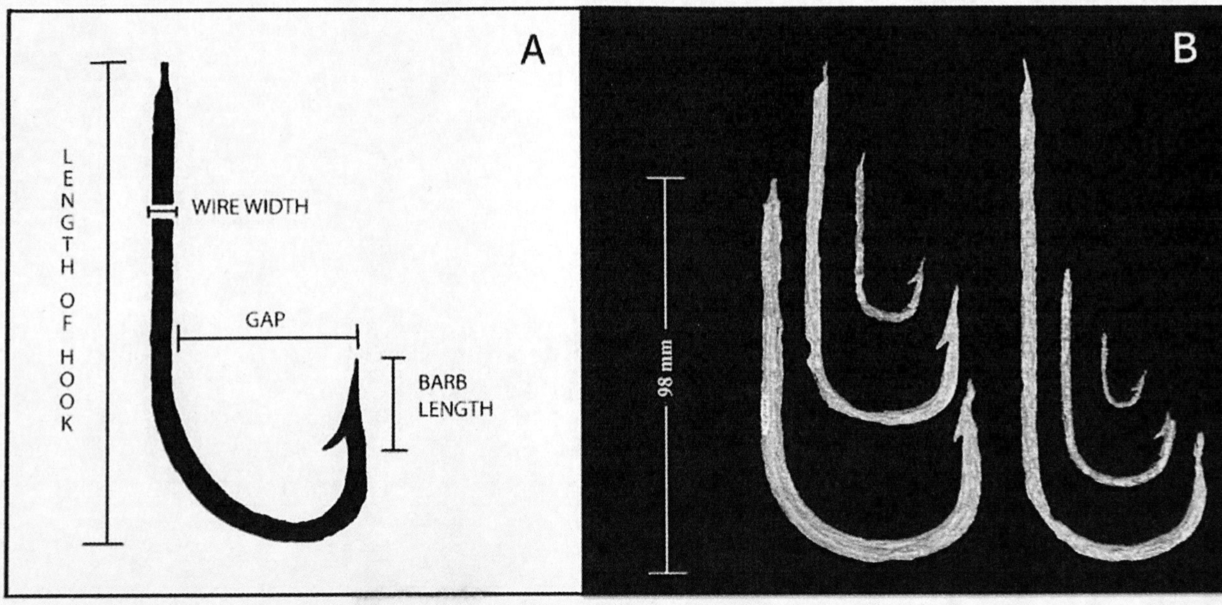

FIG. 3
Fishhook attributes and photo of iron fishhooks found at James Fort (APVA).

While fish were plentiful near Jamestown, a lack of fishing expertise and a lack of salt to preserve fish resulted in "starving times" that ultimately led to cannibalism in the winter of 1609 to 1610. SOCIETY FOR POST-MEDIEVAL ARCHAEOLOGY

No one familiar with the long Welch career would ever accuse Herb of being the shy and retiring type. Herb's arrival on the Campbell-Fairbanks stage gave him national exposure, resulting in celebrity guide status. Herb capitalized on his recognition by attaching his name to three of the dominant fly patterns of the day: the Cahill, the Pembina, and the Montréal. The Percy Tackle Company of Portland invoices from 1926 through 1949 record numerous orders for these Welch-adapted flies.

But beyond the famous name, what were the flies like? There was a reference to the Welch Montréal in J. Edson Leonard's *Flies*, but his archives contained no pattern. Perrault's exhaustive *Standard Dictionary of Fishing Flies* mentioned it, but again without a pattern. Perrault did, however, give thirteen other variations, as it seemed like every North American tier felt compelled to adapt the Montréal pattern. Doubtless, its endurance would have amazed Peter Cowan of Cowansville, Québec, the High Sheriff of Bedford, who originated the Montréal pattern in 1850.[8] Whether he would have recognized it in its various forms is another matter.

For years, we searched for some clue as to what the Welch Montréal might look like. Then we caught wind that Percy had compiled a catalog containing all the patterns in their inventory. From its inception in 1926 until its effective demise in 1971, Percy was a leading commercial fly-tying house for the Eastern Seaboard, and over the years, it employed a large staff of lady fly tiers methodically churning out droves of flies in all configurations. Surely the company must have had some way to ensure pattern consistency as tiers inevitably came and went. But where was it?

Again, for years we searched for the file catalog containing the patterns for the Welch Montréal (and its variant, the Welch White-Tipped Montréal), the Welch Pembina, and the Welch Cahill. At last, we

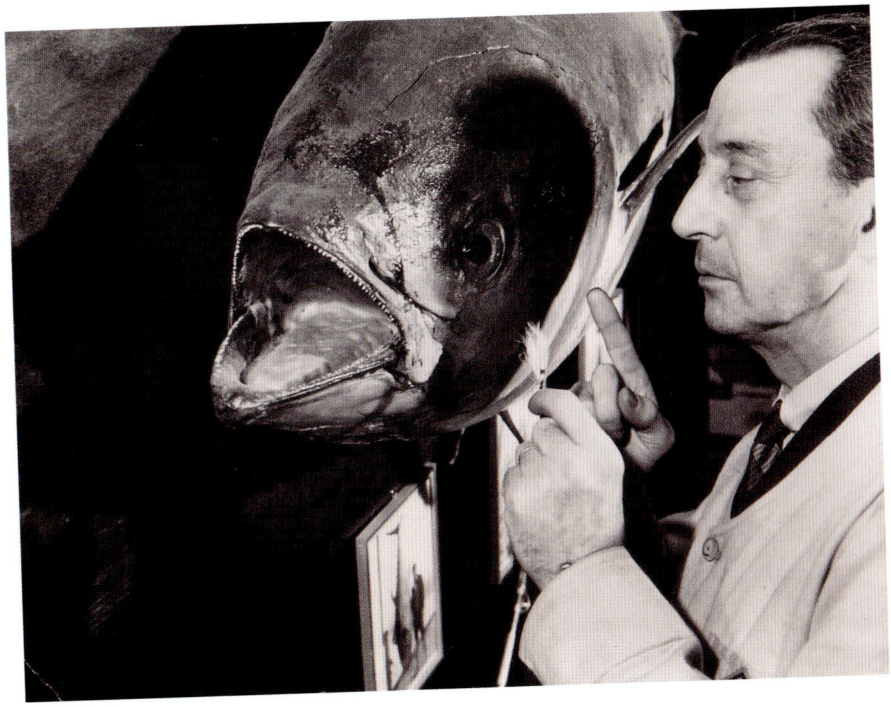

Herb lecturing a tuna on the dangers of streamers. A full-body tuna mount is rare. Due to expense and space considerations, most fishers settle for having just the tails mounted. RANGELEY SPORTING HERITAGE MUSEUM

discovered that the Percy Tackle Company, a once dominant company, had shrunk to a single owner/employee named Peter Sang. Competition from developing nations and changes in the U.S. tax code had conspired to end the American tradition of lady fly tiers at the bench. But who was Peter Sang, and where was he?

With his unusual surname, we thought Sang would be easy to find—after all, the advent of the Internet has made the notion of privacy seem quaint. But trying every possible search combination we could think of, we remained in the dark. It was only years later, through sheer serendipity, that we found the elusive Sang hiding out as a tax attorney in North Carolina. We introduced ourselves, found common ground, and eventually paid for the remaining inventory of the Percy Tackle Company: an estimated 3,000 flies and ephemera that all landed with

The Percy Tackle Company was the first to commercially tie the Black Ghost, in 1927. HILYARD COLLECTION

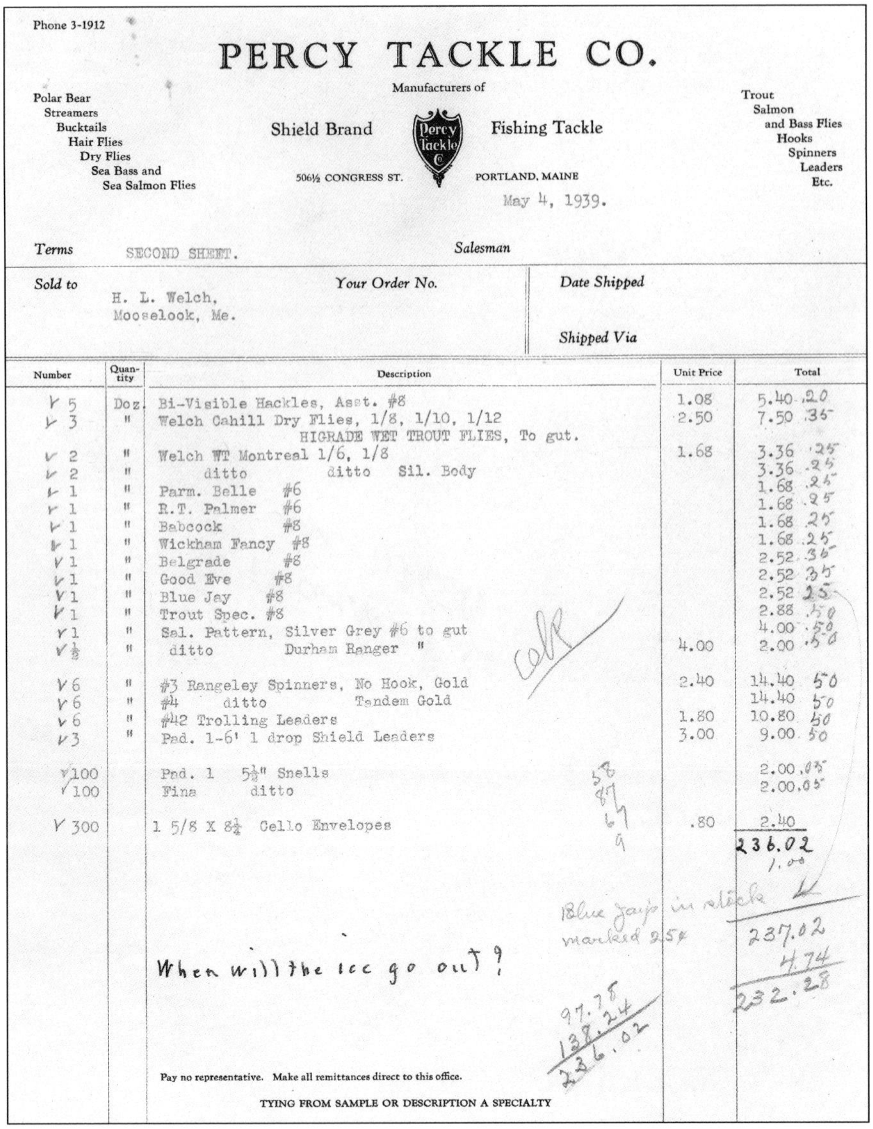

Phone 3-1912

PERCY TACKLE CO.

Manufacturers of

Shield Brand Fishing Tackle

Polar Bear Streamers Bucktails Hair Flies Dry Flies Sea Bass and Sea Salmon Flies

Trout Salmon and Bass Flies Hooks Spinners Leaders Etc.

506½ CONGRESS ST. PORTLAND, MAINE

May 4, 1939.

Terms SECOND SHEET. Salesman

Sold to H. L. Welch, Mooselook, Me. Your Order No. Date Shipped Shipped Via

Number	Quantity	Description	Unit Price	Total
5	Doz.	Bi-Visible Hackles, Asst. #8	1.08	5.40
3	"	Welch Cahill Dry Flies, 1/8, 1/10, 1/12	2.50	7.50
		HIGRADE WET TROUT FLIES, To gut.		
2	"	Welch WT Montreal 1/6, 1/8	1.68	3.36
2	"	ditto ditto Sil. Body		3.36
1	"	Parm. Belle #6		1.68
1	"	R.T. Palmer #6		1.68
1	"	Babcock #8		1.68
1	"	Wickham Fancy #8		1.68
1	"	Belgrade #8		2.52
1	"	Good Eve #8		2.52
1	"	Blue Jay #8		2.52
1	"	Trout Spec. #8		2.88
1	"	Sal. Pattern, Silver Grey #6 to gut		4.00
½	"	ditto Durham Ranger "	4.00	2.00
6	"	#3 Rangeley Spinners, No Hook, Gold	2.40	14.40
6	"	#4 ditto Tandem Gold		14.40
6	"	#42 Trolling Leaders	1.80	10.80
3	"	Pad. 1-6' 1 drop Shield Leaders	3.00	9.00
100		Pad. 1 5½" Snells		2.00
100		Fina ditto		2.00
300		1 5/8 X 8¼ Cello Envelopes	.80	2.40
				236.02

Blue Jays in stock marked 25¢

237.02
4.74
232.28

When will the ice go out?

Pay no representative. Make all remittances direct to this office.

TYING FROM SAMPLE OR DESCRIPTION A SPECIALTY

Stocking up on Welch Cahills and Welch White-Tipped Montréals. If Herb had answered the ice-out question May 14, he would have won the annual guessing contest. As Rangeley winters come early and stay late, ice-out is cause for great rejoicing.

a thud on our Ashland porch. And, yes, the Percy pattern files were among the mass of feathers, ending our decade-long quest.

As it turned out, the Percy pattern file was divided in two parts: a master file that held the patterns for corporate and catalog sales, and a client file that did the same for individuals. The organization of the files was ingenious, straightforward and designed to ward off conflict. For instance, if a Herb Welch wanted a Welch Cahill tied by Percy, he was required to supply the fly. It would be filed in a 3 x 5.5 manila envelope noting the fly name and any special instructions. On receipt of an order, a Percy lady tier would pull the Welch Cahill envelope marked Welch and duplicate the enclosed fly. If a client later complained about inaccurately tied patterns, Percy was on solid ground. We learned much of what follows from the contents of these envelopes; however, it should be noted that it is not always clear that the sender was the tier of the content. We spent hundreds of pleasant hours exploring and cataloging the Percy archives whose envelopes did, in fact, contain examples of the Welch Cahill, the Welch Montréal (and its variant, the Welch White-Tipped Montréal), and the Welch Pembina.

As it turns out, only one element differentiates the Welch Cahill from the original Cahill created in the late 1800s, presumably by a Dublin fly-maker, Daniel Cahill.[9] Welch neither added nor subtracted any materials from the original. His innovation was mechanical and consisted of pulling the traditional upright split wing together and canting it forward at a 45-degree angle.

In appearance, the Welch Cahill is the forerunner of the single-horned Bomber, originated in the 1950s by the Reverend Elmer Smith for sea-run trout on the Royal River in southern Maine.[10] Presumably, the rationale behind both flies was the same: When fished dry, the horn creates a skittering action on the swing that might entice reluctant fish to strike.

Prior to the establishment of the Percy Tackle Company, the Sportsman's Supply Company of Portland was Welch's chief source of flies. Their shop invoices show that from 1922 to 1926, Herb ordered nothing but standard Cahills, known today as Dark Cahills. However, for the first time on August 3, 1927, we find a Percy invoice listing four dozen Welch Cahills sold to Herb, giving us an approximate time for the Welch Cahill adaptation.

The Welch Cahill and Montréal were tied by Welch, and the Welch White-Tipped Montréal was tied by Leslie K. Hilyard. HILYARD COLLECTION

While the Portland merchants were his primary fly source after 1922, Herb by no means limited himself to their inventories. The Hardy Brothers of Alnwick, England, and Anderson & Sons of Edinburgh, Scotland, supplied Herb's salmon flies while Dame Stoddard and Bigelow & Dowse of Boston; Weber of Stevens Point, Wisconsin; and Boehme-Cummings of Missoula, Montana, supplied much else.

If the Welch Cahill adaptation was simplicity itself, the Welch Montréal was anything but, and the Welch White-Tipped Montréal even more complex. The most striking elements of the Welch Montréal are the addition of a claret hackled collar and the substitution of silver tinsel wraps for the traditional gold as the ribbing over a seal-fur-dubbed claret body of spiky fibers. Combining the iridescence of a turkey body feather wing with the spiky body reflecting off the silver wraps, the Welch Montréal was a highly attractive offering. As a species, wet flies tend to be rigid and diminutive, but the pulsating collar on Welch's fly would both increase the action and add a larger silhouette.

A life-size painting of Herb's Tyee salmon hangs in the Rangeley town office. HILYARD COLLECTION

Herbert L. Welch of Maine

I THINK if I was pinned down to three flies they would be the Welch Rarebit, Golden Grouse and Kennebago.

The Welch Rarebit is a fly not generally known among fly-fishermen, strangers to this section, as it is one of my own creations. In fact, I tie most of the flies with which I fish. The Welch Rarebit is a cross between a Silver Doctor and a White Streamer, with the difference that the streamers are not so long as in the usual streamer fly.

The Golden Grouse and the Kennebago need no comment, as they are very well known in Maine. It may be that I have had better luck with the three flies named because I understand fishing them. I readily admit that some fishermen have better luck with flies with which they understand how to fish. I know fishermen who have exceptional luck with the Silver Doctor, yet I have never had any great success with it, simply because I do not understand how to fish with it. On the other hand, I know how to serve up my Welch Rarebit to them to the queen's taste.

TROUT TAKEN BY MR. WELCH ON TWO-OUNCE ROD

This is the second inst... lment of the "Three Favorite Tro... lies" symposium. The first fraction ... the series appeared in the February number with Charles Zibeon Southard, ... r. Robert T. Morris, W. E. Kidder, Ellis Parker Butler, Otis E. McIntyre, ... arl Brong and Frank Darling contributing. The symposium will continue fo... some four or five months, in which time practically all the famous trout f... en of the continent will express themselves on this most delicate ... r. Henry van Dyke, Gifford Pinchot, George M. L. La Branche, ... Dr. John D. Quackenbos, Chase S. Osborn, Dan Beard, Irvin ... il B. De Mille, David Starr Jordan, General George W. Wingate, ... am C. Kendall and Ernest Thompson Seton are only a few of the an... celebrities yet to be heard.—THE EDITOR.

The upper Welch Rarebit was tied by Herb. The middle Golden Grouse and lower Kennebago were tied by Percy. The text is from *American Angler,* 1919. HILYARD COLLECTION

The Welch White-Tipped Montréal only exists because natural selection failed to anticipate the arcane needs of fly tiers. Unfortunately, all a pair of white-tipped turkey wing feathers will produce is enough proportional white tips to create three flies, usually sizes 4, 6, and 8. This made the original White-Tipped Montréal an expensive fly, which caused some tiers to substitute white-tipped squirrel, creating an undesired rigid bucktail effect.

Enter Herb Welch. As with the Welch Cahill, his adaptation for the White-Tipped Montréal was primarily mechanical. Using his Welch Montréal as the base pattern, he altered the wing by incorporating two feathers: an outer segment of brown turkey and an inner segment of slightly longer white duck. To achieve the proportional amount of white tip required, Herb simply adjusted the length of white duck. Problem solved.

A review of invoices shows that in 1924 Herb was paying $1.93 per dozen for standard White-Tipped Montréals. In 1928, his initial order of the Welch White-Tipped Montréals cost $1.68 per dozen. For a dealer such as Herb, ordering dozens of White Tips at a whack in the 1920s, this was a considerable savings. Remember also, this was a man who kept Carrie Stevens on a consignment basis until 1937. Inventory and costs were closely managed at Haines Landing.

Again, a review of Sportsman's Supply invoices finds that Herb's last order for standard Montréals was on June 12, 1922, and his first order for Welch Montréal's was on July 6, 1923, giving us an approximate origination date. However, we can only speculate, as the Welch invoices prior to 1922 are lost to us and the narrow time frame between orders leaves open the possibility of earlier orders for the Welch Montréal. Then too, Herb was a merchant determined to stay in business. If a Leonard or Hawes rod did not fit your budget, perhaps a Heddon would. Similarly, Herb continued to sell standard fly patterns alongside his adaptations. As to the Welch White-Tipped Montréal, a five-year gap between his last 1923 orders for standard White Tips and his first 1928 order makes it difficult to establish an origination date.

Another streamer of interest mentioned in Herb's 1949 letter to J. Edson Leonard is the Green Spot, which he claims to have originated. Confusion reigns over this pattern, which has been spelled as both Green Spot and Green's Pot. Per Stewart and Leeman's *Trolling Flies for Trout and Salmon*, Green's Pot is a misnomer for the Green Spot, but Perrault's definitive *Standard Dictionary of Flies* gives a different pattern for each spelling. Herb commented to Leonard in a circa 1948 letter that his Green Spot appeared to have been hijacked by J.H. Sanborn, a Waterville, Maine, dentist's 9/3 pattern. However, Percy records indicate that Herb himself consistently received orders for Green's Pots instead of Green Spots and made no apparent effort to correct the spelling.

Although Herb was fond of his Welch Rarebit, it is a difficult fly to warm up to for many of my generation who grew up in Maine. Perhaps it has something to do with the play on words for Welsh Rabbit, a cheesy dish that showed up weekly in rural school

Jane Greys as prelude to the Jane Craigs. HILYARD COLLECTION

Herb's tying style evolved over time, adding to the challenge of identifying his flies. Top row: early Jane Craigs tied by Herb Welch. Bottom row: late Jane Craigs tied c. 1948 by Herb Welch. HILYARD COLLECTION

lunch programs, with a texture ranging from soupy to crusty depending on the availability of crackers or breadcrumbs. With no other options back then, you either crunched or slurped it down while hoping that it would not come back the next week, as it often did. Culinary issues aside, the Welch Rarebit is a beautiful and effective streamer that appeared sometime prior to 1918.

While Herb's brief note to Leonard laid claim to the Jane Craig, he gave no hint of that fly's complex history. That explanation was left to our exploration of the Percy archives. As early as 1927, Welch was ordering an intriguing pattern simply called the Welch Fly, but it had dropped from sight by 1929. Luckily, we found an envelope marked "Welch Fly," and in it was a fly identical to a Jane Craig. Curious... We then found a second identical Welch Fly sewn onto a Percy demonstration tying board, which ruled out any chance of misfiling. A review of Percy orders found that the last Welch fly order was dated July 25, 1928, and the first Jane Craig order was dated August 16, 1929. Subsequent order sheets show that the two flies never coexisted. Curious... Are we to assume that Herb was smitten and had joyfully given up his surname to Jane Craig? But how to explain the presence of a mystifying Jane Grey so similar to the Jane Craig?

Nothing suggests that Herb and Jane Grey ever met. However, it is a good bet that he and Jane Craig did, as she was one-half of the vaudeville comedy duo Dalton & Craig. On December 4, 1926, the *Vaudeville News* and *New York Star* reported that in July the duo was at the Rangeley Lake water carnival. Competing against 99 other entrants, Howard Dalton distinguished himself by winning the fly-casting tournament with a cast of 94 feet. (Impressive, but not enough to get your name attached to a streamer, it seems.)

Sometime later, again while roaming the archives, we noticed an envelope marked Jane Grey-Welch. We had seen no evidence of Herb ever ordering a Jane Grey, yet, here it was in the Percy client file. Cautiously, we opened the envelope and out fell a fly that could easily be confused with a Jane Craig, identical except gray hackle had been substituted in the wing for white.

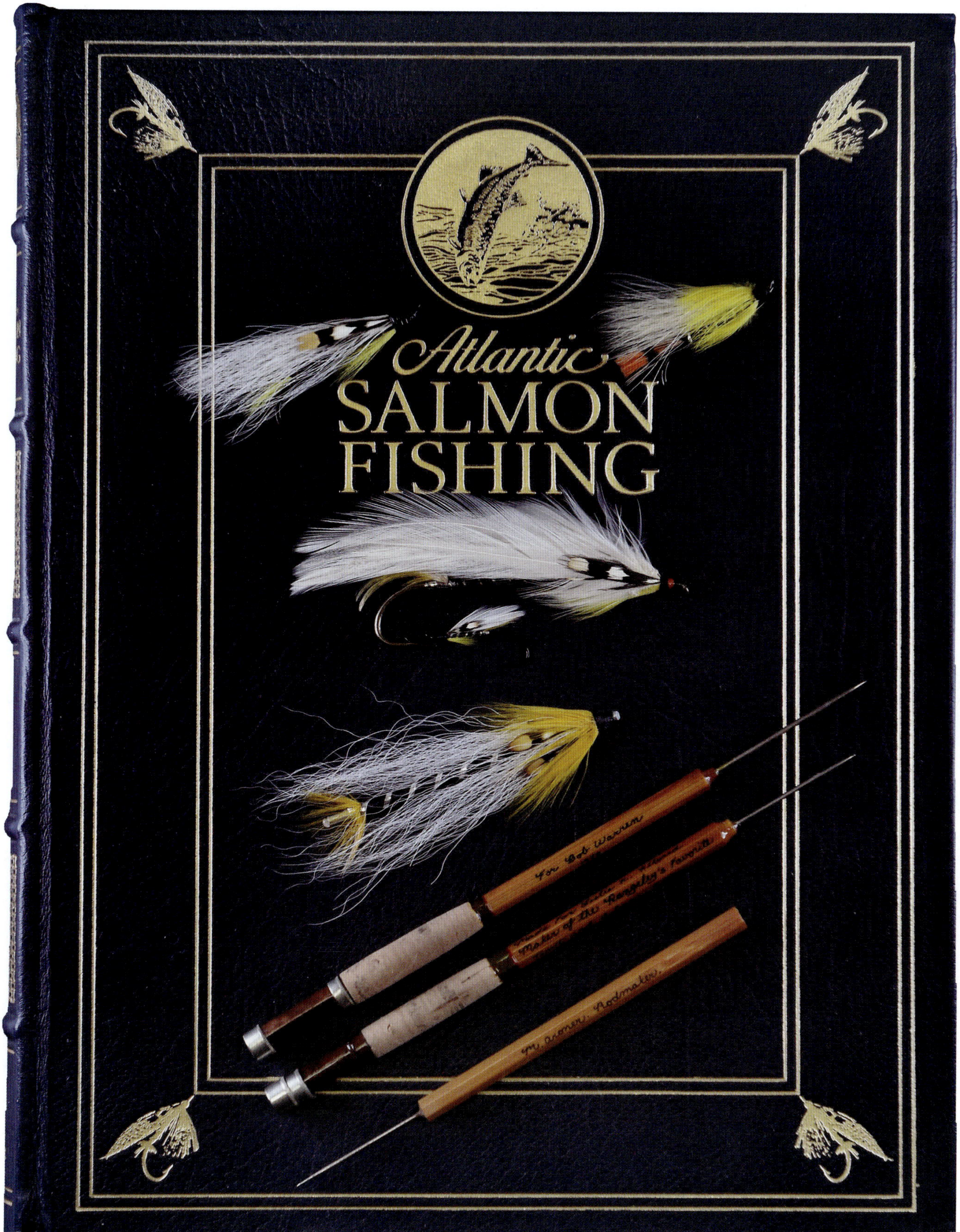

Black Ghost addaptations for Atlantic Salmon. Bodkins by Marc Aroner.

Top left: Maritime style, tied by Warren Duncan. Top right: Gaspé style, tied by Ralph Billingsley.
Center: Spring salmon style (3-inch shank), tied by Carrie Stevens; low-water style, tied by Leslie K. Hilyard.
Bottom: Tube fly, tied by Ted Patlen. HILYARD COLLECTION

A 2005 oil on canvas painting by John Swan titled "Coffee Break." The rarely seen western Black Ghosts were tied by Leslie Hilyard. HILYARD COLLECTION

Are we to believe that this young Hollywood actress from Middlebury, Vermont, with sixteen films (1915–1927) to her credit had been but a brief flirtation before Jane Craig finally stole Herb's restless heart away? Curious, indeed.

Since Herb could have added to that pattern list sent to Leonard, we can conclude that the patterns he didn't add never seriously entered his sales repertoire. Although well documented in the literature, his Kennebago and Cupsuptic streamers are not to be found on any of his order sheets. With their

Bob Knight's
"Special – the same pattern as
Colonel Bates' only the two long
streamers were white and the
two short ones yellow – with him –
it is the 'handsomest' fly I make
and he has over a hundred
patterns mounted on cards
and enclosed in cellophane
envelopes – these he does not
use for fishing."

Carrie Stevens explains. RANGELEY SPORTING HERITAGE MUSEUM

herled butts and segmented bodies, both of these striking patterns reflect an Atlantic salmon fly-tying influence.

Although Maine's Penobscot River salmon fishery was still viable, it is unclear just how much Atlantic salmon fishing Herb did. We have only found two references to him doing so: once on New Brunswick's Miramichi in 1936 with Chief Needebah and another time on the Tabusintac around 1942 with Julian Crandall.

Equally unclear is who deserves credit for adapting Herb's iconic Black Ghost streamer into the two differing hair-wing Atlantic salmon patterns, still sold by Canada's Gaspé and Maritime fly shops. The same can be said for the pattern's more recent adaptation to the tube fly, a method created in 1945 and attributed to Winnie Morawski of Aberdeen, Scotland; for the steelhead adaptation, called the Western Black Ghost and documented in Poul Jorgensen's *Book of Fly Tying*; and for the low-water version.

Several years ago, we obtained two Atlantic salmon patterns unmistakably tied by Herb that would fall into the "tribute" category. Included with them were a rare example of the Herb Welch spoon and a Welch-tied Pattern Number 11, originated by Carrie Stevens. Each of these streamers came with a small tag with writing in an unknown hand: "Herb Welch – Golden Knight – Jun, 28, 1951" and "Mrs. Andrews – Herb Welch, Jun, 28, 51." Another tag with the handwriting read "Silver Knight – Herb Welch – Jun, 28, 51," but that fly was missing. Although both flies are tied on Allcock 1810, size 6 streamer hooks, with their golden pheasant crest toppings and tails, segmented bodies, and herled butts, they are reminiscent of Atlantic salmon flies from the Victorian period. Although we cautioned earlier about the dangers of assuming, we believe that the longtime presence of the Knight brothers on Mooselookmeguntic Lake, combined with the correspondence between them and Herb, means that the Golden Knight most likely refers to Robert L. Knight and the Silver Knight to his younger brother, Howard.

Robert L. Knight (1883–1962) of Hope, Rhode Island, arrived at Mooselookmeguntic in 1932 and built a camp that could only be accessed by water at Black Point near Upper Dam. As Mooselookmeguntic was often too rough for crossing, he later bought a camp adjacent to his brother Howard on the eastern shore and renamed it Rocky Ledge Kamp, after his own initials. Meanwhile, having bought the venerable Allerton Lodge, Howard renamed it the Silver Knight.

Descended from Roger Williams, who founded Rhode Island in the seventeenth century, both brothers were wealthy, partly due to relatives who established the Fruit of the Loom cotton mills and partly due to their own entrepreneurial skills. Despite his wealth, Robert Knight preferred to go by Bob, and Carrie Stevens would name a streamer after him: the Bob Knight Special. According to Carrie, Bob had a packaged collection of 100 of her patterns,[11] although currently the Knight family has been unable to find any of his fishing collection.[12]

When Carrie needed to create a streamer for Colonel Joseph D. Bates Jr., she simply reversed the white-and-yellow hackle found in the Bob Knight Special.[13] This has led many to regard the Bob Knight Special, with its shorter yellow hackle over the longer white hackle, as a variant of the Colonel Bates streamer. We feel, however, that the term "variant" suggests a lesser work and is not fitting in this case. After all, is a Black Ghost any the lesser because it is sometimes tied with golden pheasant crests rather than the ordained yellow hackle?

Another factor to consider is the nature of commercial tying, since the bulk of tiers we collect were commercial tiers. If a paying client wanted a dozen bucktails tied with polar bear instead of deer hair (and who would not?), the client probably got what they wanted. Should the polar bear bucktail be considered a variant or just part of what a tier needs to do to make a living? Consider also that early tiers often had limited access to materials. If a paying customer was hounding you for a dozen General MacArthurs and the red floss ran out, a silver tinsel body would probably do. Either way, Carrie Stevens considered it a General MacArthur, and there is a message for us there.

Problems also arise when adding the label "custom" to describe an established pattern that mildly differs, as has often been done with Carrie Stevens. In a review of twenty-four Carrie Stevens invoices to Herb Welch dating from 1926 to 1949, involving the sale of twenty-five of her patterns, not once does

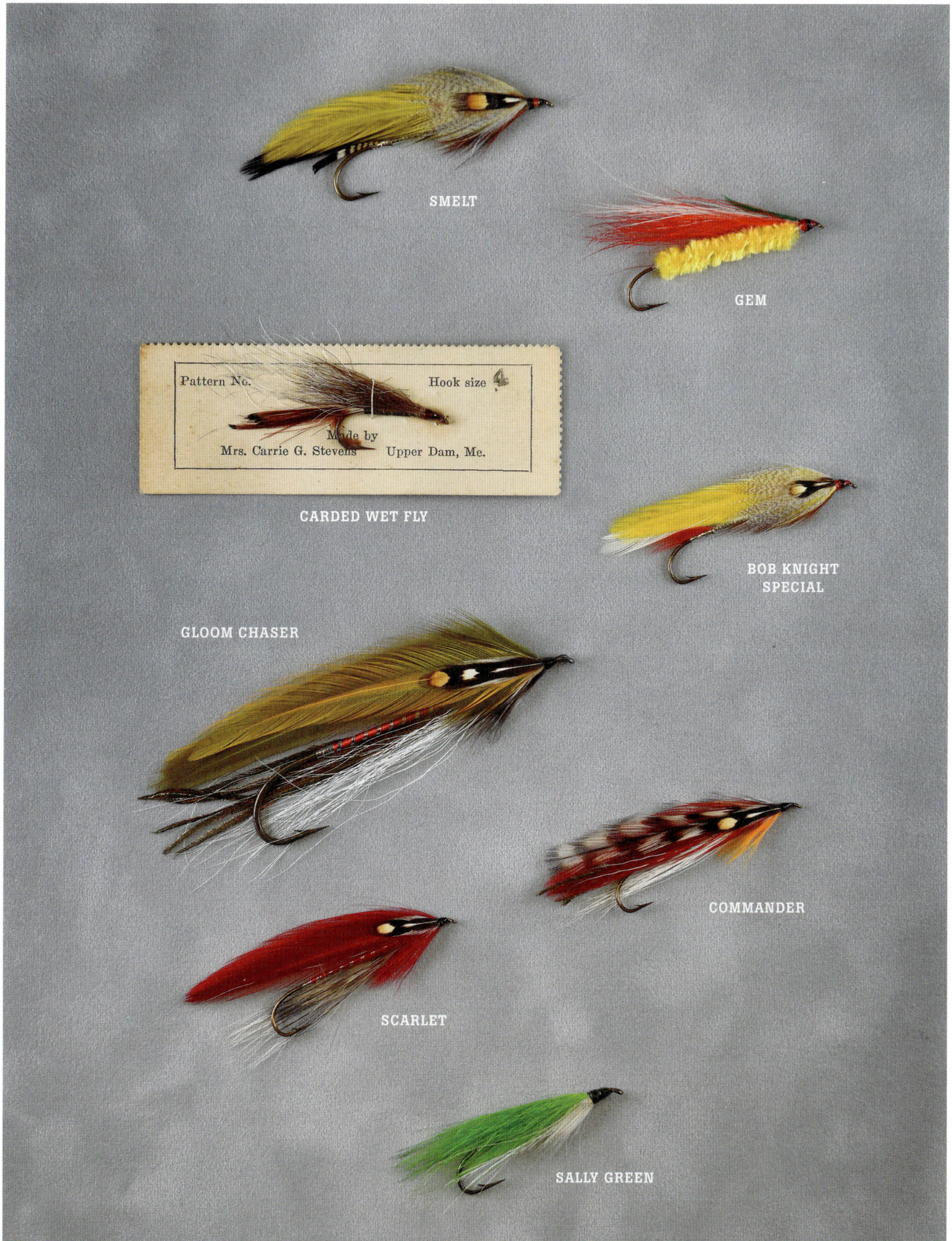

Pattern searches never end. Clockwise: Smelt, Gem, Bob Knight Special, Commander, Sally Green, Scarlet, Gloom Chaser, Carded Wet Fly, unnamed and not numbered. HILYARD COLLECTION

The Welchman (above) and Welchman's Special (below) were tied by the Percy Tackle Company, but the patterns' originator(s) are unknown. HILYARD COLLECTION

she use the word "custom." Slapping the "custom" label on a known pattern that mildly differs simply to get the body count up does not constitute research.

And that is the end of our rant. As penance, we offer up a plate of eight Carrie Stevens originations that have emerged and been identified since we originally published our book on her in 2000.

Returning to Welch's tribute patterns, we find the Mrs. Andrews. Since Andrews is a common name, trying to associate this pattern with a real person is difficult. However, there was a Zephie Andrews who operated the Whispering Winds Lunchroom in Oquossoc during the late 1940s until her death in 1957.[14]

Another streamer bears mentioning, even though as yet it has no direct link to Herb. Sublimely beautiful, this pattern has two versions and bears the names of the Welchman and the Welchman's Special. Thus far, we have only two merchants that offered them: the Welchman by Bert Quimby of South Windham, Maine, and the Welchman's Special by the Percy Tackle Company.

In Quimby's catalog, he also lists another pattern by the name of Pickel Special. One cannot help wondering if, perhaps, Bert Quimby originated both the Welchman and the Pickel and named them for the Rangeley's leading taxidermists. (See how easy it all starts, this creating facts from fancy?) Curiously, although samples of the Welchman's Special show up in the Percy file with Welch's name on the envelope, there is no evidence of Herb ever ordering any. Whether the fly was effective or not, one would think an artist like Herb would have appreciated the sheer beauty of the pattern.

While circumstances surrounding the Welchman are cloudy, the origin and the intent of the Welch Dry Fly are crystal clear. Initially, we found this dry-fly pattern in the *Book of Fly Patterns* by Eric Leiser, who had received it from Dick Frost (1930–2005), a legendary Maine Guide and owner of the Rangeley Region Sport Shop. Eventually, we would track it to George Fletcher (1900–1996), who had founded that same shop in 1945. Herb was instrumental in getting key contracts for George's start-up, and George never forgot it. As a tribute to Herb, he originated the Welch Dry Fly pattern in 1956.[15] Herb fished it so extensively on the Kennebago Lake and River that it soon became known as the Kennebago Wolf and was marketed under that name by the Percy Tackle Company.

ENDNOTES

1 Graydon and Leslie Hilyard, *Carrie Stevens: Maker of the Rangeley Favorite Trout & Salmon Flies*, Mechanicsburg, Pennsylvania: Stackpole Books, 2000, p. 21.
2 "1950 Fishing Contest Winners," *Field & Stream*, May, 1951, p. 41.
3 Raymond Camp, "Wood, Field & Stream," *New York Times*, March 15, 1950.
4 Al Pflueger Jr., interview with author, February 9, 2008.
5 R. Christensen, "Notes on the History of the Fish Hook," *Bulletin of U.S. Fish Commission*, 1884, vol. 4, p. 211.
6 Todd E.A. Larson, *The History of the Fish Hook in America*, Whitefish Press, 2007, p. 171.
7 Andrew Herd, *The Fly*, Ellesmere, UK: Medlar Press, 2003, p. 238.
8 Mary Orvis Marbury, *Favorite Flies and Their Histories*, Secaucus, New Jersey: Wellfleet Press, 1988, pp. 328–330.
9 Ibid., p. 260.
10 Dick Stewart and Allen Farrow, *Flies for Atlantic Salmon*, Intervale, New Hampshire: Northland Press, 1991, p. 14.
11 Carrie Stevens, letter to Colonel Joseph D. Bates Jr., September 24, 1949.
12 Adelaide Knight, letter to author, September 24, 2003.
13 Stevens to Bates, September 24, 1949.
14 Edward Ellis, *A Chronological History of the Rangeley Lakes Region*, Trevose, Pennsylvania: Brook Trout Press, 1983, p. 86.
15 George Fletcher, letter to author, August 13, 1993.

Percy's
Salmon d Trout
Streamers
Size.........
Pat. ....
Manufactured by
PERCY ACKLE CO.
Maine

CHAPTER 8

Saving History, Creating History

At the start of the Welch project, we were determined to establish a protocol for identifying streamers tied by Herb Welch as we had done with Carrie Stevens. Being addicted to patterns, we did not want to believe H. Wendell Folkins' cryptic December 13, 1956, line to Austin Hogan: "I have one fly made by Herb Welch himself. Claimed that he'd never made two alike, never commercially." Would that we did. Despite years of sleuthing, no treasure trove of packaged Welch flies emerged, as was the case with Carrie Stevens. Rumors of packaged flies had kept us searching for years, but the packaging turned out to be just a 4-inch, open-ended envelope marked

A (Vague) Chronology of Herb Welch's Fly Book

Welch Special	pre-1917	per Kennebago Scraps, pattern unknown
Kennebago Special	pre-1917	per Kennebao Scraps, wet fly, pattern unknown
Welch Rarebit	pre-1918	per Welch in *American Angler*, vol. 3, 1918
Welch Montréal	pre-1922	per Percy Tackle Company invoices
Welch Fly	pre-1927	per Percy Tackle Company invoices
Welch Cahill	pre-1927	per Percy Tackle Company invoices
Black Ghost	1927	per Gardner Percy, owner of Percy Tackle Company
Welch White-Tip Montréal	pre-1928	per Percy Tackle Company invoices
Welch Pembina	pre-1928	per Percy Tackle Company invoices
Jane Gray	pre-1929	per Hilyard & Hilyard extrapolation
White Jane Craig	pre-1929	per Percy Tackle Company invoices
Yellow Jane Craig	pre-1931	per Percy Tackle filing envelope
Kennebago	pre-1949	per Colonel J.D. Bates Jr.
Cupsuptic	pre-1949	per Colonel J.D. Bates Jr.
Golden Knight	pre-1951	source unknown
Silver Knight	pre-1951	source unknown
Mrs. Andrews	pre-1951	source unknown

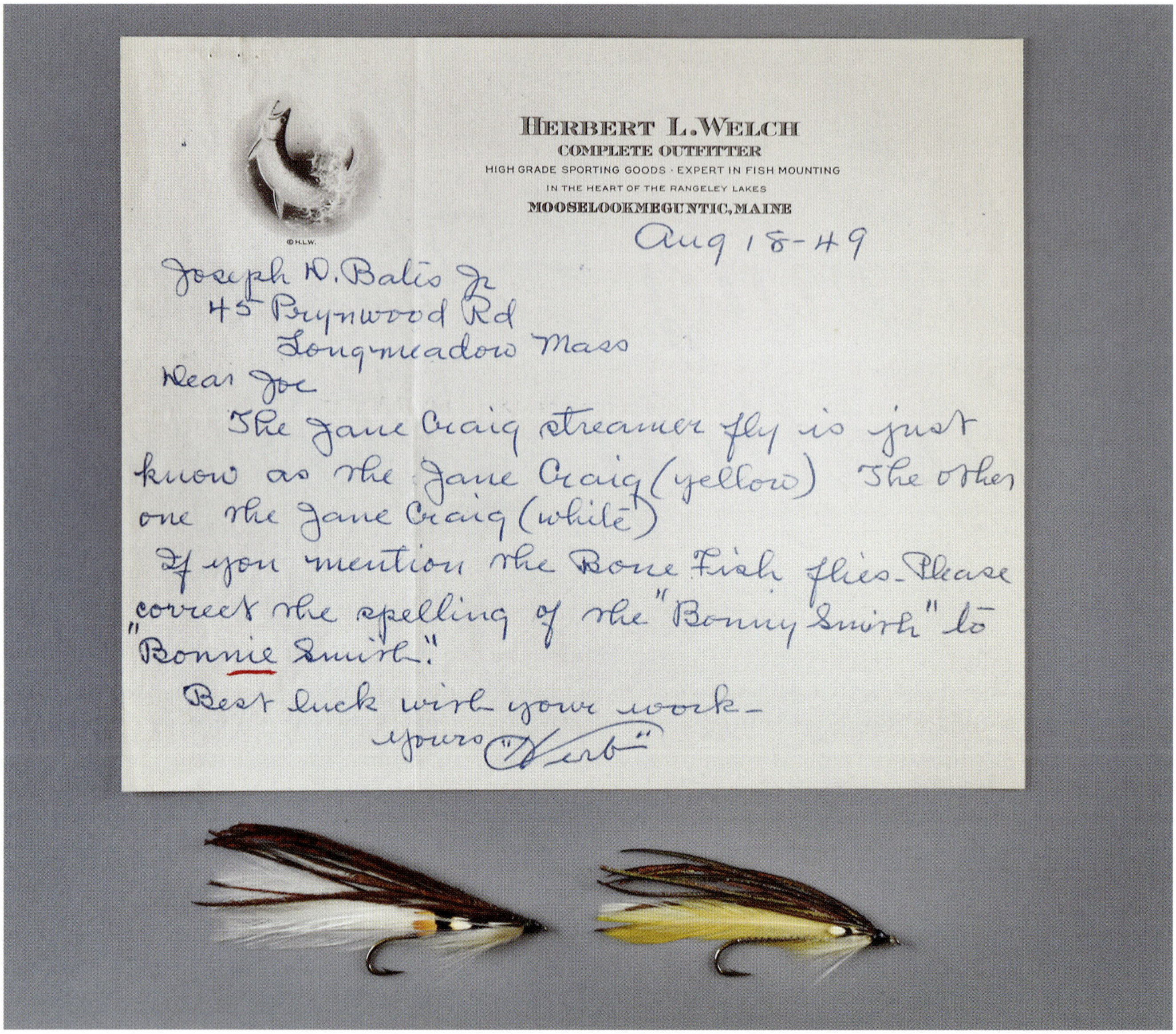

No matter the dominant wing color, a Jane Craig was a Jane Craig to Herb. Unfortunately, there is no record of the Welch bonefish fly patterns. HILYARD COLLECTION

"Welch's Sporting Goods Store, Haines Landing, Me," designed to be stuffed with snelled wet flies supplied by Hardy and Percy.

Shop records did not show orders for fly-tying materials sufficient to sustain a commercial tying operation. Undeterred, we plodded on, as the shop records for the early days when he most likely would have been tying were missing. Too late, we realized that H. Wendall Folkins, Larry Hinds, and Dave Footer were correct: Herb tied only for himself and close friends, and quite roughly at that. No sitting around waiting for multiple coats of head cement to dry. Just tie it and go.

Having determined this, we shifted our focus to finding any surviving friends who might have benefited from Herb's tying. Since forty-five years had passed, this was a rapidly telescoping search. H. Wendall Folkins could not remember where his one fly went. Dave Footer left his vintage fly roll on the banks of the Broadhead. Larry Hinds lost his flies on the bottom of the water and in the trees. Stan Bogdan never had any. Bud Wilcox and Dick Frost were commercial tiers—why would they have any? Mercifully, George Fletcher finally gave us his one Black Ghost.

Moving at a glacial pace, we discovered twenty-four streamers tied by Herbert L. Welch. Attribution did not come easy and would require Leslie's thirty-five years of experience at the bench, combined with

All of the Jane Craig streamers were tied by Herb Welch, illustrating his stylistic changes over the years. HILYARD COLLECTION

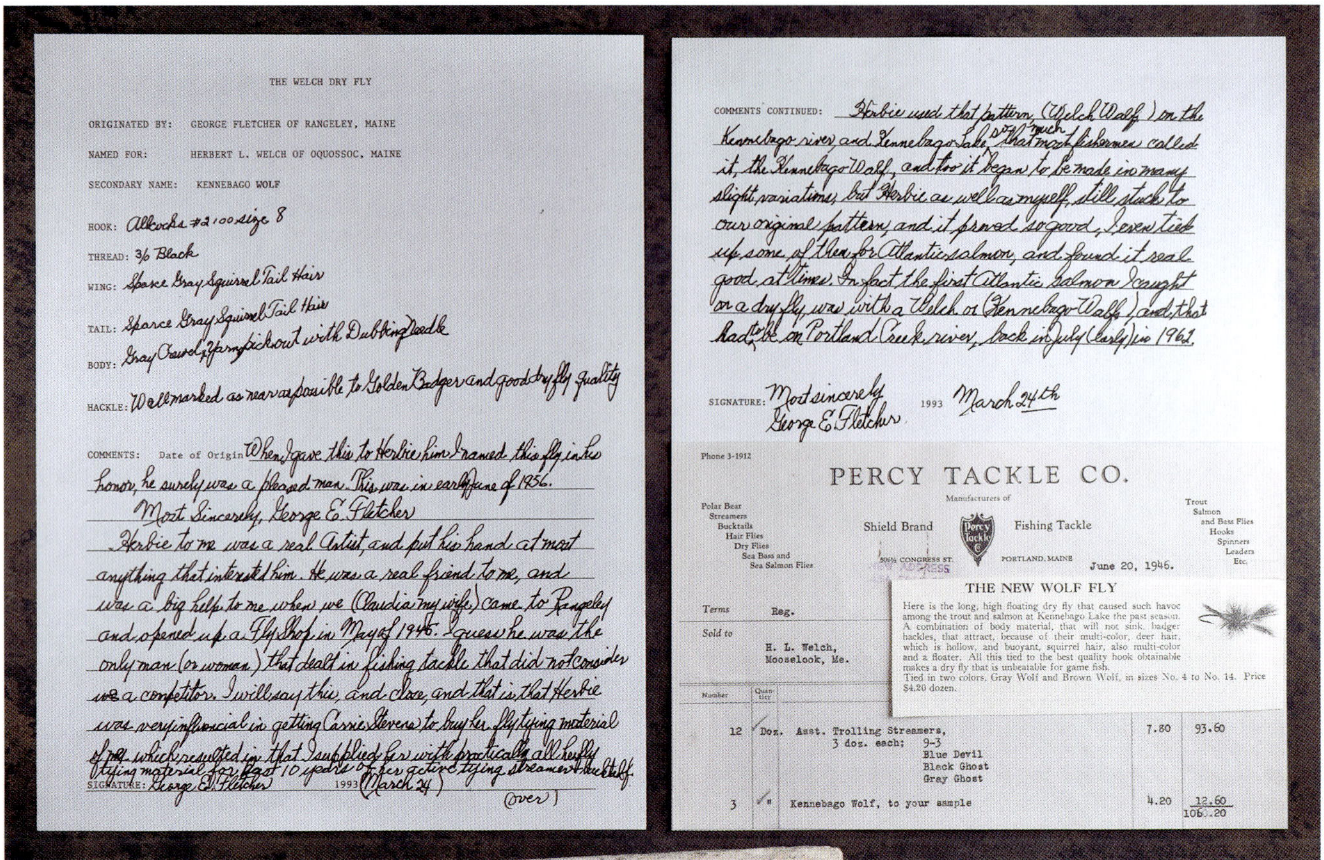

THE WELCH DRY FLY

ORIGINATED BY: GEORGE FLETCHER OF RANGELEY, MAINE

NAMED FOR: HERBERT L. WELCH OF OQUOSSOC, MAINE

SECONDARY NAME: KENNEBAGO WOLF

HOOK: Allcocks #2100 size 8

THREAD: 3/0 Black

WING: Sparce Gray Squirrel Tail Hair

TAIL: Sparce Gray Squirrel Tail Hair

BODY: Gray Crewel Yarn pick out with Dubbing Needle

HACKLE: Well marked as near as possible to Golden Badger and good dry fly quality

COMMENTS: Date of Origin When I gave this to Herbie him I named this fly in his honor, he surely was a pleased man. This was in early June of 1956.
Most Sincerely, George E. Fletcher
Herbie to me was a real Artist, and put his hand at most anything that interested him. He was a real friend to me, and was a big help to me when we (Claudia my wife) came to Rangeley and opened up a Fly Shop in May of 1946. I guess he was the only man (or woman) that dealt in fishing tackle that did not consider me a competitor. I will say this, and close, and that is that Herbie was very influencial in getting Carrie Stevens to buy her fly tying material of me, which resulted in that I supplied her with practically all her fly tying material for last 10 years of her active tying streamers & bucktails.

SIGNATURE: George E. Fletcher 1993 (March 24)

(over)

COMMENTS CONTINUED: Herbie used that pattern, (Welch Wolf) on the Kennebago river and Kennebago Lake so very much that most fishermen called it, the Kennebago Wolf, and too it began to be made in many slight variations, but Herbie as well as myself, still stuck to our original pattern, and it proved so good, I even tied up some of them for Atlantic salmon, and found it real good at times. In fact the first Atlantic Salmon I caught on a dry fly, was with a Welch or (Kennebago Wolf) and that had to be on Portland Creek river, back in July (early) in 1962.

SIGNATURE: Most sincerely George E. Fletcher 1993 March 24th

Phone 3-1912

PERCY TACKLE CO.

Manufacturers of

Shield Brand Fishing Tackle

Polar Bear Streamers, Bucktails, Hair Flies, Dry Flies, Sea Bass and Sea Salmon Flies

Trout, Salmon and Bass Flies, Hooks, Spinners, Leaders, Etc.

506½ CONGRESS ST. PORTLAND, MAINE

June 20, 1946.

Terms Reg.

Sold to H. L. Welch, Mooselook, Me.

THE NEW WOLF FLY

Here is the long, high floating dry fly that caused such havoc among the trout and salmon at Kennebago Lake the past season. A combination of body material, that will not sink, badger hackles, that attract, because of their multi-color, deer hair, which is hollow, and buoyant, squirrel hair, also multi-color and a floater. All this tied to the best quality hook obtainable makes a dry fly that is unbeatable for game fish.
Tied in two colors, Gray Wolf and Brown Wolf, in sizes No. 4 to No. 14. Price $4.20 dozen.

Number	Quantity			
12	Doz.	Asst. Trolling Streamers, 3 doz. each; 9-3 Blue Devil, Black Ghost, Gray Ghost	7.80	93.60
3	"	Kennebago Wolf, to your sample	4.20	12.60
				106.20

The Welch Fly takes on a new identity. Over time, both names and patterns can change, leading to confusion. HILYARD COLLECTION

No tribute streamer patterns have been clearly linked to Herb, so we offer up the Herbert L. Welch (left) and Chief Black Hawk (right), originated and tied by Leslie K. Hilyard. HILYARD COLLECTION

sixty years' worth of insight on tying for Maine's rivers from Bob Warren of Princeton, Massachusetts.

During the 1990s, a flurry of interest in Welch streamers resulted in prices from two to three hundred dollars each. Any collector who was tempted would need to have a competent tier inspect the fly to rule out other tiers, if not confirm origination. Since Herb only tied for friends, provenance takes on enhanced importance. Family lore may often be shaky stuff, but knowing a fly's possible connection to Herb may give the collector some comfort.

But, in the final analysis, it is the quality and style of work that identifies the maker, not the oral provenance or some words on paper. Herb was not a

Memories of a Maine Game Warden

I don't remember the first time I met Herb Welch. In my early days, Oquossoc was a long way from Rangeley, to say nothing about Haines Landing, but I had heard a lot about him and his shop at Haines Landing. After the Second World War, I joined the Maine Fish and Game Department as a warden and was later assigned to the Oquossoc district. Herb Welch's shop was in this area located at Haines Landing. Most of the fishermen who fish on the big lake would stop in at his shop to swap tales with Herb and talk fishing.

To me, his shop seemed a little dark inside. The walls were painted a green color, not quite as dark as a fir tree, and I always wondered if this made Herb feel he was in the outdoors. He had a stock of fishing equipment and also coats and jackets, as well as a good stock of Pendleton clothing. If the weather took a change from hot to cold, the heavy clothing would be a hot item on the sales. He also sold Carrie Stevens flies. One of the times I was in there, he asked me if I ever went into Parmachenee. I told him that I did once in a while. Over fifty years ago now, and I don't remember the exact words he used, something like when things quiet down I would like to go in there with you.

I picked him up sometime in October and we went up the Lower Cupsuptic and into Parmachenee. He took his gun along, and I feel sure we got some partridge. It was late in the afternoon when we got back. He thanked me for taking him in there with me. A long tromp for a sixty-seven-year-old man, but it didn't seem to bother him.

The next time I was out with Herb was either in 1955 or 1956. I had gotten through being a warden and was guiding out of the Kennebago Lake Camps. He called in there, and I guided him and a man who he introduced to me by the name of Rou. Herb said he had something do with the sports shows. We fished on the lake, Herb in the bow of the boat, standing up most of the time. He would cast a long line, and if he saw a fish, he would bring his fly in and tell the client to get his fly near it. Herb would stop his fly in the water and the other man would start moving his fly and the fish would go after it. I don't remember how many fish we caught, but the man told me it was one of the best days fishing he ever had. As I recall, his casting had much to learn.

Bud Wilcox
Rangeley, Maine
2002

Warden Bud Wilcox rescuing a small dog c. 1947. His streamers, the Tri-Color (originated in 1946) and the Kennebago Smelt (originated in 1951), are still found in New England fly shops.
HILYARD COLLECTION

As with Welch's Jane Craigs, there is some confusion about the proper way to tie Chief Needebah's patterns. Streamers tied by Leslie K. Hilyard. HILYARD COLLECTION

commercial tier, and so he did not have the consistency and discipline bred by thousands of hours at the bench tying standardized patterns. Certainly, he did not tie in the so-called Rangeley Style, for the good reason that no such style exists. That misnomer seems to have entered the literature in the 1950s as a way to describe the work of regional streamer tiers. However, a careful review of the Maine tiers, including Herb, reveals that they all tied in the eastern method, which is characterized by tying all material in at the head. Only Carrie Stevens differed with her approach of staggering the material. Because everyone else used the eastern method, it alone is of little use in identifying tiers.

While by no means definitive, perhaps our following observations will guide the collector through Herb's maze of streamer-tying inconsistencies:

HOOK: Usually Allcock's 2811s, but sometimes 1810s.

HEAD: Ranges from balls and long tapers to the blunt and boxy. Often a reveal shows between where the throat is tied in and where the head begins. Windings often show due to minimal coats of lacquer.

Portland Sunday Telegram And Sunday Press Herald—Portland, Maine—September 15, 1940

And Show Wardens Fine Points Of Fly Fishing And

By Staff Photographer

Two well-known Maine fly-fishing experts, who also happen to be angling pals, had the "time of their lives" in a backwoods pond in the Allagash Region a few days ago. The men, Herb Welch of Rangeley and "Chief" Needahbeh, Penobscot Indian, are shown in the group of photos above as they fished in Big Pleasant Lake. Top, left, Chief tries to raise a Pleasant Lake togue by plug casting; right, Chief, at left, and Herb, starting roll casts almost in unison (the over-size appearance of the lines in this photo is caused by blurring, the camera shutter being too slow to stop the motion); below, left, Herb holds up a two pound trout before putting it back in the lake; right, Chief and a pair of square-tails taken from the springhole.

Never a fashion statement, tucked-in pants were a defense against the bloodthirsty black fly known as the Maine state bird.

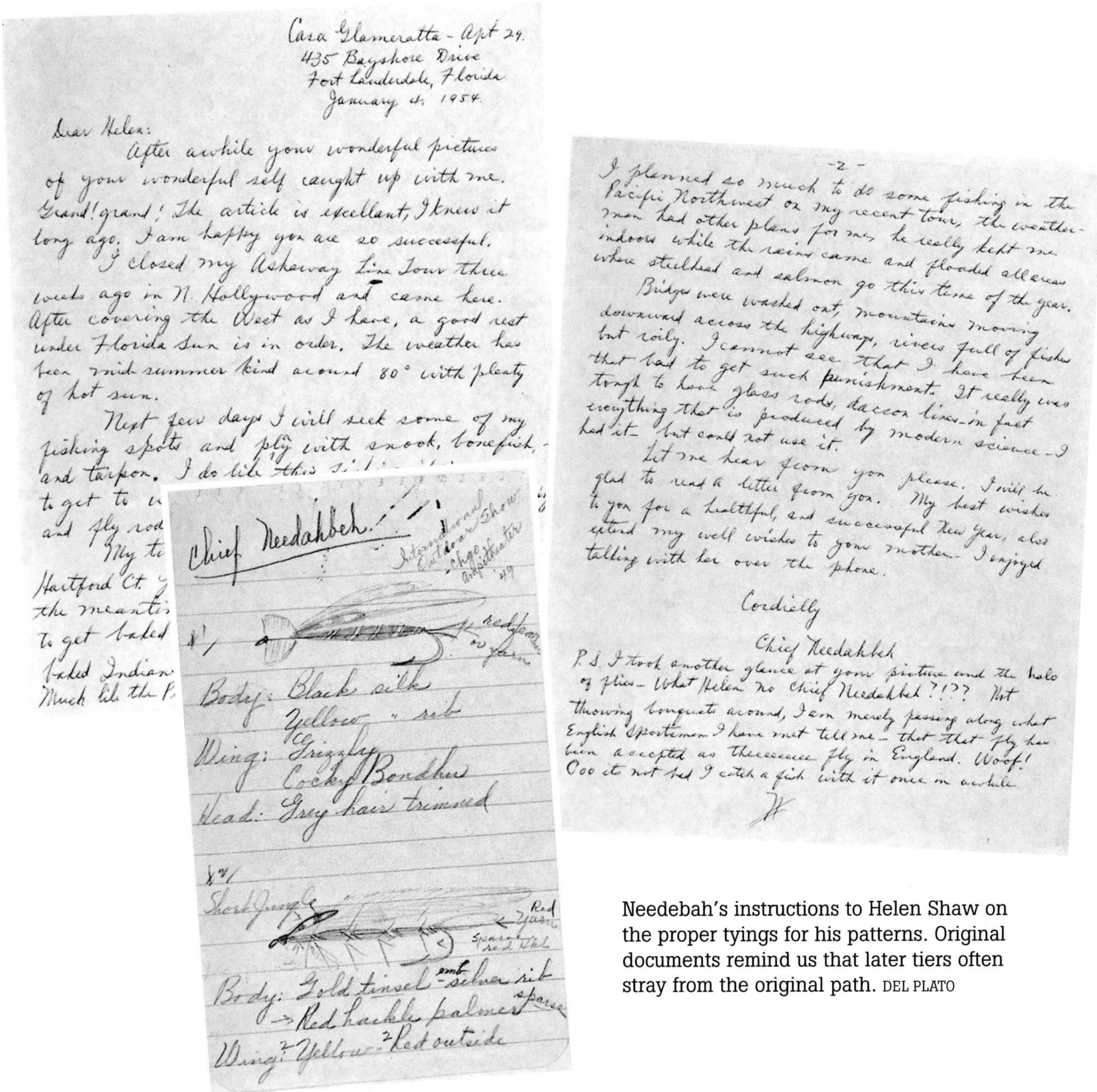

Casa Glameratta - Apt 24.
435 Bayshore Drive
Fort Lauderdale, Florida
January 4, 1954.

Dear Helen:

After awhile your wonderful pictures of your wonderful self caught up with me. Grand! grand! The article is excellant, I knew it long ago. I am happy you are so successful.

I closed my Ashaway Line Tour three weeks ago in N. Hollywood and came here. After covering the West as I have, a good rest under Florida Sun is in order. The weather has been mid-summer kind around 80° with plenty of hot sun.

Next few days I will seek some of my fishing spots and ply with snook, bonefish, and tarpon. I do like this ... to get to ... and fly rod ... My te... Hartford Ct. ... the meanti... to get baked ... faked Indian ... Much like the P...

-2-

I planned so much to do some fishing in the Pacific Northwest on my recent tour, the weather man had other plans for me, he really kept me indoors while the rains came and flooded all area where steelhead and salmon go this time of the year.

Bridges were washed out, mountains moving downward across the highways, rivers full of fish but roily. I cannot see that I have been that bad to get such punishment. It really was tough to have glass rods, dacron lines-in fact everything that is produced by modern science-I had it-but could not use it.

Let me hear from you please. I will be glad to read a letter from you. My best wishes to you for a healthful, and successful New Year, also extend my well wishes to your mother-I enjoyed talking with her over the phone.

Cordially

Chief Needahbeh

P.S. I took another glance at your picture and the halo of flies-What Helen no Chief Needahbeh?!?? Not throwing bouquets around, I am merely passing along what English Sportsmen I have met tell me-that that fly has been accepted as theeeeeee fly in England. Woof! Ooo it not bad I catch a fish with it once in awhile

N

Chief Needahbeh

International Outdoor Show Chgo Amphitheater '49

#1

red yarn

Body: Black silk
Yellow " rib
Wing: Grizzly
Cock of Bondhu
Head: Grey hair trimmed

#2

Short Jungle

Red Yarn

Sparse red hackle

Body: Gold tinsel - emb. silver rib
→ Red hackle palmer sparse
Wing: 2 Yellow - 2 Red outside

Needebah's instructions to Helen Shaw on the proper tyings for his patterns. Original documents remind us that later tiers often stray from the original path. DEL PLATO

THROAT: Throats on Herb's own patterns are usually long, extending nearly to the hook point. Herb seems to have preferred throats to underbellies, which are consistently absent.

SHOULDER: When present, shoulders are large, often half the length of the wing. Jungle cock, if used, is usually long.

WING: Always very long, sometimes as much as a hook length beyond the hook point, and always tied in on top.

RIBBING: Usually narrow flat silver tinsel, closely spaced.

TAIL: Usually present.

TAG: Always present on floss bodies.

OBSERVATIONS: Herb liked peacock herl and golden pheasant crests, which many tiers avoid, as they are hard to work. When using peacock herl as a topping, he would typically use 12 to 15 strands. When tying with marabou, he used whole plumes. On his Black Ghosts, he preferred a fuller body. When tying others' patterns, Herb respected the recipes and proportions of the original tier.

All told, identifying Welch flies is tricky business because it hinges on subtleties that do not lend themselves to a formulaic protocol. Even with this guidance, collectors will often require a degree of faith when collecting the flies of Herbert L. Welch.

The Welch canon: an impressive body of work that remains relevant to this day. HILYARD COLLECTION

Left column, top to bottom: Cupsuptic (tied by Hilyard), Jane Craig variant (tied by Welch), Welch Pembina (tied by Percy Tackle Co.), Welch Rarebit (tied by Welch). Right column, top to bottom: Kennebago (tied by Hilyard), Jane Craig (tied by Welch), Welch Montréal (tied by Percy Tackle Co.), Welch White-Tipped Montréal (tied by Hilyard).

Left column, top to bottom: Mrs. Andrews (tied by Welch), Green's Pot (tied by Percy Tackle Co.), Welch Cahill (tied by Percy Tackle Co.). Right column, top to bottom: Golden Knight (tied by Welch), Jane Grey (tied by Welch), Jane Craig, marabou (tied by Welch), Black Ghost (tied by Welch).

1. Smelt

Tied by Carrie Stevens
Hook: Size 4 sproat Allcock 1810, 2X stout
Tag: Flat silver tinsel
Tail: Narrow strip of wood duck
Body: Flat silver tinsel
Wing: 2 black hackles flanked on each side by a slightly shorter yellow hackle
Shoulders: Each a gray mallard flank feather
Throat: Brown hackle feathers
Cheeks: Jungle cock
Head: Black with red band
Note: Allcock was bombed out during WWII and never recovered. As such, Carrie's preferred 110 and 2811 model hooks are rare finds. Tiers may substitute hooks of their choosing.

2. Wet Fly (unnamed and not numbered)

Tied by Carrie Stevens
Hook: Size 4 Allcock 4991, 2X long
Tail: 2 Amherst pheasant crests with pronounced black tips
Body: Flat silver tinsel
Wing: Gray squirrel tail
Head: Red
Note: This carded wet fly is the earliest known Carrie Stevens work.

3. Gem

Tied by Leslie K. Hilyard
Hook: Size 6 sproat Allcock 1810
Tag: Flat silver tinsel
Body: Yellow chenille
Wing: Red, then white goat hair
Topping: Short strip of emerald green goose shoulder
Head: Red with black band
Note: This atypical design includes a chenille body and a short topping, but lacks many standard Stevens components, such as jungle cock cheeks, a throat, and an underbelly.

4. Gloom Chaser

Tied by Leslie K. Hilyard
Hook: Size 1/0 extra stout Allcock 2811
Tag: Flat silver tinsel
Body: Red silk floss
Rib: Flat silver tinsel
Underbelly: White bucktail under peacock herl of equal length
Throat: Natural grizzly hackle fibers
Wing: 4 olive hackles flanked on each side by a single orange hackle
Cheeks: Jungle cock
Head: Black with red band
Note: The use of a size 1/0 hook indicates that this pattern was intended for spring Atlantic salmon fishing. Other known Carrie Stevens patterns in this size are the Gray Ghost, Black Ghost, Blue Devil, and Green Beauty.

5. Bob Knight Special

Tied by Carrie Stevens
Hook: Size 6 sproat Allcock 1810
Tag: Flat silver tinsel
Tail: Red hackle fibers
Body: Flat silver tinsel
Wing: 2 white hackles flanked on each side by a slightly shorter yellow hackle
Shoulder: Each a gray mallard flank feather
Throat: Brown hackle fibers
Cheeks: Jungle cock
Head: Red with a black band
Note: This pattern was named for Robert L. Knight (1883–1962) of Hope, Rhode Island.

6. Scarlet

Tied by Leslie K. Hilyard
Hook: Size 6 sproat Allcock 1810
Tag: Flat silver tinsel
Body: Scarlet floss
Rib: Flat silver tinsel
Underbelly: Gray squirrel tail
Throat: Scarlet hackle fibers
Wing: 4 scarlet hackles
Cheeks: Jungle cock
Head: Black with red band
Note: We could not determine body material from the framed presentation at the Anglers' Club of New York, but for purpose of tying, assume scarlet floss ribbed with flat silver tinsel.

7. Commander

Tied by Leslie K. Hilyard
Hook: Size 6 sproat Allcock 1810
Body: Flat silver tinsel
Underbelly: White goat hair
Throat: Orange hackle fibers
Wing: Peacock herl, then 2 reddish orange hackles flanked by 2 grizzly hackles
Cheek: Jungle cock
Head: Black with red band
Note: We could not determine body material from the framed presentation at the Anglers' Club of New York, but for purpose of tying, assume flat silver tinsel.

8. Sally Green

Tied by Carrie Stevens
Hook: Size 6 sproat Alfred Willis, 6X long
Body: Flat silver tinsel
Wing: Green goat hair
Underbelly: White goat hair
Throat: White hackle fibers
Head: Black
Note: When Allcock hooks were scarce, Carrie would substitute Alfred and John Willis hooks and, more rarely, Mustad.

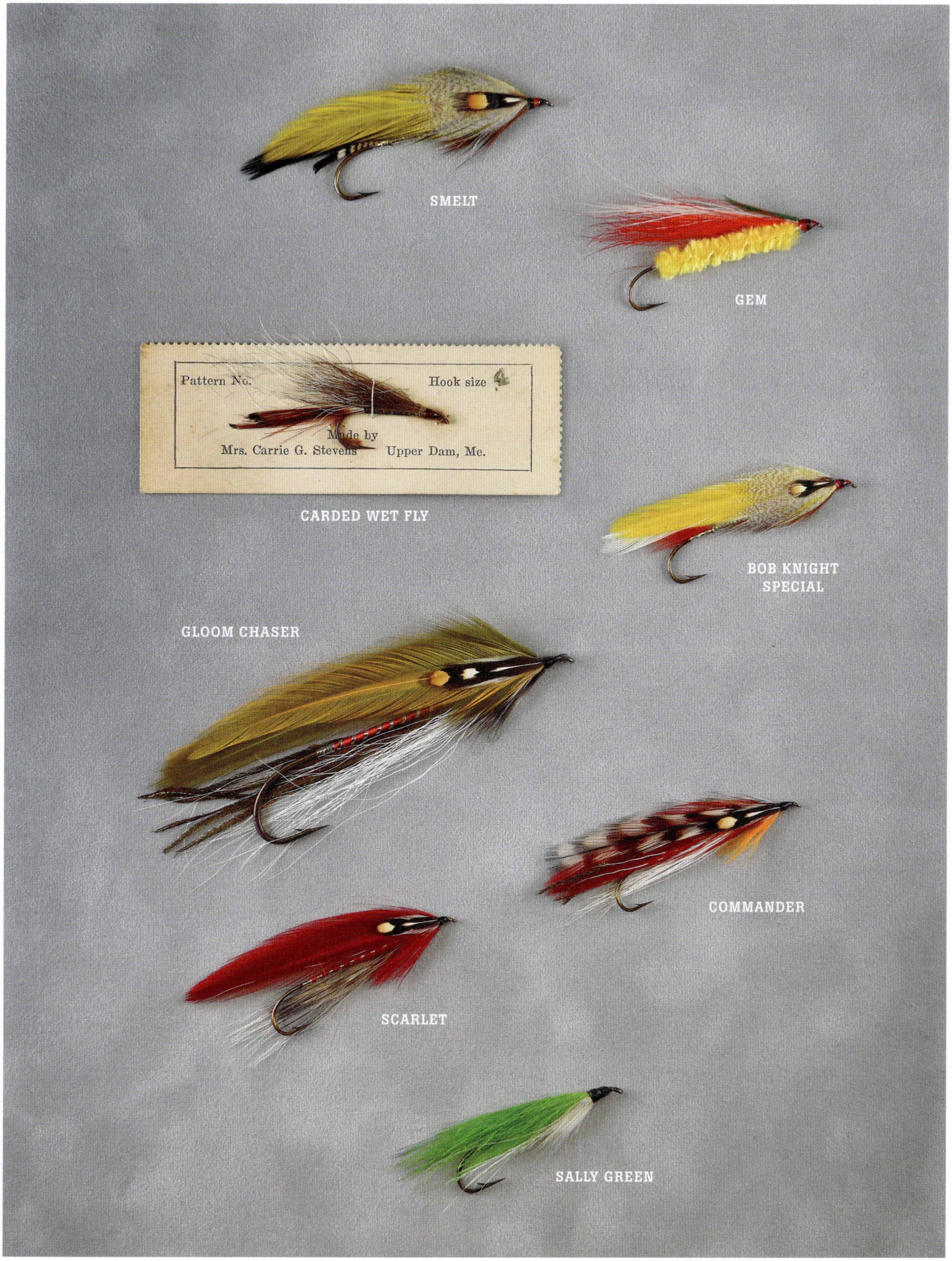

Carrie Stevens Plate.

BIBLIOGRAPHY

Allerton, R.G. *All About Brook Trout*. New York: Perris & Browne, 1869.
Barber, Lynn. *The Heyday of Natural History (1820–1870)*. Garden City, New York: Doubleday, 1980.
Barker, Capt. F.C. *Lake and Forest As I Have Known Them*. Boston: Lothrop, Lee, and Shephard, 1903.
Bierly, Paul E. *John Phillip Sousa, American Phenomenon*. Ohio: Integrity Press, 1973.
Bourque, Bruce J. *Twelve Thousand Years: American Indians in Maine*. Lincoln: University of Nebraska Press, 2001.
Campbell, A.J. *Classic & Antique Fly-Fishing Tackle*. New York: Lyons & Burford, 1997.
Cook, Robert W. *Chasing Danforth: A Wilderness Calling*. New Hampshire: Wilderness Books, 2005.
Dixfield Bicentennial Committee. *The Early History of Dixfield, Maine*. Dixfield Historical Society, 1976.
Douglas-Lithgrow, R.A. *Dictionary of American-Indian Place and Proper Names of New England*, Salem Press, 1909.
DuBois, Donald. *Fisherman's Handbook of Trout Flies*. New York: A.S. Barnes, 1960.
Ellis, Edward. *A Chronological History of the Rangeley Lakes Region*. Trevose, Pennsylvania: Brook Trout Press, 1983.
Ellis, Edward. *The Journal of Squire James Rangeley*. Horsham Valley Graphics, 1990.
Encyclopedia of Minor League Baseball Team Histories—American League. Meckler: Westport-London, 1997.
Grenville, Donham. *1902 Maine Register*. Portland, Maine, 1902.
Gribben, Peter E. *First Century of Portland High School Football 1889–1989*. Portland, Maine, 1989.
Haines, Zenas T. *Squire Rangeley's Township. The Early Days—1837–1849*. Edited by Barbara Bruce. Rangeley, Maine: Highland Publishers, 1970.
Hall, Elizabeth and Max. *About the Exhibits*. Cambridge: Harvard Museum of Comparative Zoology, 1985.
Herd, Andrew. *The Fly*. Ellesmere, England: Medlar Press, 2003.
Hilyard, Graydon R. *Bogdan*. Portland, Oregon: Amato Books, 2006.
Hilyard, Graydon R. and Leslie K. *Carrie Stevens: Maker of Rangeley Favorite Trout & Salmon Flies*. Mechanicsburg, Pennsylvania: Stackpole Books, 2000.
Hoar, J. Sherman. *Pioneer Days of Rangeley Maine*. Rangeley, Maine: self-published, 1950.
Hurum, Hans Jørgen. *A History of the Fish Hook*. New York: Winchester Press, 1977.
Hutchinson, Doug. *The Rumford Falls and Rangeley Lakes Railroad*. Dixfield, Maine: Partridge Lane Publications, 1990.
Hyde, Durwood. "Kennebago Scraps." c. 1921.
Jorgenson, Poul. *Book of Fly Tying*. Johnson Books, 1988.
Karp, Walter. *Charles Darwin and the Origin of Species*. New York: Harper & Row, 1968.
Kauffmann, John Michael. *Dear Old Kennebago*. Freeport, Maine: Freeport Village Press, 1992.
Krohn, William B. *Joshua Gross Rich (1820–1897): The Life and Works of...* Orono, Maine: Maine Folklore Center, 2010.
Larson, Todd. *The History of the Fishhook in America*. Whitefish Press, 2007.
Leiser, Eric. *The Book of Fly Patterns*. New York: Alfred A. Knopf, 1987.
Leonard, J. Edson. *Flies*. New York: A.S. Barnes, 1950.
Marbury, Mary Orvis. *Favorite Flies and Their Histories*. Secaucus, New Jersey: Wellfleet Press, 1988.
Masta, Henry Lorne. *Abenaki Indian Legends, Grammar and Place Names*. Odanak, P.Q., 1932.
McCauley, Brian. *The Names of Maine*. Beverly, Massachussetts: Commonwealth Editions, 2004.
Milgram, Melissa. *Still Life: Adventures in Taxidermy*. Boston: Houghton Mifflin Harcourt, 2010.
Morris, P.A. *A History of Taxidermy: Art, Science and Bad Taste*. Ascot, UK: MPM Publishing, 2010.
Netherton, Cliff. *History of the Sport of Casting: Golden Years*. Lakeland, Florida: American Casting Education Foundation, 1983.
Perrault, Keith. *Standard Dictionary of Fishing Flies*. Orlando: Daniels Publishing, 1984.
Pick, Nancy. *The Rarest of the Rare: Stories Behind the Treasures at the Harvard Museum of Natural History*. New York: HarperCollins, 2004.
Priest, Gary. *The Gilded Age of Rangeley, Maine*. North Reading, Massachussetts, 2009.
Rangeley Lakes Historical Society. *Bemis, Birches, Barker, the Sporting Camps of Captain F.C. Barker*. Cheshires Press, 2011.
Ranlet, Phillip. *Enemies of the Bay Colony (Andros)*. Lenham, Maryland: University Press of America, 2006.
Rasles, Sebastian. *Dictionary of the Abenaki Language in North America*, vol. 1. New Delhi: Isha Books, 2015, reprint.
Reed, Charles K. and Chester A. *Guide to Taxidermy*. New York: Skyhorse Publishing, 2012, reprint.
Reguart, Antonio Saez. *Diccionario Histrico De Los Artes De La Pesca Nacional*. Madrid, 1753.
Schullery, Paul. *Fly-Fishing Secrets of the Ancients*. Albuquerque: University of New Mexico Press, 2009.
Sellers, Charles Coleman. *Mr. Peale's Museum*. New York: W.W. Norton, 1980.
Shirrefs, Herbert P. *The Richardson Lakes: Jewels in the Rangeley Chain*. Randall H. Bennet, ed. Bethel, Maine: Bethel Historical Society, 1995.

Stewart, Dick, and Allen Farrow. *Flies for Atlantic Salmon*. Intervale, New Hampshire: Northland Press, 1991.
Stewart, Dick, and Bob Leeman. *Trolling Flies for Trout and Salmon*. Vermont: Stephen Greene Press, 1982.
Toone, Thomas E. *Mahonri Young: His Life and Art*. Salt Lake City: Signature Books, 1997.
Trask, Kerry A. *Black Hawk: The Battle for the Heart of America*. New York: Henry Holt, 2006.
Trumbull, J. Hammond. *The Composition of Indian Geographical Names*. England: Dodo Press, reprint.
Ward, David C. *Charles Willson Peale, Art and Selfhood in the Early Republic*. Berkeley: University of California Press, 2004.
Wert, Hal Elliot. *Hoover: The Fishing President*. Mechanicburg, Pennsylvania: Stackpole Books, 2005.
Whitney, J. Parker. "Reminiscences of a Sportsman." *Forest & Stream*, 1906.

Percy's
Streamers
Size
Pat.

CHAPTER 9

Welch Canon: Seventeen Originations and Adaptations

The following includes all of the patterns for the Welch canon and the newly minted Kennebago Tribe originations. Saving history and creating history, it seems, is sometimes closely joined. Also included are Welch-related patterns by tiers, past and present. Some of these patterns are well established while others have faded from view. Others are being presented here for the first time.

The Black Ghost streamer etched in time. Top (from left to right) tied by Carrie Stevens, Herb Welch, and Leslie K. Hilyard. Lower, left to right, versions tied by Lew Oatman, Bob Warren, and Stan Bogdan.

1. Black Ghost

Tied by Herbert L. Welch
Hook: Size 6 sproat Allcock 2811
Tag: Flat silver tinsel
Tail: Yellow hackle fibers
Body: Black silk floss
Rib: Flat silver tinsel
Throat: Yellow hackle fibers
Wing: 4 white saddle hackles
Cheek: Jungle cock
Head: Black
Note: Herb used black wool, black rayon floss, and black silk floss for his Black Ghost bodies, which are often distinguished by their cigar shapes.

2. Cupsuptic

Tied by Leslie K. Hilyard
Hook: Size 6 limerick Allcock 1810
Tag: Flat silver tinsel
Tail: Yellow hackle fibers
Body: Butt of peacock herl, then white floss, then another peacock herl butt all comprise the back third; the front two-thirds are red silk floss
Rib: Flat silver tinsel over the red silk floss
Wing: 2 red hackles flanked on each side by a golden badger hackle
Throat: Yellow hackle fibers
Shoulder: Gray saddle hackle
Cheek: Jungle cock
Head: Black

3. Golden Knight

Tied by Herbert L. Welch
Hook: Size 6 Allcock 2811
Tag: Flat gold tinsel
Tail: White hackle fibers
Body: Butt of peacock herl, then wraps of red silk floss, then another butt of peacock herl, then pale blue silk floss
Rib: Narrow flat gold tinsel over the pale blue floss
Wing: 2 yellow saddle hackles flanked by 2 grizzly saddle hackles of equal length
Topping: Golden pheasant crest
Throat: White hackle fibers
Shoulder: Golden pheasant tippet feather
Cheek: Jungle cock
Head: Black

4. Green Spot

Tied by Percy Tackle Company
Hook: Size 6 Allcock 2811
Body: Flat silver tinsel
Rib: Oval silver tinsel
Wing: Bunch of white bucktail, then bunch of pale green bucktail, then 4 dark olive hackles
Cheek: Jungle cock
Head: Black

5. Jane Craig (Yellow)

Tied by Herbert L. Welch
Hook: Size 6 sproat Allcock 2811
Body: Flat silver tinsel
Rib: Oval silver wire
Wing: 4 yellow hackles
Topping: Multiple strands of peacock herl the length of the wing
Cheeks: Jungle cock
Head: Black
Note: Although Welch did not give clear pattern identities to the Craigs, Percy Tackle Company did. Early invoices list the Jane Craig (white) and the yellow Jane Craig implying that the white came first. With all due respect to Welch, we hope to avoid further confusion by sticking with Percy's version.

6. Jane Craig (White)

Tied by Herbert L. Welch
Hook: Size 6 sproat Allcock 2811
Body: Flat silver tinsel
Throat: White hackle fibers
Wing: 6 white hackles
Topping: Multiple strands of peacock herl the length of the wing
Cheeks: Jungle cock
Head: Black

7. Jane Craig (Marabou)

Tied by Herbert L. Welch
Hook: Size 4 Allcock 2811
Body: Flat silver tinsel
Wing: 2 full marabou plumes
Topping: Multiple strands of peacock herl the length of the wing
Cheeks: Jungle cock
Head: Black

8. Jane Grey

Tied by Herbert L. Welch
Hook: Size 3 Carlisle streamer (offset)
Body: Flat silver tinsel
Throat: Light gray hackle fibers
Wing: 4 light gray hackles
Topping: Multiple peacock herl strands the length of the wing
Cheeks: Jungle cock
Head: Black

9. Kennebago

Tied by Leslie K. Hilyard
Hook: Size 6 limerick Allcock 1810
Tag: Flat gold tinsel
Tail: Orange hackle fibers
Body: Butt of peacock herl, then pale blue silk floss, then another peacock herl butt, all comprising the rear third of body; front two-thirds are flat gold tinsel
Rib: Oval silver tinsel over the flat gold tinsel
Wing: 2 red hackles each flanked by a golden badger hackle
Throat: Orange hackle fibers
Cheek: Jungle cock
Head: Black
Note: With their segmented bodies and herled butts, the Kennebago, Cupsuptic, Golden Knight, and Mrs. Andrews all show a strong Atlantic salmon tying influence.

10. Kennebago Special Wet Fly

Tied by Percy Tackle Company
Hook: Blind eye gut snelled wet fly hook
Tag: Fine oval gold tinsel
Tail: 2 narrow sections of bronze mallard
Butt: Blue seal fur
Body: Dark orange seal fur
Rib: Fine oval gold tinsel
Collar: Dark grouse
Wing: Oak turkey, then bronze mallard
Head: Black
Note: An early Welch pattern was referenced in the 1917 Kennebago Tribe archives.

11. Mrs. Andrews

Tied by Herbert L. Welch
Hook: Size 8 Allcock 2811
Tail: Golden pheasant crest
Tag: Flat silver tinsel
Butt: Peacock herl, followed by wraps of red silk floss, followed by another peacock herl butt
Body: Black silk floss
Rib: Narrow silver tinsel over black silk only
Throat: Red hackle fibers
Wing: 4 white saddle hackles
Topping: Golden pheasant crest
Shoulder: Widgeon body feather
Cheek: Jungle cock
Head: Black

12. Welch Cahill Dry Fly

Tied by Herbert L. Welch
Hook: Dry fly
Tail: Lemon wood duck fibers
Body: Gray muskrat body fur
Wing: Single wing of lemon wood duck flank fibers
Hackle: Brown hackle
Head: Black
Note: Tie the wing in at a 45-degree angle so that it extends beyond the eye of the hook.

13. Welch Fly

Tied by Herbert L. Welch
Hook: Size 3 Carlisle streamer (offset)
Body: Flat silver tinsel
Wing: 4 white saddle hackles
Throat: White hackle feathers
Topping: Multiple strands of peacock herl the length of the wing
Cheeks: Jungle cock
Head: Black
Note: Tiers often borrow from themselves, and Herb was no exception. His Welch Fly pattern became the template for his later Jane Grey/Craig series. While the Welch Fly was consistently tied on a Carlisle #3 hook, Herb abandoned this hook for Allcocks in the conventional Jane Grey/Craig series.

14. Welch Montréal Wet Fly

Tied by Herbert L. Welch
Hook: Blind-eye wet fly snelled with gut
Tail: Red goose shoulder
Body: Claret seal fur
Rib: Flat gold tinsel
Wing: Copper wild turkey body feather segment
Collar: Claret hackle tied full
Head: Black

15. Welch Pembina Wet Fly

Tied by Herbert L. Welch
Hook: Gut snelled on an eyed wet fly
Tag: Flat silver tinsel
Tail: Married strips of goose shoulder, red over yellow
Body: Flat silver tinsel
Rib: Silver twist
Collar: Claret hackle
Wing: Oak mottled turkey, veiled by married strips on each side of red over yellow goose shoulder
Head: Black
Note: Pembina translates from the Algonquin as a species of viburnum, the low bush cranberry.

16. Welch Rarebit

Tied by Herbert L. Welch
Hook: Eyed wet fly
Tag: Flat silver tinsel
Tail: Narrow strips of married yellow and blue goose shoulder with the yellow strip above; 2 or 3 strands of peacock sword fibers laid beside; and a narrow strip of red goose shoulder, all of equal length
Body: Flat silver tinsel
Rib: Narrow silver twist
Throat: Liberal amount of natural guinea feather
Wing: Single dark red hackle flanked by a white hackle on each side
Topping: 7 strands of peacock herl
Head: Black
Note: An early Welch origination, it was first documented in a March 1919 issue of the *American Angler*.

17. Welch White-Tipped Montréal Wet Fly

Tied by Leslie K. Hilyard
Hook: Blind-eye wet fly with a gut snell
Tag: Flat gold tinsel
Tail: Narrow strip of red goose shoulder
Body: Claret seal fur
Rib: Flat gold tinsel
Collar: Claret hackle
Wing: Tied in two parts: inner wing of white goose shoulder; outer wing of oak mottled turkey tied shorter to allow the white tip of the inner wing to show
Note: Due to a glaring oversight by natural selection, turkeys provide few white-tipped feathers suitable for tying in the smaller sizes. Welch's adaptation incorporates additional feathers to circumvent that problem and cut costs. Per Percy Tackle Company invoices, Welch often ordered the Welch Montréal and the Welch White-Tipped Montréal with a silver body.

Kennebago Tribe Patterns

All patterns are originated and tied by Leslie K. Hilyard.

1. Chief Sleeping Bear

Tied by Leslie K. Hilyard
Hook: Size 4 sproat Allcock 2811
Tag: Flat silver tinsel
Body: Orange polar bear underfur
Hackle: Palmered black hackle gathered at the throat
Wing: Large bunch of peacock herl
Head: Black
Note: Tiers may substitute hook style and sizes at will.

2. Chief Black Hawk

Tied by Leslie K. Hilyard
Hook: Size 4 sproat Allcock 2811
Tag: Flat silver tinsel
Tail: Golden pheasant crest
Butts: Rear of wrapped peacock herl, then embossed copper tinsel, then a forward butt of wrapped peacock herl
Body: Orange silk floss
Rib: Embossed copper tinsel
Wing: 4 black hackle feathers
Throat: Black hackle fibers, then a bunch of blue hackle fibers
Cheeks: Jungle cock, then a blue kingfisher scale at the base
Horns: Each a strip of scarlet macaw tail
Head: Black

3. Chief High Bear

Tied by Leslie K. Hilyard
Hook: Size 4 sproat Allcock 2811, 2X stout
Tag: Embossed silver tinsel
Tail: Slip of barred wood duck flank
Body: Double wrapped embossed silver tinsel
Wing: Large bunch of natural polar bear, then 2 royal blue hackles flanked on each side by a black hackle
Cheeks: Jungle cock
Throat: Blue peacock breast feather fibers
Head: Black

4. Chief Dustmaker

Tied by Leslie K. Hilyard
Hook: Size 4 sproat 2811 Allcock 2X stout
Tag: Flat silver tinsel
Body: White silk floss
Rib: Flat silver tinsel
Hackle: Blue-eared pheasant substitute, palmered, extending over the front half of the body
Throat: Dyed green mallard flank feather, wrapped as a collar
Wing: 2 lavender hackles flanked by 2 black hackles
Cheeks: Jungle cock
Head: Black

5. Chief Kicking Bear

Tied by Leslie K. Hilyard
Hook: Size 4 sproat Allcock 2811, 2X stout
Tag: Flat silver tinsel
Body: Blue silk floss
Rib: Flat silver tinsel
Underbelly: Blue bucktail
Wing: 4 dyed blue grizzly hackles
Shoulders: Each a blue peacock breast feather
Throat: Blue hackle fibers
Cheeks: Jungle cock
Head: Black
Note: Historically called *beards*, throats can be any length, causing confusion. Underbelly is what we call the elongated throat that extends the length of the hook.

6. Chief American Horse

Tied by Leslie K. Hilyard
Hook: Size 4 sproat Allcock 2811, 2X stout
Tag: Flat silver tinsel
Tail: Peacock sword fibers
Body: Double-wrapped flat silver tinsel
Wing: 4 royal blue hackles flanked by a pale golden badger
Throat: Peacock sword fibers
Cheeks: Jungle cock
Topping: 2 silver pheasant crests
Head: Red then white then blue

7. Chief Red Cloud

Tied by Leslie K. Hilyard
Hook: Size 4 sproat Allcock 2811, 2X stout
Tag: Flat silver tinsel
Butt: 2 strands of wrapped peacock herl to be concealed by the body
Body: Staggered bunches of peacock sword fibers forming a tube over the entire shank
Wing: 2 claret hackles, flanked by a slightly shorter silver badger hackle on each side
Collar: Peacock sword fibers
Head: Black

8. Chief Spotted Horse

Tied by Leslie K. Hilyard
Hook: Size 4 sproat Allcock 2811, 2X stout
Butt: Dubbed red Davy Wotton SLF
Body: Rear quarter uses red Davy Wotton SLF dubbing; front three-quarters uses golden olive Davy Wotton SLF dubbing
Wing: 2 grizzly hackles dyed yellow each flanked by a slightly shorter pale golden badger hackle
Shoulders: Golden pheasant yellow flank feather
Throat: Small bunch of red Davy Wotton SLF dubbing
Cheeks: Jungle cock
Head: Black

9. Big Chief Zibeon

Tied by Leslie K. Hilyard
Hook: Size 4 sproat Allcock 2811, 2X stout
Tag: Flat gold tinsel
Body: Black silk floss
Rib: Flat gold tinsel
Wing: 4 badger hackles dyed bright green
Shoulders: Golden pheasant red body feather
Cheeks: Jungle cock
Throat: Bunch of grizzly hackle fibers dyed red
Topping: Golden pheasant crest dyed green
Head: Black

10. Chief Sitting Bull

Tied by Leslie K. Hilyard
Hook: Size 2 limerick John Willis loop eye
Body: Embossed copper tinsel
Wing: 6 strands of peacock herl then 4 golden badger hackles
Throat: Small bunch of orange hackle fibers, then small bunch of red hackle fibers
Shoulders: Male ruffed grouse (partridge) ruff feather
Cheeks: Jungle cock
Head: Red with black band

11. Chief Eagle Elk

Tied by Leslie K. Hilyard
Hook: Size 4 sproat Allcock 2811, 2X stout
Tag: Flat silver tinsel
Tail: Claret hackle fibers
Body: Pale mauve alpaca yarn
Rib: Flat silver tinsel
Underbelly: White goat hair
Wing: 2 black hackles flanked on each side by a slightly shorter grizzly hackle dyed blue
Shoulders: Amherst pheasant white-barred rump feather
Cheeks: Jungle cock
Throat: Claret hackle fibers
Head: Black

12. Chief White Buffalo

Tied by Leslie K. Hilyard
Hook: Size 4 sproat Allcock 2811, 2X stout
Body: Double-wrapped using embossed copper tinsel
Underbelly: Peacock herl then white goat hair
Wing: 2 olive hackles flanked on each side by 2 slightly shorter golden badger hackles
Throat: Orange hackle fibers, then golden pheasant crest dyed red
Cheek: Jungle cock
Head: Black

13. Chief Thunder Cloud

Tied by Leslie K. Hilyard
Hook: Size 4 sproat Allcock 2811, 2X stout
Tag: Flat silver tinsel
Body: Black silk floss
Rib: Flat silver tinsel
Underbelly: White goat hair
Wing: Peacock herl under 4 black hackles
Shoulders: Blue peacock breast feather
Throat: Peacock sword fibers
Cheeks: Jungle cock
Head: Black

14. Chief Wolf Robe

Tied by Leslie K. Hilyard
Hook: Size 4 sproat Allcock 2811, 2X stout
Tag: Embossed silver tinsel
Tail: Narrow slip of red goose shoulder
Body: Spun gray wolf body fur
Rib: Embossed silver tinsel
Wing: 4 brown hackles
Throat: Brown then orange hackle fibers
Shoulders: Double golden pheasant tippet feathers overlaid so that the top band of the second feather aligns with the second band of the first feather
Cheeks: Jungle cock
Head: Red

15. Chief Little Bird

Tied by Leslie K. Hilyard
Hook: Size 4 sproat Allcock 2811, 2X stout
Body: Flat silver tinsel
Underbelly: White goat hair under peacock herl
Wing: 2 orange hackles flanked by 2 bright green hackles flanked by 2 natural grizzly hackles
Throat: White hackle fibers
Cheeks: Jungle cock
Head: Black

16. Chief Little Bear

Tied by Leslie K. Hilyard
Hook: Size 4 sproat Allcock 2811, 2X stout
Tip: One wrap of embossed silver tinsel
Tag: One wrap of royal blue silk floss
Tail: Narrow slip of red goose shoulder
Body: Double wrapped with embossed copper tinsel
Hackle: Silver badger, palmered to throat
Wing: Natural polar bear, then light green polar bear, then bright orange polar bear, then burnt orange polar bear, then yellow polar bear
Topping: 2 jungle cock nails, very long
Head: Black

17. Chief Turning Eagle

Tied by Leslie K. Hilyard
Hook: Size 4 sproat Allcock 2811, 2X stout
Tag: 2 turns of silver twist
Tail: Golden pheasant crest dyed green
Body: Flat silver tinsel, double wrapped
Rib: Silver twist
Wing: 2 yellow hackles flanked by a dusty silver badger hackle on each side
Throat: Several strands of unraveled silver twist
Cheeks: Jungle cock with a blue kingfisher scale at the base
Head: Black

18. Chief Swift Dog

Tied by Leslie K. Hilyard
Hook: Size 4 sproat Allcock 2811, 2X stout
Tag: Flat silver tinsel
Body: Rear half is orange silk floss; front half is black silk floss
Rib: Flat silver tinsel over the entire body
Wing: 7 strands of peacock herl under 2 orange hackles and flanked by 2 black hackles on each side
Shoulders: Peacock pheasant feather, small eyed
Throat: Black hackle fibers
Head: Black

Welch-Related Patterns

The following patterns, originated by tiers past and present, relate to Welch's story, the Rangeley region, the Canadian Maritimes, and the Gaspé. Some of these patterns, like the Black Ghost Atlantic salmon adaptations, are established, while others have either faded from view or are being presented here for the first time.

1. Captain Barker

Originated and tied by Leslie K. Hilyard
Hook: Size 6 Allcock 1810
Tag: Orange silk floss
Tail: Several strands of golden pheasant tippet fibers
Body: Rear two-thirds is flat silver tinsel; front third is blue silk floss
Rib: Medium silver oval tinsel over entire length of body
Hackle: Yellow, palmered over blue, tied heavy at the throat and pulled down
Wing: 4 brown furnace hackles
Shoulders: Married strips of red, white, and blue goose nazurias, with the red on top
Head: Red

2. Otis Bean .38 Special

Originated and tied by Leslie K. Hilyard
Hook: Size 6 Allcock 1810
Tag: Flat silver tinsel
Body: Rear half is red silk floss; front half is black silk floss
Rib: Flat silver tinsel
Underwing: 2 golden pheasant crests, extending beyond the hook bend
Wing: 2 black saddle hackles flanked by 2 blood red saddle hackles
Throat: Peacock sword fibers tied full
Cheeks: European starling white-tipped purple flank feather, then a shorter kingfisher scale revealing the white tip
Head: Black

3. Black Ghost (Atlantic Salmon Hairwing, Maritimes Style)

Tied by Warren Duncan
Hook: Size 1/0 Mustad 36890
Tag: Oval silver tinsel
Tail: Yellow bucktail
Body: Black wool
Rib: Oval tinsel
Wing: White bucktail
Throat: Yellow bucktail
Cheeks: Jungle cock, very long
Head: Black

4. Black Ghost (Atlantic Salmon Hairwing, Gaspé Style)

Tied by Ralph Billingsley
Hook: Size 2 Mustad 36890
Tail: Golden pheasant tippets
Body: Black floss
Rib: Oval silver tinsel
Wing: White polar bear
Collar: Yellow hackle
Head: Black

5. Black Ghost (Atlantic Salmon, Low Water)

Tied by Leslie K. Hilyard
Hook: Size 8 Wilson low water
Tag: Narrow flat silver tinsel
Tail: Golden pheasant crest
Body: Black silk floss
Rib: Narrow silver tinsel
Wing: 4 white hackle tips
Throat: Yellow hackle fibers
Cheeks: Jungle cock
Head: Black

6. Black Ghost (Atlantic Salmon, Tube Style)

Tied by Ted Patlen

Hook: Single, double, or treble per local regulations
Tube: Metal
Tag: Oval silver tinsel
Tail: Yellow hackle fibers
Body: Black silk floss
Rib: Wide flat silver tinsel
Wing: White bucktail
Hackle: Yellow, collared
Cheeks: 4 jungle cock
Head: Black

7. Black Ghost (Western)

Tied by Leslie K. Hilyard

Hook: Size 6 Allcock 9441
Tail: Yellow hackle fibers
Body: Black chenille
Rib: Oval silver tinsel
Wing: White bucktail
Collar: Black hackle
Head: Black

8. Chief Needabeh 1

Tied by Leslie K. Hilyard (per Chief's recipe sent to Helen Shaw, dated 1949, International Outdoor Show at the Chicago Amphitheater; see pages 108–10)

Hook: Size 2 sproat Allcock 2811
Tail: Red feather or red yarn
Body: Black silk
Rib: Yellow silk
Wing: 2 long cock-y-bondhu hackles flanked by 2 shorter natural grizzly hackles
Cheeks: Jungle cock
Head: Trimmed gray deer hair

9. Chief Needabeh #2

Tied by Leslie K. Hilyard (per Chief's recipe sent to Helen Shaw, dated 1949, International Outdoor Show at the Chicago Amphitheater; see pages 108–10)
Hook: Size 2 sproat Allcock 2811
Tail: Red yarn
Body: Flat gold tinsel
Rib: Embossed silver tinsel
Hackle: Red, sparsely palmered
Wing: 2 yellow hackles flanked by 2 red hackles
Cheeks: Jungle cock
Head: Black

10. Senator Frye Lake Fly

Originated and tied by Leslie K. Hilyard
Hook: Size 6 wet fly, 5X long
Tag: Oval silver tinsel, medium
Tail: Red goose nazuria and lemon wood duck
Hackle: Olive, palmered, and finished at the throat
Body: Rear two-thirds is blue alpaca wool; front third is Davy Wotton red SLF dubbing
Rib: Fine silver wire
Wing: Each a golden pheasant tippet feather with a jungle cock nail at the base
Head: Wrapped with Davy Wotton red SLF dubbing and finished with black thread

11. General Ike

Originated by George Fletcher and tied by Leslie K. Hilyard
Hook: Size 2 sproat Allcock 2811, 10X long
Tag: Gold tinsel
Tail: Scarlet wing quill
Body: Yellow chenille
Throat: Scarlet hackle fibers
Wing: 4 brown olive hackle feathers
Shoulders: Widgeon body or breast feather
Cheeks: Jungle cock
Head: Black

12. Golden Grouse Wet Fly

Tied by Percy Tackle Company
Hook: Size 8 eyed with a gut snell
Tail: Narrow strip of tan goose shoulder
Body: Gray muskrat
Hackle: Orange, palmered over the body
Collar: Dark grouse body feather
Wing: Oak turkey under bronze mallard
Head: Red
Note: Fishers were slow to accept eyed hooks, leading manufacturers to adopt a transitional "belt and suspenders" approach, by attaching the traditional gut leader to the eye.

13. Pickel Special

Tied by Percy Tackle Company
Hook: Size 8 sproat Allcock 2811
Tag: Flat silver tinsel
Tail: Maroon wool
Body: Flat silver tinsel
Rib: Silver twist
Underwing: Clump of white bucktail
Wing: 2 natural grizzly hackles
Cheeks: Jungle cock
Head: Black

14. Welch Dry Fly (Kennebago Wolf)

Originated by George Fletcher
Hook: Size 8 Allcock 9441
Thread: Black
Wing: Sparse gray squirrel tail hair
Tail: Sparse gray squirrel tail hair
Body: Gray crewel yarn, picked out
Hackle: Golden badger

15. Stanley Streamer

Originated and tied by Leslie K. Hilyard
Hook: Size 6 Allcock 2811
Body: Embossed silver tinsel
Wing: 2 lavender hackles flanked on each side by a slightly shorter golden badger hackle
Topping: Golden pheasant crest
Cheek: Jungle cock eye with a South American kingfisher scale at the base
Throat: Peacock sword fibers
Head: Black

16. Welchman

Tied by Percy Tackle Company
Hook: Size 6 sproat Allcock 2811, 2X stout
Tag: 3 turns of flat gold tinsel, medium
Tail: Golden pheasant crest
Body: Peacock herl, thickly wrapped
Wing: Short bunch of pale yellow polar bear, then 2 yellow hackles flanked by 2 royal blue hackles flanked by 2 burgundy hackles
Topping: Golden pheasant crest the length of the wing, then a short bunch of peacock sword
Cheeks: Jungle cock
Head: Black

17. Welchman's Special

Tied by Percy Tackle Company
Hook: Size 6 sproat Allcock 2811, 2X stout
Tail: Golden pheasant crest
Body: Flat silver tinsel
Rib: French silver twist
Wing: 2 red hackles flanked by 2 yellow hackles flanked by 2 pale blue hackles
Throat: Brown hackle fibers
Topping: Peacock herl
Cheeks: Jungle cock
Head: Black

18. Herbert L. Welch

Originated and tied by Leslie K. Hilyard
Hook: Size 4 Allcock 2811
Tag: Embossed silver tinsel
Body: Blue chenille
Rib: Embossed silver tinsel
Wing: 2 black hackles flanked by a dyed green badger hackle on each side
Topping: Golden pheasant crest
Cheeks: Jungle cock
Throat: Peacock sword fibers
Head: Black

INDEX

N

O

P

Q

R

S

T

U

V

W

Y